John Edmund Cox

Musical Recollections of the last Half-century

Vol. I

John Edmund Cox

Musical Recollections of the last Half-century
Vol. I

ISBN/EAN: 9783337107079

Printed in Europe, USA, Canada, Australia, Japan

Cover: Foto ©ninafisch / pixelio.de

More available books at **www.hansebooks.com**

MUSICAL RECOLLECTIONS

OF

THE LAST HALF-CENTURY.

" And MUSIC shall untune the sky."
DRYDEN AND HANDEL.

IN TWO VOLUMES.

VOL I.

LONDON:
TINSLEY BROTHERS, 18, CATHERINE ST. STRAND.
1872.

TO

SIR MICHAEL COSTA, KT.

ETC., ETC., ETC.,

TO WHOSE UNIVERSALLY ACKNOWLEDGED TALENT AND INDOMITABLE
ENERGY THE ADVANCEMENT OF MUSIC IN ENGLAND
OWES SO MUCH,

AND

BY WHOSE ACTIVE EXERTIONS AND UNWEARIED LABOURS THE PER-
FORMANCE OF THE WORKS OF THE GREATEST "MASTERS"
HAS BEEN SO LARGELY PERFECTED,

THESE

"MUSICAL RECOLLECTIONS OF THE LAST HALF-CENTURY"

Are Dedicated,

WITH EVERY EXPRESSION OF THE SINCERE ESTEEM AND REGARD
OF HIS OLD AND ATTACHED FRIEND,

THE AUTHOR.

PREFACE.

About two years ago, whilst conversing with a friend with reference to the progress of music in England, and —after my wont—being somewhat of a "*laudator temporis acti*"—comparing past with present "celebrities," by no means with advantage to the latter, he hazarded the remark, that "he was surprised I had not long ago written my "Recollections, inasmuch as I must have made notes respecting the several incidents and individuals I had been talking of, which, if thrown together, might become generally interesting." Being put upon the *qui vive* by this remark, I at once hunted up those materials, and after a lengthened search I found them stowed away in an old chest; the greater part covered with the dust of many years' accumulation, and stained with age. It was no very easy matter to bring this "rude matter into due form." Not only was a large portion of those jottings desultory, from having been pencilled down more for amusement than even as a means of refreshing my memory in after times, and, most assuredly, with no view whatever to

future publication, but they were far from being conse-
cutively perfect. When I had almost wholly determined
to put them back into the place whence they had
been unearthed, I happened to mention their existence to
Mr. WILLIAM TINSLEY, the proprietor of *Tinsleys'
Magazine*, who encouraged the idea of causing them to
take shape and substance. Upon commencing my task,
with no very clear idea of the amount of labour and
research its fulfilment would demand, I speedily discovered, that unless the purpose were extended, any-
.thing but a satisfactory conclusion would be arrived at,
as well by myself as by the public. It had been one
of my most persistent assertions—reiterated, without
doubt, *usque ad nauseam* to very many friends less
enthusiastically imbued than myself, and prone to be
bored by repeated references to " dear, happy hours
that can return no more "—that England may justly
be classed as a musical nation, in spite of its being
the fashion in many circles, both home and foreign,
to deny that conclusion. If, therefore, a combination
of proof in this direction could be effected, accompanied by a *résumé* of events and circumstances running over the last half-century, that would tend, in
some degree at least, to establish that assertion, an advantage seemed to be " looming in the distance," which
might not be altogether unacceptable alike to musicians
in particular, and to the public in general. Taking,
therefore, my own personal " notes " as the basis of the

work upon which I had been induced to meditate, I determined to fortify whatever statements I might make, whatever opinions I might express, and whatever facts I might relate by means of authentic documents, the value, importance, and veracity of which are indisputable. This decision once taken, it only remained to search for such documents, and, " when found," to use them as advantageously as possible, whilst acknowledging both their source and their value.

At the period from which my own personal " Recollections " date, musical literary publications had not become so numerous as they now are; but for the details of that period I had the special advantage of being able to refer to one of the most accurate and perfect " musical records " extant, in which the advance of the science, the progress of the art, and the criticism concerning events and individuals were treated with the utmost discernment and discrimination, as well as with that large amount of acumen, only to have been expected from the well-known talent and honestly earned reputation of the gentleman who was himself amongst the first and foremost, of his day and generation, to maintain that " England deserves a place amongst all those other nations, wherein music has always been fostered and cultivated." In the earlier portions of the " Recollections," it will be, therefore, discovered that I, have drawn largely, in explanation and confirmation of my own views, upon the *Quarterly Musical Magazine* *and Review,*—a work now, unfortunately, out of print, but of which the value and importance are acknowledged by every person laying claim to musical information and intelligence. Of the character of that work, I have no hesitation in speaking in the strongest terms of admiration and regard; for it was amongst the many—musical and otherwise—privileges of my youth to be acquainted with, and, in a measure, instructed by its accomplished proprietor, editor, and critic in chief, the late Richard Mackenzie Bacon, a man for his literary, musical, and political attainments universally looked up to, and admired, although always working in a provincial district, and never residing in the metropolis.* By the judgment of this remarkable man I am, therefore, indeed proud to have been fortified in the opinion I have expressed concerning events and individuals during the earliest period over which my " Recollections " extend.

In passing onwards, however, from that period, after much consideration and a careful examination of other reliable sources of information, I discovered, as I had anticipated, that I could meet with no better " authority " than *The Harmonicon,* the existence of which extended from the year 1823 to 1830. The editor of that musical periodical was Mr. Ayrton, a son of the late Dr. Ayrton, organist of Westminster Abbey, and tutor of Sir George

* Mr. Bacon was one of the first of the literary critics of his day to discern and encourage the talent of Lord Lytton, to whom he also gave much useful advice, when he was commencing his brilliant, and—happily for the world— still unfinished career.

Smart,*—who, although not himself a musician by profession, had been—as the term is—" regularly built," and
was thus thoroughly competent for the office he had
undertaken—much more so indeed than he proved himself to be for operatic management, in which, with the
exception of having brought out *Il Don Giovanni* at the
King's Theatre in 1817, he had little to show in the way
of success, either musically or financially.   Mr. Ayrton's
criticisms were marked throughout with a considerable
amount of asperity, but in the relation of facts as connected with the period over which his labours extended,
he is most reliable.   I have, therefore, been able to avail
myself of repeated references to his writings, as, for the
most part, confirming the impressions my own personal
Memoranda have supplied.   From the year 1830 to 1867
—at which I have deemed it advisable to close my
"Recollections"—I have had the advantage of continued
reference to *The Athenæum*, the musical criticisms of
which deservedly popular journal were from the pen of
the late Mr. Henry F. Chorley, to whose capabilities,
honesty of purpose, and thorough reliableness—having
had occasion to mention each and all of those qualities
in the body of the work—I need not again refer.†

Although the authorities have been most useful,
upon which I have had the advantage of drawing for
the establishment of such facts and circumstances as

---

* See vol. i. pp. 80, et sqq.   † See vol. i. pp. 160, 179, 181.

needed larger confirmation than my own personal
" Recollections " afforded, I have not failed to call to my
aid several other publications,—especially the *Times*, the
Spectator,* and such well-known journals, wherein the
subject of music has invariably been made a feature,
and the opinions therein expressed concerning its development, have been, for the most part, fair and
appropriate.

In prosecuting the task which has now come to a conclusion, I may be permitted to remark that the chief
difficulty I have had to contend against has been, not a
paucity of details, but a positive *embarras de richesses.*
Had I been inclined to travel beyond those events and
circumstances which my own memory furnish, I might
have produced an extended and comprehensive " history,"
that might perhaps have served as a sequel to the
standard works of Dr. Burney and Sir John Hawkins.
Inasmuch, however, as I have not been able to undertake so important a task, I yet venture to hope I may
have the satisfaction of discovering that, until such a
work may appear, these " Recollections," written from
month to month, *currente calamo*, for serial publication
in *Tinsleys' Magazine*, in the first instance, but now
brought together in their present form, after revision
and emendation, may be accepted as a narrative of

* Many of the musical criticisms of the *Spectator* were generally believed
to have been written by the late Mr. Edward Taylor, the Gresham Professor of
Music. See vol. i. p. 208.

events and individuals that will be not only of interest, but of use, whenever a larger work be may undertaken. I trust too it will be found, that, in speaking of *artistes*, both of the past and of the more immediate time, I may be found to have avoided any remarks that might have a tendency to wound the most susceptible, for whilst I have been at the pains "nothing to extenuate," I have most earnestly striven not " to set down aught in malice."

In closing these prefatorial remarks there is one duty, however, that I would by no means omit to discharge— to tender my best thanks and acknowledgments to very many friends, who have most kindly assisted me by their advice, and to numerous journals, both metropolitan and provincial,—as well as American also,—which have issued most flattering notices whilst the several portions were passing through *Tinsleys' Magazine*. Amongst the former I should indeed be guilty of a dereliction of duty were I not specially to acknowledge the invaluable aid afforded me by Mr. Charles Lewis Gruneisen, a well-known accomplished and honest critic, who has most kindly read the proof sheets, and added most important information that can but enhance whatever value may attach to my own personal " Recollections." To Sir Julius Benedict I equally owe no small debt of gratitude for his having furnished me with the details of his active life and eminent career; to Mr. W. G. Cusins, the able and energetic " director of Her Majesty's state and

private bands, and the Philharmonic Society's concerts,
for his arrangement from Handel's score of the music to
the motto I have selected for my work; and to Mr. S.
Hall, the learned and indefatigable librarian of "the
Athenæum Club," who has never been at fault, whenever
a reference, difficult to be met with, or comparatively
unknown, has been needed. I might easily extend this
list of names, but I forbear, although I venture to express
the hope that each and all of those, who have so ably
assisted me, will be assured that I equally value, and
shall never cease to remember, their generous support,
although I am unable more particularly to enumerate
. them.

ATHENÆUM CLUB,
October 9th, 1872.

CONTENTS.

INTRODUCTION.

CHAPTER I.

CHAPTER II.

CHAPTER III.

CHAPTER IV.

CHAPTER V.

CHAPTER VI.

CHAPTER VII.

CHAPTER VIII.

CHAPTER IX.

CHAPTER X.

CHAPTER XI.

PART I.

VOL. I.

MUSICAL RECOLLECTIONS OF THE LAST HALF CENTURY.

INTRODUCTION.

"THE character of a nation has been thought to be in no small degree influenced by its amusements." It was a truth enforced long, long ago, before refinement in taste or improvement in morals had made any great mark upon the then so-called civilised nations of the world:

"Didicisse fideliter artes emollit mores, nec sinit esse feros."

But the ancients certainly were in one respect utterly ignorant of one great means to such an end—the knowledge of musical science in its theory and practice. Little reliable information has reached us as to the use of musical instruments in times when Greece supplied the most polished evidences of those centuries during which it stood foremost in the production of classic poetry, and reached a height in the extension of dramatic force and excellence which has since been rivalled, but can scarcely be said to have been excelled. Of Roman musical tastes or science the details are less than those which have been acquired from her greater rival in the grand work of civilisation. Indeed, it is only in reference to modern times that we have any information as to progress in this direction. Not until the decline of the Roman Empire had well-nigh approached its entire decadence was music reduced to anything like a science, or the rude melodies, of which every nation must have been more or less possessed, reduced into form and rhythm. To the church as established upon the ruins of paganism, and from which she was at this period of Roman declension borrowing many of its meretricious forms, ritualistic practices, and gorgeous ceremonies, must be attributed this pleasant and gratifying result ; for it was speedily perceived by those who undertook first to raise, and then to elevate, the platform of ecclesiastical religion, that without the means which would please the ear and gratify the senses through the adoption of "the concord of sweet sounds," preaching alone would not influence the rude and unlettered minds upon which it was then brought to bear, whilst the repetition even of increasing ceremonial would only weary and afterwards disgust them.

It is no part of my present purpose to attempt to illustrate "the manner how" music advanced from the simple notation of Gregorian and Ambrosian puerilities to a larger and more extended science. Interesting as it would be to trace how in Italy, its birth-place, it took form and combination, until it found in Palestrina, Luca Marenzio, and other composers of unqualified skill and originality, its best and worthiest exponency, that field is much too wide to enter upon, and too large to be traversed except by attempts at its investigation which it would take more than a lifetime properly and thoroughly to complete. All that can indeed be satisfactorily done is to localise, as it were, musical progression in one particular spot ;

and to show, with as much precision and with as clear explanations as limited means and curtailed space will permit, how it originated, what it has since done, and what it is still likely to produce. Even in this direction the materials are so extensive, the details so remarkable, and the information so varied, that little else than the surface can be touched. Our own country is rich indeed in each of these particulars, abounding and running over with resources of which but few are cognisant, and concerning which the most part is indifferent.

The ridiculous assertion that "the English are by no means a musical people," has been repeated so "many a time and oft," and has so resolved itself into something closely akin to a proverb, if not actually into form and substance, that even the better informed and more experienced seem to believe that it is so, or at least are unwilling to stand up in defence of a contradiction as positive in fact as it is easy of demonstration. All that is required is the will to undertake the explanation, combined, of course, with sufficient knowledge on the one hand and industry on the other to conduct an investigation, the process of which will become one of increasing interest as it is continued, and the results of which cannot but be useful and satisfactory.

But upon this repeated assertion—so constantly urged from want of due consideration—that "the English are by no means a musical people," it may raise "a smile if the attempt to remove an imputation so injurious to ourselves be attributed to an identification of musical taste with national character. But this must arise from a deplorable blindness to the interest we have in maintaining that the English are a musical people ; for it is very obvious that the odium which our great dramatist has, no doubt justly, attached to 'the man that hath no music in himself,' must most materially affect the reputation of a community of such individuals. It is not within our province to attempt to unveil the physical causes of distaste for music, wherever it may, if it ever does, exist, as the most delightful of all sciences. We cannot affirm whether it arises most from our sedulous application to dull, plodding, money-getting acts, or to the influence of a cold and foggy climate on our material and immaterial character; yet we may safely aver that our climate deprives us of what may be termed the poetry and romance of music, and therefore of those associations which would in the breasts of most people insure it a place." It is not within our power to indulge in those voluptuous moonlight concerts on the calm

> "Bosom of the dark-blue sea,"

of which the ideas alone are sufficient

> "To steal young hearts away;"

when

> "Music is the food of love,"

and when

> "Delicious dream-like harmonies"

speak but of the most devoted passion, and the soul is, as it were, dissolved in the intensity of its bliss. Such embodiments of sound are, comparatively, denied to us

> "Children of the wintry North."

But when we consider the prodigious pains and expense employed to supply, encourage, and maintain musicians—when we reflect upon the prominent part music bears in our diversions, public and private, and how successfully it aids the noblest, kindest, and best of charities that warm the human breast—

no one can surely be disposed to accuse the English of apathy towards this most charming of all pleasures. It may, however, be urged, that music has become a prominent fashion of the day, and that it is not exactly just to infer the character of a great society from any peculiar traits exhibited by a few of its members. Our views must rather be directed towards the majority of the people, and our decision arrived at according to the bias of their inclinations. And here we shall undoubtedly discover that the masses are beginning at last to have a strong liking and predilection for "the concord of sweet sounds." For how else is it that our churches, in which plain, simple, but assuredly cold parochial services prevail, are comparatively deserted, in spite of the efficiency of the preachers, whilst those where a choral or cathedral service has been introduced over-flow with congregations? Will not the most illiterate and unthinking answer, that it is owing wholly to the abundance and superiority of the music of the latter? How is it that our theatres are also filled by means of operatic and melo-dramatic performances — which species of entertainment has of late usurped the places of the noblest efforts of dramatic genius— whilst the tragic and the comic Muses exert their powers vainly before

> "A beggarly account of empty boxes"?

What nation in the world is so wont to express conviviality and to heighten it by music, as our own? Are not our streets crowded with itinerant performers, to the disgust of not a few, and the annoyance of a host of residents? Are not the cries of our costermonger classes given out distinctly in recitative? And how many a drowsy bachelor and crabbed old maid loudly lament the peculiar taste and love for the sound of, as they think,

> " Sweet bells, jangled, out of tune, and harsh,"—

a taste inherent amongst all classes of their countrymen, and invariably exhibited on particularly festive occasions. Shall it then be asserted that ours—the first of nations—is unmusical ? But it may be said, that the taste of the present time goes no great way towards establishing us in the honour for which we contend, and that the distinguishing features of a people must be stamped by the hand of ages. " Let us survey, then, the days which have been of old, and see whether these, so fraught with agreeable and romantic associations, come to the mind connected with aught of the love and charm of song. Let us return to the years when

> ' Fingal lived and Ossian sung ; '

and whose imagination does not revel here in the harpings of those ancient fathers of song—the bards ? Do we not see them, ' in our mind's eye,' leading their countrymen forth to battle ? Do we not hear the tender melodies wherewith they soothed the excited spirits of the ardent combatants, and induced such as were bent on destruction to return in peace and tranquillity to their homes? Who views them not at a later period pre-eminent in the households of our ancient princes, nobility, and gentry,

> ' High placed in hall,'

and forming a striking feature in the rude sports and solemnities of the times ? And who that remembers how bards, minstrels, and troubadours were courted and caressed of old, what vast privileges, immunities, and liberties were granted them, can doubt what has been the taste of the English nation from the earliest of times ? "

" In the Middle Ages," says Strutt, " the courts of princes and the residences of the opulent were crowded with minstrels ; and such large sums were expended for their maintenance, that the public treasuries were often drained." He states also elsewhere the esteem in which music was held during the sixteenth and seventeenth centuries, and ascribes the origin of three places of public resort—Vauxhall, Ranelagh, and Sadler's Wells—to the " music clubs or private meetings for the practice of music," in which the opulent and the fashionable greatly delighted at that period. The curious reader may, indeed, be referred to Strutt's* most interesting sketch of the music of England, both as a matter of amusement, and as affording a decisive proof of the high estimation in which the science and its professors, of all descriptions, had been held by the English nation of every rank and in every age. Indeed, the present taste or fashion for music, call it what we may, seems to be rather a revival of former love than the commencement of a novel passion.

" Whence, then, arises the idea that we are not a musical people? It may perhaps have its origin in the fact of our having fewer national melodies than almost any other nation on the face of the globe. Do we not hear daily of the Scotch, the Irish, and especially the Welsh—of the French, the Italian, the Spanish, the American, and even ' nigger '—melodies? But where are we to look for the English? The fact is, that,

---

* See Strutt's *Sports and Pastimes,* b. iii. c. iii., b. iv. c. i., for a brief account of the bards, gleemen, joculators, jongleurs, trouvers, minstrauls, &c., of old, down to the blind harpers, fiddlers, pandean pipers, and ballad-singers of the present day, now the only remnants of the olden itinerants above named.

of all the world, we exhibit perhaps the most curious picture of pride and discontent.   Absent from his country, an Englishman sees united in her all beauty and perfection, thinks of her with enthusiasm, and speaks of her as the mistress of his soul. Returned, the scene is totally changed: every country he has visited has something to recommend it above his own.   English manners, dress, dancing, cookery, are not to be endured after the French; nor may English music be listened to, or our fine arts and natural scenery be viewed with common complacency, after those of Italy and Switzerland.   It is to this dissatisfied spirit that we owe our fashions, ever varying and ever drawn from all but home resources.   And that this evil extends to our music and our theatrical representations who can doubt that beholds the ·airs of Italy and Germany, and the dramas of France, in a manner naturalised amongst us ?   The higher classes receive them first"—not perhaps so much as heretofore, but still to a considerable extent; whilst the middle and " the lower quickly imbibe them from the same spirit of adoption which actuates their superiors in rank and fortune in matters of amusement and taste; and we may hear hummed and whistled in our streets by the most illiterate those airs which have delighted us at the theatre or music-hall, or ravished our very senses in the opera-house."

But it may also be remarked, that Scotch, Irish, and American —especially "nigger"—melodies supersede the English; whilst the Welsh—those strongly marked and delicate melodies—seem to be no great favourites with the commonalty; for which one probable reason may be assigned—that they are chiefly in the minor mode, and therefore highly unpalatable to an uncultivated taste.

Why, then, are not English melodies taken under the protection of rank and genius? One cause has been assigned, as existing perhaps in that desire for change, that anxiety for novelty, and that spirit of adoption, and perchance, as a commercial people, that pleasure received from every new importation so prevalent amongst us; but a second and no less efficient one arises from the painful associations they bring to the elegant and refined mind. Many an exquisite English melody is banished without recall from what is called genteel society because of the senseless verbal accompaniment to which it has been deemed necessary to annex it; so that not even the most skilful and original composers could wholly obliterate therein every trace of its primal and unmitigated vulgarity. Thus much, then, for the utter fallacy, so constantly paraded, of decrying our national possession, no less than our taste and facility of musical creation.

Before, however, it is ventured to record any "Recollections" of the progress of music during so recent a period as the last fifty years, it is perhaps scarcely necessary to enter upon an elaborate elucidation of earlier times than those before the writer saw the light. Nevertheless, previously to the particulars of such "Recollections" being entered upon, a brief *résumé* of the rise and progress of music in England may perhaps be pardoned.

Before the monk Augustine, A.D. 596, was sent by Gregory, surnamed the Great, to undertake the conversion of our forefathers, there exists no clear, satisfactory, or reliable authority as to the prevalence of music in this country according to the strictest requirements of rule and method. Wild and simple melodies may have existed; for then, as now, those ignorant of everything else than sound doubtless could "hum a tune," and bring it into something like shape and substance, even as they "might whistle" it, "for want of thought." Augustine and his attendant monks undoubtedly brought with them as much of the Gregorian musical system as had then been developed by their great master and authority ere they left Rome, to settle amongst a people upon the designation of whose children, accidentally met with in the slave-market, he had played—or rather, as we should say, punned—by turning *Angli* into *Angeli.* In setting up the platform of the church which these earnest-minded men had come over to a waste and barbarous island to establish, it is not likely that they omitted to use every legitimate resource for reaching the minds of hearers, by no means less impressionable than those of other nations with whom they had hitherto been better acquainted. As intercourse was kept up between England and Rome, and as success, after the first few years of opposition, attended upon the efforts to Christianise first the king and nobles, and then the rude kerns who were their vassals and dependents, information would naturally be transmitted concerning the progress music was making at the latter place, no less than instruction as to the increasing use of form, so as to make even the rude progressions of the Gregorian tones a more and more attractive means of influence. Whether, however, even in progressive years the music of the church advanced or not, it is not easy to discover; but to all intents and purposes it skilfully extended very little, if at all, beyond the precincts of the sanctuary, until the Reformation cleared off the long oppressive mists of superstition and error, and opened the path for the growth of intellect, the march of mind, and the advance of civil and religious freedom. From that time to the present, the way is plain for ascertaining what music did among our forefathers ; and the facts are patent, that, like every other means of mental education and improvement, it then took that start from which the achievements of the nineteenth century may positively be dated. In what condition Thomas Tallis, the father of the church-music of the Reformation period, found it, may be discerned from the anthem, "O Lord, the Maker of all things," a composition generally attributed to Henry VIII., which, as a youthful exercise, conclusively indicates that had that king been called on to follow an evidently natural bent, he would have been as great therein as he certainly was, according to modern illustration, as a king.*

Whilst, however, the music of the church held its ground as "the mother and mistress" of sound, it also produced a daughter, as it were, by means of the stage. And no long time transpired before both the one and the other proceeded, as it were, *pari passu*, increasing in force and vigour, and improving in style and method, till at length the greatest musical genius of his times, Henry Purcell—who died at the early age of thirty-seven, A.D. 1695—so welded the two together, that it was impossible to discern which were the more excellent.

From that time to the settlement of GEORGE FREDERICK HANDEL in England, the science of music ebbed and flowed, making no rapid progress, and by no means emulating the stride which Henry Purcell had caused it to make, and with whose works it, to all intents and purposes, had culminated. Although not strictly speaking an English composer, Handel from that time to the present has always—and most deservedly —remained the first and most continual object of English ad-

---

* See Froude's *Hist. of England*, vols. i. ii.

miration. "He not only laid the foundation," says an eminent professor and writer so long ago as fifty years before our "Recollections" are to date;* "but he lived long enough to complete it. So that Handel's music may with justness be called English music, and every musician the son of Handel; for whatever delicacies and improvements have been made by them, they are all owing to, and took their rise from, a perusal of his works. What had we to boast of before he settled in England and new modelled music? Nothing but some good church music. He joined the fulness and majesty of the German music, the delicacy and elegance of the Italian, to the solidity of the English, constituting in the end a style of magnificence superior to any other nation." The reasons why this was so are to every sound and "well-built" musician obvious.

"Handel was a composer of great majesty and strength; even his elegancies partake of sublimity. His style is great, and yet is simple in the degree which most contributes to such an end. From a singer he requires more legitimate and genuine expression than any other master. In the hands of mere ordinary or common-place executants his best efforts will be heavy, and perhaps fatiguing; but when heard from those who are alive to their subject"—such as were some of those to whom our earliest "Recollections" will constantly refer—"they awaken the noblest and best feelings of humanity. They produce a reverential awe for the power they celebrate, while they elevate the soul into adoration and thanksgiving." Accompanied by such sensations, this dignified simplicity of manner, and that pure elocution that "spoke so sweetly and so well," revive the finest accordance of sentiment and sound, combined

* Potter, on Music, &c.

with emotions of the sublime, with which not unfrequently even a certain kind of terror is mixed. " When, for example, we hear and feel such specimens of elevated piety and wondrous grandeur as ' I know that my Redeemer liveth,' ' The trumpet shall sound,' or any specimen of a similar cast, ideas of death, of resurrection, and of judgment fill the mind, which cannot dwell upon such subjects without the strongest emotion. The sensation produced is too sublime and too awful; and when it has passed away, we are not solicitous to recall it, except on certain solemn occasions. Such are the genuine effects of Handel's glorious sacred strains. And even in his lighter compositions something of the same grandeur is always prevalent. In his *Acis and Galatea,* in despite of music so exquisitely graceful, beautiful, descriptive, original, and impassioned, the mind is strained beyond its ordinary tension; so that the hearers are not so much affected by the tenderness of the lovers, in the same manner and in the same degree, as they are by the amatory productions of other masters. In the story itself of that work, love is mingled with apprehension, and pathos with ideas of the bulk, the ferocity, the strength, the hideous form, and the rage of Polyphemus,—grand features, which serve to give the mind a contrary determination, and prevent it from sinking into that delicious languor which it once was, but is now no more, the sovereign art of the Italian school to produce."

Thus Handel may be said to have effaced all recollection, except amongst such as are acquainted with, or versed in the practice and performance of, the works of such earlier English composers as Purcell, Croft, Blow, Green, and Boyce, who, although all eminent and high in the estimation of sound taste, are now but seldom heard beyond the cathedral minster. Their style it has become the fashion to consider obsolete and tedious, simply because it is deficient in the rapidly progressive improvements and adornments of modern art and taste ; which had been much the same even with Handel himself, giant as he was in strength compared with others, had not Mozart given an impulse, by his unrivalled wind-instrumentation, to the *Messiah*, which in our immediate times has been quite as successfully imitated by "the greatest *chef-d'orchestre* of the world," Sir Michael Costa. Such accompaniments have blended and incorporated with the happiest success the sweetness, the tenderness, and the variety of Italian illustration with the strong and natural character of the original score, which Handel himself could not possibly have equally adorned, although it was his custom, by presiding at the organ, to fill up the harmonies according to his taste and tact, in the absence of those appliances which are now available by means of improved wind-instrumentation.

But if the modern English school of music owes and must attribute such advantages as these to the great naturalised composer of the last century, it ought not to be lost sight of, that another source of progress has been, perhaps in less degree, derived from the works of two other masters of German birth and education—Haydn and Mozart, and especially the former. These certainly take rank among the highest order of genius; and so truly do their notions of expression accord with what is real and beautiful, that it may be asserted without fear of contradiction, that no composers have treated the illustration or the elucidation of most peculiar subjects with similar eminent propriety. No Englishman could desire or conceive a more exquisite consent between sound and sense than is to be met with in the works of each of these rightly acknowledged masters The *Creation* of Haydn certainly contains very many singular imitations, not a few of which, if one is inclined to be hypercritical, must be said to be as weak as they are fanciful,—take, for example, the attempt to represent the plungings of the whale in the *terzetto* of the second part of the *Creation*, "How beautiful appear,"—and, although by no means to be compared for simplicity, solemnity, and grandeur with either the *Messiah*, or the *Israel in Egypt* of Handel,—works which are addressed to a totally different class of thoughts and perceptions,—it is nevertheless full of beauty, tenderness, and grace, and has tended to form the style of many of our own writers at the beginning of the present century, as the later works of Mendelssohn have furnished our more modern *alumni* with ideas so closely similar as to cause the accusation of positive plagiarism to be as rife as it is applicable. After all, however, it is most unfair to attempt to draw a parallel between Handel and Haydn. All that can be advantageously done is to contrast them, inasmuch as in works, no less than in style, they are as totally opposite as they are distinct, and, therefore, ought never to be treated as objects of comparison. It has been not inappropriately said, that "their beauties are as distinct and different as the poetry of *Paradise Lost* and the *Seasons*, to which, in point of style, they bear some analogy. The *Creation* of Haydn, then, if it seldom rises into magnificence, is full of elegance and invention, and does not contain an uninteresting melody," even although there be a certain amount of weakness or commonplace about it ; as, for instance, in the opening of the chorus, "The heavens are telling," of which the late Dr. Crotch, with more accuracy than good taste, said, that "it began at the Opera House and ended at Vauxhall." "Joy and gratitude, benevolence and love, are expressed with as much purity and ecstasy in the *Creation* as are the sublime emotions which inspire all the hopes and terrors of religion—all 'the blessing and honour, glory and power,' that are assigned to the great Creator and Preserver of mankind in the *Messiah*."

In spite, however, of the manifest advantages which the English school of music derived from the genius of Handel, the elegance of Haydn, the versatility of Mozart, and in our own time from the fancy of Mendelssohn, the present race of composers is certainly not to be compared with our predecessors, even within the "Recollections of the last fifty years." And yet musical taste has grown in the largest proportions, in spite and in defiance of this fact; whilst musical accomplishments amongst the masses have taken a stride which has not been equalled in any other country of the world—not even in Germany itself.

Whilst, however, it will be seen, as the "Recollections of the last fifty years" are unravelled, that composers and vocalists—the same may not be said of instrumentalists—were far in advance of those at present before the public, it is a fact neither to be gainsaid nor denied, that to the works of the masters whom we have named England owes its present musical position. Where fifty years ago executants could be numbered scarcely by tens, they may now be computed by thousands. Nor does the metropolis alone supply the best-instructed musicians of the day. Time was when the oratorios of Handel and Haydn could not be given in any of the country cities or provincial towns, not even in the "grand"—as they were called—"triennial meetings of Birmingham, York, and Norwich," without aid being had from the London Ancient Concerts, the Lenten oratorios held in Covent Garden and Drury Lane Theatres and the Opera House, for leading "the attack," and keeping the local choristers together in the exponency of choral effects, that even then were but weak, rough, and imperfect in execution. Such is no longer the case. But very few London engagements are now made for the singing of choruses in the country, inasmuch as the body of local vocalists consists chiefly of members of well-trained Choral Societies, the members of which begin their practice immediately a festival terminates, and never cease to keep up their proficiency by such means, so as to be as ready three years hence as they are to-day. Massive, grand, and also refined as are the great choral effects of the performances of the Sacred Harmonic Society—thanks to the energy, the skill, and the precision of its inimitable conductor—it is an undoubted fact that in the provinces, especially in Lancashire, Yorkshire, and the Midland Counties, no less than at Norwich, those effects are rivalled. The test of this assertion has several times been offered at the great Handel Festivals within the Crystal Palace, where the various provincial Societies act in combination with the metropolitan Handel choir, and show as much skill in reading, steadiness in interpretation, and as nice an observance of "light and shade," as are ever attainable at Exeter Hall; whilst in addition to such perfection there is a freshness about the voices —especially the female voices—which is not, and we believe cannot be, heard at any time in London. Such excellence has been attained and kept up, simply because the works of the great instructors and improvers of the English school of music are constantly studied and interpreted with unremitting zeal and earnestness, the appreciation of their value and excellence being "increased by what it feeds upon."

Whilst, however, in choral and instrumental effects such excellence has been attained, it is painful to have to state that the qualities of vocal principals, as solo singers are called, are a thing wholly of the past. The old race has passed away, it is to be feared, for ever, unless the rising members of the profession be induced —we might say, be driven—to resort to the same means which made their predecessors appear like giants in the presence of the present race of musical pigmies—patient study and application not only in the matter of vocal execution, but in that of theory and sight-singing. The present race of English public vocalists—and of foreign also—with but one or two rare and singular exceptions, is like fruit, which might, sooner or later, have become ripe and luscious had it been permitted to hang until it was fit to be gathered, but which, having been plucked much too soon, is crude and sour, and never comes to perfection ; for, in plain terms, singers, both male and female—and especially the latter —nowadays rush before the public ere their style is formed, their voices settled, or their education completed. As for learning the scales so as to distinguish each tone and half-tone as distinctly as if given out by the clarionet, the flute, or the oboe, as we have heard them, and as by marked instances it will be specified, no such result, we fear, is again to be expected. Such scale passages are heard in perfection only on the rarest occasions, and even then are, unhappily, generally so little appreciated by the public, in spite of the musical progress of the times, that it has come to be believed both by modern teachers and pupils to be an effect "more honoured in the breach than in the observance." In their place and room a mischievous and miserable system of tremulousness is substituted, as a mere meretricious attempt at producing feeling, the only apt explanation of which is to be found in the words of the satirist—

> " And seizing on innocent little B flat,
> She shook it like terrier shaking a rat."

All nature, feeling, sentiment, style, and method are thus discarded ; whilst purity of tone is sacrificed for mere sensational screaming ; a "final close," contrary to all rules of rhythm or of art, being substituted for the composer's intention ; and a vulgar shout—as if from lungs of forty-horse steam-engine power—adopted merely to "split the ears of the groundlings," and to obtain the demand of an uproarious encore, whether that equivocal compliment is intended to be acknowledged or not.

Under such circumstances as these, patent at every Festival, manifested in every concert-room, everywhere persisted in with the utmost obstinacy and determination, in defiance of good taste, in ridicule of earnest entreaty, and in the teeth of that most rare quality, honest criticism—it may be taken by not a few to be a truism, that "England is not a musical nation." Yet, whilst there are " Recollections " to be unfolded which all point in a contrary direction, and there are facts constantly being brought out, both in the provinces and in London, in the opposite direction, testifying to the growth of progress in defiance of " heavy blows and great discouragement," hope is perchance but deferred that the best effects and specimens of the olden times may be restored, so that we may " enjoy our own again," in the future excellence of individual principal singers, as well as in the present competency of instrumentalists on the one hand, and choral executants on the other. That immediate improvement is to be expected is not likely ; for this is indeed true for the present, no less than for all time— that "whoever would reform a nation, supposing a bad taste to prevail in it, will not accomplish his purpose by going directly against the stream of its prejudices. Men's minds must be formed to receive what is new in them. Reformation is a work of time. A national taste, however wrong it may be, cannot be totally changed at once, and we must yield a little to the prepossession that has taken hold of the mind. We may then bring people to adopt what would offend them, if endea- voured to be introduced by violence."

CHAPTER I.

1817-1820.

THE preceding "introductory remarks" upon this subject will have, in a great measure, intimated the nature of the musical school in which I was nurtured. From the earliest period to which my memory dates back, I was thrown in contact with musicians, both professional and amateur. So soon also as my little fingers could be made to move, I was put down to a piano-forte ; and as if not enough of torture were inflicted upon a child of between four and five years of age by the painful drudgery of having to play scale passages hour by the hour together, their tips were made as sore as they well could be and cramped to form the tones—no, that would have been an impossibility, but something as much unlike them as it is possible to conceive—of a viola, between which and my small self there was a daily struggle of some hour and a half's duration which should have the mastery—whether I should beat that goodly-sized fiddle, or it should beat me. This struggle did not continue very long—scarcely, I should say, more than three or four months—because of my progress with the latter instrument being much smaller than my improvement on the former. Besides, unhappy child that I was, I was beginning to give indications of a voice, which unwittingly I had made known by frequently piping out any popular tune my ear had caught up; and *that* was therefore to be cultivated, that I might become, so far as possible, a proficient " boy soprano." My father had been a chorister himself of the cathedral church of ——, and had obtained in his youth a large amount of musical instruction from a former organist—one of the most competent pupils of the Dr. Hayes' (of Oxford) school; and at the time I can first remember to have heard it, possessed a counter-tenor voice, the quality of which more nearly resembled that of Mario than of any other male singer I have since listened to. He was my first master, and a stern and severe one indeed he was; for not only did he insist upon the constant practice of my fingers upon the pianoforte keys, but upon vocal scale and division passages, with the utmost pertinacity, the remembrance of which calls up many a sad moment of childish grief and lamentation. That I hated the drudgery was but natural; yet it had its pleasant side, because it gave me the means of becoming acquainted with musicians—professional and amateur—very early indeed in my career, to listen to whose performances, either vocal or instrumental, which even then I greatly enjoyed, was the offered and the granted reward of perseverance. The early training to which I was subjected might have disgusted many another child, and driven him in after-time to have detested and abhorred everything musical, whatever might have been its nature or its character. That it had not this effect upon a mind not a little sensitive, and somewhat precocious, I can attribute only to the praise I continually obtained from my father's friends; to the predictions—which I could not fail to overhear—that I should be an excellent pianist, if not altogether so satisfactory a singer; and, above all, to the delight I even thus early took in listening to the performance of Corelli's trios, Haydn's earlier symphonies, interspersed with one or two of the less difficult of those of Mozart, which were practised weekly by amateurs in a private concert-room, with two first and second violins, one viola, one violoncello, and a double bass—the violoncello being scraped by an ambitious plasterer, with such an absence of tone and taste as would have made dear old Bob Lindley's hair stand on end; and the double bass rasped at a frightful rate by an eccentric clergyman, with so small an idea of the nature of a *nuance*, that it would have made Dragonetti swear, "*She!* dirty blackguard!"* The wind instruments were of the like proportion as to number and quality, save as to one exception, the oboe—which was played by a brother of the eccentric contre-basso, with a tone and execution not even surpassed in much later days by a Barret or a Nicholson. To these rehearsals were now and then added public performances, to which London *artistes* lent their aid, and who indicated what was the state of music in the great metropolis, to reach which it then took a day and a night, instead of, as now, but a few hours. At my father's house many of these *artistes* were welcome guests; and well do I remember—can I ever forget it?—the first impressions I received of what really dramatic singing consists. I could not have been more than six years of age—perhaps a month or two less—when Bartleman spent an evening under my father's roof —an event which is imprinted upon my mind with as much intensity as my having been taken about a month previously to the dark and dingy little theatre of my native town, redolent with the sickening smell of oil and orange-peel, to witness Miss

---

* This was a well-known expression of Dragonetti concerning any one with whom he thought he had cause to be offended.

O'Neil's personation of Belvidera in Otway's *Venice Preserved;* the remembrances of which would have been assisted by my having been supported in my father's arms through the crush into the pit—it was in that part of the house where the *savans,* in those days, "most did congregate"—and by his having had his coat-tails torn off, were not the sound of that actress's bell-like voice still ringing in my ears, as she called Jaffier twice before making her *entrée ;* and did I not also continue to see, "in my mind's eye," her last great mad scene, in which every one of the other performers upon the stage stood weeping like children, wholly forgetful of their business.

Well, I say, when about six years old I heard Bartleman—a little man, of no very prepossessing appearance, neatly dressed, somewhat stiff and formal in his manner, and not at all indisposed, in spite of his proverbial ill-health, to enjoy a glass or two of sound old fruity port. Trained under Dr. Cooke, in the choirs of Westminster Abbey and the Chapel Royal, where so many of our best musicians in former days obtained their education, this remarkable baritone not only possessed the utmost purity and roundness of tone, but manifested an amount of feeling in his interpretation of the older masters which I believe, without desiring to be a *laudator temporis acti,* has never since been rivalled, not even by Santley, who, so far as I can remember, more resembles him in point of style and finished execution than any singer of this class I have ever listened to between 1817 and 1872. Of this remarkable man it was said by one of the most competent and judicious critics that ever wrote,* that he possessed "a fancy lively to an extreme degree,"

---

* Mr. Richard Mackenzie Bacon, the proprietor and editor of the *Quarterly Musical Magazine and Review,* vol. i. pp. 326-7.

which, from his career having commenced in the church, "there received a chastening and a temperance which had been the more important, inasmuch as his natural vivacity must have always exposed him to the strong temptations by which the keen sense of dramatic effect, visible in everything he did, proved him to be assailable. His execution of the song of Polypheme (Handel's *Acis and Galatea*), "O, ruddier than the cherry," which before his time had always been held to be a rude, heavy, and unmanageable composition, was truly theatrical, yet equally just. It was really gigantic. . . . To the last movement of Pergolesi's exquisitely-pathetic air, set to the words, 'O Lord, have mercy upon me,' he also imparted the exact measure of animation which the subject required and would bear." It was this latter song which I heard him sing at my father's house, standing as it were upon tiptoe, as was his wont, to give height to a somewhat diminutive stature, entrancing the ear with the pious fervour of the entreaty of the first *motivo* of that song, and elevating the spirit by the enthusiastic burst of joyous assurance in the second, "But my hope hath been in Thee." I was caught up weeping by my mother at the close of this song, and hurried away by her to bed, where I sobbed myself to sleep. No marvel that the impression of that night has never been obliterated. I never saw or heard Bartleman afterwards.

From the circumstance of my being located in a cathedral town at the beginning of my career, I naturally heard much more of church than of secular music. ·Indeed, I should have known little or nothing of the latter, had I not been taken up to London, after hearing Bartleman, with a view to my being placed in Westminster Abbey, St. Paul's or the Chapel Royal, for musical training, and with a view to my future means of livelihood. From some cause or other, which I never heard distinctly explained, the idea of my being permanently placed in one or other of those great musical schools fell through; and, much to my own, as well as to the gratification of my family, I was taken back considerably wearied and very much bewildered with all I had heard and seen; for my father having put up at a small lodging in the immediate vicinity of Cockspur Street— not a stone of which now remains—I had to accompany him wherever he went; and on not a few evenings—our stay did not exceed a fortnight—I was roused up from a sound sleep, stowed away in a hackney-coach, wherein I again slept, in spite of an amount of indescribable alarm at the seven- or eight-caped topcoats of sundry jarvies, till I was taken out more dead than alive, and put to bed, heartily glad to rest therein, and earnestly hoping, if not praying, that I might soon be back again in old ——, never again to leave it. Of all the music I heard at the Abbey, St. Paul's, and the Chapel Royal—at the latter a shilling was then paid to enter, and another shilling for a most uncomfortable seat—in the daytime, and at concerts at night, I have but the most indifferent reminiscences. I remember well that I was taken to the Catch and Glee Clubs, then, as now, held at the Freemasons' Tavern; but I know nothing more about what was said or sung there, or anything else, than that some of the young chorister-boys who assisted at the latter laughed at my strange provincial dress and my stranger dialect; plagued me mightily by pulling my ears, twitching my hair, and kicking my unoffending shins; threatening all the while that if I dared to make a noise, I should be taken up into the dark gallery at the end of the room, and left there for ever and ever. I would as soon have thought of going to be hanged as to have called out to my father in my trouble, for he belonged to the severe school of the times, and believed that Solomon was not so far wrong, as we of the present time believe him to have been, when he wrote and talked about " sparing the rod and spoiling the child." There is one event, however, which will never be obliterated from my memory—the hearing of *Don Giovanni* at the King's Theatre, whither I was taken on an early evening after my arrival in London. Of the cast of that opera the world has heard much ever since; and I doubt, so far as principals are concerned, whether it has at any time been given in England with a more perfect *ensemble*—Camporese, Fodor, Ambrogetti, Angrisani, Begrez, and Naldi—the influence of whose respective qualities was well-nigh matchless.

The bewilderment and excitement of a mere child's introduction into such a house as the King's Theatre may be imagined. It literally took away my breath, and " brought my heart," as the saying is, " into my mouth." Accustomed as I had been to be taken occasionally to our provincial theatre, and naturally expecting nothing more exciting or grand, I was literally overwhelmed. It happened occasionally to be a brilliant occasion in more respects than one—from what cause I have no remembrance, any more than I have of the date of this, to me, ever memorable night— the ladies being elegantly dressed in court costume, as I was told they were, in which feathers and diamonds largely predominated. I was also much puzzled why, between the acts, in an open space between the seats, gentlemen strolled up and down, talking loudly to one another and to the members of the orchestra, their conversation being interspersed with certain strong expletives, of which I had already gained some understanding. This was then the fashion both in town and country —and an abominable fashion it was, one which, I regret to say, young as I was, I had not been slow to imitate. But to the performance of *Don Giovanni;* and of this my "Recollections" are more intensely vivid than they are of its more recent presentations under Sir Michael Costa's admirable direction, before he was compelled to leave the Royal Italian Opera, and the management of that house learned, doubtlessly most unwillingly, although it ought not to have been unexpectedly, that it lost its chief prop and mainstay with that *maestro's* departure.† Of Fodor, I can say but little, since she left no impression upon my mind.* Of Camporese I have the liveliest recollection, most probably on account of my having become personally known to her shortly afterwards, as I shall presently relate. This accomplished lady, who was of good birth and parentage, was the wife of Signor Giustiniani, a gentleman also of family and respectability. She had been principal chamber-singer at the court of Napoleon Bonaparte, and had never appeared as an actress until she made her *début* at the King's Theatre in Cimarosa's now wholly forgotten opera, *Penelope.* Although never a great actress, she was perhaps, at the time of her appearance,

* The Earl of Mount Edgcumbe, a noted musical connoisseur of his day, says of this "prima donna" in his *Musical Reminiscences* (ed. 1828) : "It is true Fodor was an improvement upon Sessi, but she never greatly pleased me. Her voice had sweetness, but she injured and confined it by not opening her mouth, and singing through her teeth. Her style was not truly Italian, nor could it be expected, for she was a Russian married to a Frenchman, had lived much in Paris, and never been in Italy. . . . . Yet she was much liked by many, and became almost a favourite after her performance of Zerlina in *Don Giovanni*, which opera was brought out for the first time in the second year of her engagement " (pp. 134-5).

the most genuine Italian singer the Opera had heard for several
years, " her superiority having consisted in her style, or rather
in the sensibility she manifested, the delicacy in which she
modified and refined, and in the force and truth with which she
conveyed sentiment and passion."* It was impossible not to
have been struck by the grace and elegance of this *prima
donna's* manner and deportment, any more than it was to be
uninfluenced by Ambrogetti's personation of the profligate
Spanish Don; of which character, with the exception of Garcia
—even excluding Tamburini—there has not since been such a
representative either at home or abroad. In person this remarkable Italian was tall and well made, and although, at the
time I am referring to, he was no longer in his *premier jeunesse,* and his voice was decidedly on the wane, he was to all
intents and purposes the very *beau-idéal* of the gentleman,
whatever might be the characteristics of the notorious *roué*
whom he had to represent.† Whilst Ambrogetti failed as a
singer, and relied upon his acting for his fame, Angrisani was
just the reverse; for he possessed a fine and powerful bass

* The Earl of Mount Edgcumbe says, " Of Camporesi's voice and manner of
singing, . . . the former, if not of the very finest quality, is extremely
agreeable, of sufficient power and compass, and capable of considerable ability;
and of the latter, that it is regulated by good taste, and is full of feeling and
expression " (pp. 140-1).

† Of Ambrogetti the same nobleman's opinion is worth recording, especially
as it confirms my own early impressions. " He was an excellent actor, with a
natural vein of humour peculiarly his own; but he was sometimes put into
characters unsuited to his turn, to his want of voice, and deficiency as a singer,
Yet he acted extremely well, and in a manner too horribly true to nature, the
part of the mad father in Paer's beautiful opera of *Agnese,* taken from Mrs.
Opie's tale of the *Father and Daughter* " (pp. 135-6). I recollect distinctly
having heard Mrs. Opie herself, as well as the late Gresham professor of music,
Mr. Edward Taylor, confirm this opinion.

voice, resembling a rich and full diapason in tone, in combination with a chaste and refined method. Naldi also was certainly one of the most consummate buffo-singers to be remembered in England before the appearance of de Begnis, Lablache, and Ronconi. The amusement he afforded me—I suspect, for I cannot tell at this distance of time that it was so—in the celebrated "Madamina" will never be forgotten. He was said, however, by those most competent to speak advisedly of his qualities, to have been defective in his intonation, which was nasal, and that he had a persistent tendency to break the *tempo* of everything he sang, lagging behind with a most painful persistency. Of Begrez's singing "Il mio tesoro" it would be impossible to be forgetful. It was, to my juvenile mind, one of the greatest charms of that eventful night's influence and enjoyment. His voice was then at its best. Although he was a Belgian by birth, he had thoroughly succeeded in mastering the true Italian method—one of those precious possessions, except in a few rare instances, now wholly lost, and in all human probability never to be regained. About the time to which I am referring, this *artiste* was said "to form, produce, and sustain his voice in a manner superior to any other tenor in London, whilst his tone was at the same time more pure and perfect." It is doubtful, however, whether he can be said to have ever reached a higher position than would now be called "tip-top mediocrity."

Of the orchestra of that period, as of the vocalists, not one survives. The leader, or *chef d'attaque*, was Weichsl; the principal second violin, Cotton Reeve; the viola in chief, R. Ashley; whilst Bob Lindley and Dragonetti were at the first-violoncello and double-bass desk. The principal oboe was Griesbach, who, with Mrs. Billington and Sir George Smart, settled what is called the Philharmonic orchestral pitch—a medium tone between that of Handel's tuning-fork and the present recognised Paris Conservatoire diapason. Willman was the first clarionet; Holmes and Tully, the bassoons; while the horns were in the hands of the brothers Petrides—two of the quaintest beings that ever entered an orchestra, and who, in the interval of a bar or two's rest, amused themselves by kicking each other's shins, since they could not quarrel more uproariously. This was a strong phalanx of instrumental talent for the period, which has been very little improved upon, in individual instances, in even more recent times.

My brief and exciting visit to London had removed whatever amount of distaste I had previously begun to feel for the drudgery to which I had had to submit for some time before that first remarkable event of my life ; and no young peacock was ever more proud in displaying his variegated tail than I was in relating to my schoolfellows—I fear with some amount of exaggeration—what I had seen and heard in the great metropolis. It was then so unusual an event in a mere boy's life to go so far from home—indeed, children of an older growth scarcely ever omitted to make their wills before doing so—that I was looked upon by those of my own age, and by many older, as something far beyond the ordinary race of mortals ; and most assuredly I was at no small pains to " improve the occasion." A time was, however, at hand when I had to begin to learn that " all is not gold that glitters "—or, in other words, that, however gratifying to the sense and pleasant to the ear it might be to listen to a cathedral service, to " assist " at an evening concert as a hearer, or to have been present in London at so grand an operatic performance as that of *Don Giovanni,* the training for taking a thoroughly practical position in either the one or the other is by no means attended with the same pleasurable associations. The intention of my being entered as a chorister in one of the London cathedral schools having failed, I was very soon after my return admitted into the cathedral choir of my native town; and from that moment my sorrows, which were to last for six long years, may be said to have begun. Having received, as I have said, some musical instruction previously to this time, I might have been relieved from a repetition of its first elements. These, however, I had to go over again, and with all the more severity, because my new master—the organist, and musical teacher of the choristers —was somewhat jealous of any one but himself being supposed to be competent to impart instruction. Under the superintendence of that master I must confess to have gone with no very pleasurable feelings. He, like many other of the town's musical celebrities—and there were some real celebrities in that place, amongst whom he was himself admitted merely upon sufferance, inasmuch as he had succeeded to his office, as it were, by what is vulgarly termed "a fluke"—was a frequent visitor at my home, and had been often and often at the pains to let me see and feel that he disliked me; for not only had he pinched my ears whenever he could do so by stealth, but he was excessively fond of saying to my parents and others in my hearing, that "little pitchers had wide ears"—which, young as I was, I construed as an insult as offensive as it was intentional. This individual was so strange a compound of conceit and cleverness, that from a description of him and of his peculiarities I cannot possibly refrain. At the time when I came under his immediate superintendence and tuition he was about twenty-

five years of age, and had not long emerged from his apprentice-
ship with the organist, whom he most unexpectedly succeeded,
that gentleman having but a few years previously followed his
father to the grave—one of the most competent musicians and
genial men that ever lived, as I always heard those say who
knew him best. This young and fortunate choir-master had
himself been a member of the cathedral as a boy, and was remarkable for a very fine voice; but upon its breaking, and his
having no resources, he sought and obtained employment from
my own father—which in itself was not conducive to there
being anything in common between us. After this he became
a member of the theatrical company which "went the ——
circuit"—a step that so greatly annoyed the cathedral authorities, that the then organist took him into his house gratui-
tously, and trained him, so that he might have, as was thought,
a more respectable means of livelihood. Independently, however, of my dislike to this individual, his personal appearance
was by no means prepossessing. Scrupulously neat in his dress,
and precise and formal in his manners, there was yet something
about him which caused a general dislike to prevail amongst his
boy pupils; whilst, somehow or other, he always managed to
win the good opinion of those of the softer sex who employed
him as their instructor. By a kind of innate perception, the
elder choristers, at the time of my joining them, had come to
the conclusion that he was by no means so competent a musician as he wished to be esteemed; indeed, one or two of those
whose term of service had nearly expired openly set him at
defiance, and successfully resisted a novel system of tuition
which deprived them of the little time permitted for recreation,
and kept them hard at practice not unfrequently until a very

late hour of the night, and long after the other labours of the day had terminated. Up to the time of his appointment the excellence of the —— choir—and it was one of the very best in the whole kingdom—consisted in the competency of its senior members. Not only did the lay vicars thoroughly understand their work—for as men and boys they had been well trained by an eminent predecessor, with whom this newly-appointed organist had never been acquainted—but the minor canons, with only one exception, were also competent to, and constantly did, take their share in the daily services, not only in chanting the prayers, but in singing their respective parts in the concerted music of *Te Deums, Jubilates, Magnificats, Nunc dimittis*, Creeds, Anthems, &c. This was now, however, to be broken down; and the means used for that end were, first, the selection of the best boy voices that could be met with in the town, and then by an entirely modern method of training, which would sooner or later—as it effectually did—supersede the necessity of reliance upon the full choir for musical effects. Speedily did I encounter all the annoyance of such an innovation, against which my spirit revolted.

It was not sufficient, however, that I had to endure this kind of drudgery day after day, but the weight of my bondage was increased by my being placed under my tormentor as a private pupil for the pianoforte. Those were the days of flogging—and to excess—and I had indeed my full, if not more than my full, share of incessant castigation. To such an extent indeed was this kind of punishment carried towards us all, that the sacred building itself was not free from its execution; until, on one occasion, one of our number, a lad of considerable determination, refused to take the beating with which he was threatened, and reminded the would-be inflictor where he then was, and that it was only in a proper place that he would submit to such an indignity, and even then that he would appeal to the prebendary in residence for redress. As might have been anticipated, that chorister was never flogged again either in church or school; but he was ever afterwards, so long as he remained, neglected, and, so far as music was concerned, learned nothing.

In a very short time the knowledge of vocalisation I had gained before entering upon my cathedral serfdom promoted me to the rank, not of a solo-singer, but of a second treble. About two years after my admission into the choir, it being then the custom to give an oratorio or miscellaneous performance in the autumn Assize week in the cathedral for the benefit of a highly useful county and city charity, Mrs. Salmon and Mr. Pyne, the uncle of Miss Louisa Pyne, were brought down from London as "the great guns of the occasion." At the same time, and, I believe, by the same coach, came Messrs. Harper and Hyde, the celebrated trumpet-players; the first notes of whose instruments, as they echoed through the vaulted roof of that sacred building at the rehearsal of Handel's Dettingen *Te Deum*, caused not only the boys, but the whole orchestra and the few strangers who were admitted, to stare at them with astonishment. The band on the instant stopped; but almost immediately perceiving the ridiculous figure they cut, one and all burst into a loud fit of laughter, which reverberated through the building. Mr. Harper, good-natured creature as he was, unused to such a reception, made a short speech from the place where " he stood up aloft," which was supposed to be of a deprecatory nature; but silence was more speedily restored by the voice of the precentor—a grave and peculiarly severe style of the *genus* cathedral minor canon of the old school—calling from the floor of the choir, and reminding us, one and all, that we were in God's house, and not in a theatre ! This rebuke having speedily restored the general gravity, the *Te Deum* was again commenced, and went from beginning to end without a hitch, although to me it seemed to take up an interminable length of time—a circumstance, in all probability, arising out of my knowledge of the fact that I was set down to sing the second line of the duet, " O lovely peace ! " from Handel's *Judas Maccabæus*, the *repetition* of which I naturally wished to get over as speedily as possible. The *Te Deum* finished, on and on went the rehearsal ; but no Mrs. Salmon put in an appearance, notwithstanding messenger after messenger had been dispatched to her lodgings to say that her presence was most earnestly desired. Just as we had come to the end of our work that lady lounged into the choir, and calling to the leader of the band— there were no conductors in those days—told him with the utmost nonchalance that she was not well enough to sing that morning, and that what she had to do the next day must take its chance. It was of no use that the leader of the band descended to the floor of the choir to entreat and to expostulate. Not being a London celebrity, but only a provincial musicseller, he made not the slightest impression. At last he bethought him that, if the man could have no influence, the child might move the feelings of the conceited upstart.

I had been looking on from my perch of the orchestra overhead all the while this scene was going on, when, on a sudden, the despairing leader, catching sight of me, beckoned me down, and planting me—a poor little frightened white-headed boy—before that *grande dame*, said,—

"Well, madam, if you will not rehearse anything on your own account, pray do go through 'O lovely peace!' with this child, who is to sing second to you."

Never shall I forget the look of contempt the "grand lady" cast upon me, and the way in which, after gathering up her dress and making the leader a profound curtsey, she said, "No, I shall not!" and forthwith waddled away. Young as I was, I had shrewdness enough to see that the dear old man, whom I greatly liked, was pained; but, aided by sundry words of advice at home, and by my father going through the duet several times with me, making me understand how I was to wait upon the lady and " nurse " her, so that she might have all the prominence she required, I went boldly to the front the next day, made my bow to the audience, and then turning to Mrs. Salmon, repeated that act of courtesy most solemnly, as wholly admitting her overwhelming superiority, but as not in the least abashed by her presence or dignity. She looked down upon me with some astonishment ; but I fancied that I remarked " a lurking twinkle" of good-nature in her eyes. There was, however, " no time for observation now."

The symphony had begun, and then came the voice—and such a voice ! It seemed to run through my frame like the shock of an electric current, and for the moment confused me completely. When she had finished, and I had to take up the lead, she whispered, " Steady now, boy !" That was enough. I went to my work with a will; and *we*—I was not ashamed then, and am not now, to say *we*—did our part so well, that a murmur of applause when *we* had finished ran through the whole audience, all louder demonstrations of pleasurable feeling being—as it always ought to be at the performances of sacred music, wherever those performances take place, and especially in churches—strictly prohibited. Our bows made—first to the audience and then to one another—the lady did then condescend to acknowledge this act of propriety on my part—I retired to my place, and became immediately so frightened at what had taken place, that the building spun round and round with me, and so prevented my knowing what else happened, that it might have in truth been said of me that I

> "Back recoiled, I knew not why,
> E'en at the sound myself had made."

It did not take long, however, to make me feel and understand that I had been successful. Sundry shillings given to me on my way home were proofs positive in that direction ; but the greatest assurance of all—and that which I valued most—was the reception my mother gave me, whose glistening eyes, rather than her "faltering utterance" of praise, were more to me than if the whole world had poured out its richest treasures at my feet.

I must not forget, however, in this manifestation of so much apparent egotism, to say something of the impression which Mrs. Salmon's vocal skill and powers made upon me. Young as I was, my ear was most sensitive. The eighth of an inch of a note out of tune—if I may use such an expression for the definition of musical sound—even then drove me nearly wild. It was my defect in producing a pure tone upon the viola which made me feel the relinquishment of my practice on that instrument to be nothing less than a positive blessing. The instant, therefore, that Mrs. Salmon began to sing " O lovely peace !" I perceived the purity of her intonation, which had not then become in the least degree impaired by the sad habit of intemperance into which she afterwards unfortunately fell. Of her execution I had then no opportunity of judging—indeed I could have been by no means competent at my then age to form an opinion thereon. This I was able to do afterwards; and therefore what I shall say in that respect, as in every other, about the vocal qualities of this "queen of song"—as I must always designate her—is to be taken as the result of a more matured decision.

Mrs. Salmon was, to all intents and purposes, an oratorio and concert-room singer. There was nothing dramatic about her manner, her appeals being made not to the passions, but to the sensibility of her audiences. Her method was of the purest; the embellishments she added to the various songs she sung being but few and always appropriate, never at variance with good sense or an outrage upon true taste. Her execution was flexible, her rapid vocal passages being so evenly sung, that every note of the chromatic scale could be as distinctly heard as if it had been drawn out by the most accomplished violin-player from his perfect instrument—the very king indeed of instruments. It was, however, in Mrs. Salmon's tone that delight chiefly lay—for delight it certainly might be called. Her voice possessed neither extraordinary compass nor volume, and came perhaps nearest to the sound of musical glasses, if their clearness could be imagined to be somewhat more rounded and refined. "How," said the accomplished critic to whom I have already referred, and with whose remarks I entirely agree,*— "how shall we find words to convey any notion of the siren who steals away the soul by tones so liquid, resonant, and delicious, that it leaves us scarcely any power to search beyond

* See above, p. 26.

the pleasure we derive from the mere pulses of the sound ?
Of all the singers we have ever heard, Mrs. Salmon the most
readily and the most felicitously disabled the severity of judgment. Her voice was to the sense of hearing what verdure is to
the eye, what the odours of the rose are to the smell, what the
delicate yet luxurious taste of the richest fluids convey to the
palate. Far from Catalani * in fulness, power, and force of
execution, she was yet scarcely less surprising for the astonishing facility, rapidity, and articulation with which she introduced
ornaments most exquisitely imagined, yet still more exquisitely
performed. Though certainly without majesty either of tone
or elocution, we heard her, and were not sensible that these
great attributes could be necessary to the song. Her intonation
was so fine, and her manner of taking passages so peculiarly
beautiful—she apportioned the degrees of loud and soft with
such exactitude of art—that it compensated for qualities of
very different use. Had Mrs. Salmon commanding dignity?
No. Had she polished enunciation ? No. Had she melting
pathos ? No. Had she anything peculiar in fire, force, feeling, or
expression ? We must still answer, No. What, then, had she?
A nameless charm to steep all senses in forgetfulness, except
the sense of the delight her voice awakened and enraptured.
It was like the gifted tones of Nourmahal,—

> ' And then her voice—'tis more than human.
>   Never till now had it been given
> To lips of any mortal woman
>   To utter notes so fresh from heav'n ;
> Sweet as the breath of angel sighs,
>   When angel sighs are most divine.' "

Of Mrs. Salmon's execution, the same critic assures us—and

* I shall have to refer to this great *artiste* in the next chapter of these
" Recollections."

I myself can also vouch for it—that "it was of the same cast and order with the voice which was its ministering agent." Whilst her great predecessors Madame Mara and Mrs. Billington—whose praises were poured in my ear so soon as they were sufficiently opened to understand anything of sound or sense, my father having sung in public with the latter, as I did with Mrs. Salmon, and at about the same age—and her contemporary Madame Catalani, "conveyed something of the notion of the practice and elaboration by which that execution was acquired and supported, appearing to sing from the chest (Mara in particular), and exerting great muscular force in the production and deep-seated articulation of the various divisions which made part of the song itself, Mrs. Salmon, on the contrary, seemed to execute—to warble rather—with an ease the hearer ascribed wholly to nature. It seemed to be more like what is understood by the vulgar term a "gift" than the operation of any artificial process. It appeared to proceed entirely from the organs of the throat, whilst she showed no more symptoms of effort in the most rapid, protracted, and difficult musical phrases than in those of the plainest and commonest structure. The choice of her ornaments likewise bore but small resemblance to those of her predecessors. Her sweetness, velocity, and brilliancy were astonishing, and certainly not surpassed by the most finished, delicate, and articulate violinist of our times."

Although Mrs. Salmon was chiefly remarkable for her manner of rendering sacred music, and especially that of Handel, her talents were not confined to this or any other particular school. "From mighty kings he took the spoil"—and especially the second movement, "Judah rejoiceth"—from Handel's

Judas Maccabæus, she gave with such energy, truth, and ease, as were not less surprising than beautiful. Variations upon airs, such as " My lodging is on the cold ground," and " Cease your funning," from the *Beggar's Opera*, for example, afforded a perfect species of gratification that delicacy and facility of execution and ornament could alone convey. " Clearness, beauty, rapidity, polish, invention, and taste—the chiefest attribute of vocal perfection—were her attributes; and with these she made so perfect a combination of what was delightful to the ear without being offensive to the judgment, that she took a rank far beyond that which it had been usual to allot to qualities which have been held rather to pertain to organic than to intellectual superiority. Although never grand, and seldom, if ever, pathetic or touching, although never extorting the tribute of applause by sudden, powerful, and irresistible appeals to the imagination or to the heart, she was nevertheless always sure of her object. She captivated by sweetness, delicacy, and variety, by exquisite ornament, and by uncommon ease. She left the judgment free; but she won the senses, and compelled the sternest, the most just, and the least easily satisfied critics of her day "—who were then honest, fair-dealing, and independent as a proverbial rule, and not biassed by personal feelings and motives, captious, unreliable, or acting together as a clique, as far too many now-a-days do—" to admit her talent, and her claims for admiration, no less than that they were as much the victims as the slaves of a fascination they could neither resist nor overcome."

Mr. Pyne, as I have said, was the London male singer who was present on the occasion of the —— cathedral oratorio performance, when I made my *début* with Mrs. Salmon in public.

That gentleman, although an excellent musician, never attained to any position of eminence. He was a member of a class who were often most undeservedly considered as of inferior quality and position because they were chiefly to be heard at such places of amusement as Vauxhall or at public dinners. I well remember that the chief exposition Mr. Pyne had to give of his quality on this occasion was the opening of the *Messiah.* The Recitative, "Comfort ye, my people," he sang, to my young ears, far better than the Aria, "Every valley shall be exalted," which immediately follows it. The circumstance weighed against him of his having been engaged to appear at the public gardens of —— during the assize week—at that time always made a season of general festivity and rejoicing, without the slightest reference to, or consideration for, the prisoners, whose trials were day by day going on, many of whom were " cast for execution," the laws being then more deeply written in blood than, happily, they are now. The " purists "—and there was no small number amongst the " best-built" musicians of —— at that time— were loud, for instance, in their complaints that a man who had to shout such roistering songs as, " If the heart of a man is depressed with care," in the open air at night at the top of his voice, to make himself heard at least half a mile off, should be called upon to sing Handel in the morning within a consecrated building ; forgetting, on the score of consistency, that Braham, who was justly admitted on all hands to be the greatest tenor England had ever reared, was not only invariably forgiven for shouting—not singing—almost exclusively to the shilling galleries of the London patent theatres such trash as " The Bay of Biscay, O !" " The Death of Nelson," and other similar monstrosities, but was always tolerated, whether he appeared in church or theatre, in concert-room or public garden. But between Braham and Pyne there was a wide and deep gulf, both as respected voice and method, and "the weaker" of the two, as is always proverbial, naturally "went to the wall." I had every reason to feel kindly towards Mr. Pyne, for he showed me much sympathy during the trying time I was in expectation of "coming out" in "O lovely peace!" and he warmed my heart immensely when I overhead him remark to a brother professional on the morning of rehearsal, that "Mrs. Salmon ought to be ashamed of herself for placing that boy in such a dilemma as to sing with her without knowing how they would go together." I did not fail to observe, on the morning of the oratorio performance, that the lady wholly ignored Mr. Pyne's presence, taking no more notice of him than if he had been the big drum or one of the far-distant pipes of the great organ, at which my master presided—happily for my peace of mind, so far out of sight that I could neither see him nor he me. When the affair was all over and I had again to enter that would-be great man's presence, not a word of praise or encouragement did he utter ; but from the additional severity he immediately exercised upon my unfortunate body, and for many weeks afterwards continued to practise, I was then thoroughly persuaded in my own mind, and am so still, that he would have been far better pleased had I wholly broken down than that I succeeded. The chief source of his opportunity for inflicting increased punishment arose out of my having been put to him with the farther object of studying theory; and as I hated thorough-bass, and infinitely preferred to make harmonies by means of my own ear than from the various figures of rhythmetical indication, there was no need of seeking for occasions, I will not say "to kill me," but most assuredly " to thrash me.'   I took the infliction, however, stoically, because my self-vanity convinced me that my chords were all right, and I was confident that if he and I could exchange places, his blunders would have been seen to be greater than my own.   This arose out of a little piece of impertinence on my part, for which I undoubtedly merited all the castigation that might have been laid upon me.   Doubting the accuracy of a correction he had made in my version of a chord of " the diminished seventh," I showed it to a young friend, a chorister in the next principal church to the cathedral at ——, whose master was one of the soundest contrapuntists I ever was acquainted with, and asked his opinion.   He thought I was right and my master wrong.   So he took it to his instructor, and the decision being given wholly in my favour—not at all to my credit, for I had as usual depended upon my ear instead of working by rule—I was not wise enough to conceal my feeling of triumph.   Much did that moment of joy and exultation cost me ; but, for a time at least, I was relieved from the oppression against which I kicked, by a coldness rising up between my father and my music-master, which I suspected was on my account, although not the breath of confirmation was ever—till many years afterwards—permitted to assure me that I had been right in my suspicion and surmises.

And now a new phase in my earliest " Musical Recollections " is dawning, the narration of which, however, must be postponed to another chapter.

CHAPTER II.

1820-1823.

ON account of the attention which, it may be inferred from the preceding chapter, was almost exclusively given in —— Cathedral to the development of the vocal gifts and powers of the " boy choristers," it must be equally apparent that their education in other respects suffered considerably. By the wisdom of founders and benefactors, it was determined that cathedrals should not merely be the nursery of musicians, but that " the young idea " to be trained therein should be fitted to supply the places both of minor-canons and lay-vicars, or clerks, when they attained to man's estate. By the statutes of the cathedral church of ——, it was expressly enacted that this state of things should for ever prevail. Not only were all the boys to be educated in reading, writing, and arithmetic, but they were also to be instructed in the Greek and Latin classics, the four senior or most gifted boys being exclusively named as to be so cared for that they might be sent to one or other of the universities, and there trained eventually to take " holy orders." The ultimate purpose hereby intended was that such boys should then have the preference as to those cathedral offices, the duties of which could not be properly discharged without their being clergymen. An ample " maintenance " for the times in which those statutes were made and confirmed was further provided ; and had the value of money remained at its standard of two or three hundred years ago, they would have been in their youth sufficiently provided for, and their incomes in the future placed beyond the necessity of being supplemented by thoroughly unsatisfactory means. There is no cathedral throughout the length and breadth of England wherein similar provisions were not made ; but at —— the statutable directions could not have been by any possibility more positive than they still remain ; inasmuch as not only were the choristers to be classically educated and relays of them sent to Oxford and Cambridge, but they were also to be taught the theory of music, and rendered proficient in the use of musical instruments. In the memory of man these directions have never been obeyed either at —— or elsewhere. At Westminster the Abbey choristers were so thoroughly considered by the foundation statutes, that they were beyond others to receive instruction at the collegiate school. So far, however, from such an injunction having been obeyed, they are to this day totally deprived of this privilege ; and whenever a parent has been rash enough to insist that his boy should partake of it, the school has immediately been made, both by masters and scholars, too hot to hold him, so that removal has been rendered absolutely necessary. In spite, however, of this fact, when the Parliamentary commissioners a few years ago examined into the condition of Westminster school, they totally ignored the Abbey choristers' privileges, leaving them to gather such knowledge as the little time allowed them from musical practice permits, or a servant of the body could impart—that servant having been nominated to his office by the sub-dean, and placed in a school-room built in sudden haste at the bottom of the organist's garden; that garden having been diminished for the purpose without this official ever having been asked for his consent, or so much as consulted. The commissioners, in fact, endorsed all that the Abbey authorities had done; and up to this very hour, in defiance of the strict injunctions of the statutes to the contrary, a Westminster choir-boy would be better off in every respect were he sent to any adjacent National school, so far as his education for any practical purpose is concerned.

In many of the other cathedrals there has been undoubtedly of late some improvement in this respect, and especially so at ——. But in no one instance has it yet been reported that a thoroughly classical education is afforded, or that the commands of the statutes are strictly obeyed. Of all the classes of which society is composed, not one remains so much—it might even be said more—neglected, than those boys, whose unhappy lot it is to be drilled into mere singing-machines, and then, when their voices are broken, cast out only half educated upon the world. In London there are openings, it is true, for the prosecution of music as a means of livelihood; but in cathedral cities and towns this is by no means the case. Much too often have lads of a sensitive disposition been hopelessly ruined. When they can no longer—their voices being gone—afford amusement to persons of good position, by whom they had been hitherto petted and spoiled, and especially by the wives and daughters of such persons, they have suddenly been subjected to neglect, if not to insult; and a bitter lesson indeed it has been when, much too frequently, they have had practically to feel the force of the old adage, "No longer pipe, no longer dance." Should any of "the authorities" have been goaded into doing something for the permanent benefit of cathedral choristers—as several of our modern deans and chapters have of late years been—it may fearlessly be said there is not a single instance wherein they have been induced thoroughly to fulfil their duty in this direction. They have to a certain extent salved their consciences. Not only to their choristers, but also to their minor canons and their lay-vicars or clerks they have refused to mete out that justice those members are statutably entitled to receive; nor have they so paid them as to render their circumstances even easy. That such circumstances should ever be independent seems to be wholly out of the question. Earnest cathedral reformers—than whom none were more sincere and courageous than the late Gresham professor of music, Mr. Edward Taylor—have striven might and main to induce a better state of things to be compassed in the Chapel Royal, St. Paul's, Westminster Abbey, and other cathedrals; but they have invariably met with little else than failure. The imperfect and insufficient condition of the cathedral chorister's education still remains at the lowest ebb; and in no direction whatever is there any indication of a better state of things being likely to obtain, save in such high-church establishments as All Saints', Margaret-street, St. Andrew's, Wells-street, and in one or two others of prominent notoriety in other parts of the country. It seems to be "to hope in hope's despite" that the day will ever dawn when the noble and generous purposes of "founders and benefactors" will be to the very letter fulfilled.

Looking upon cathedrals as the chief nurseries of musical training, it would be a joyous time indeed if ever they were rendered equally important seminaries for the highest class of education, whence many a promising lad might proceed to

Oxford, Cambridge, or Durham, and, making his mark by his proficiency and good conduct there, be ever after able to exult in life—instead of now all but cursing the hour in which he ever became a chorister—that he spent the most promising years of his boyhood in a cathedral choir. No " Musical Recollections " that are connected with a cathedral—as are the earliest portions of these—can be divested of feelings such as are now expressed. Never can they be anything else than bitter. We turn, however, "more in sorrow than in anger," from this painful subject to one more agreeable, although by no means of similar importance.

In the summer of 1821, Madame Catalani, after an absence of six years, returned to London, as it was said, "greater than when she left it." Her voice, which had, during those six years, been considerably taxed by continuous engagements at Paris and Berlin, Hanover and Stuttgart, Munich and Vienna, as also at St. Petersburg and Moscow, was at this period somewhat worn ; but the grandeur of her method and the breadth of her style more than compensated for a defect which had always been apparent to ears of the most extreme acuteness, to which her intonation was said to be imperfect. To ordinary hearers, not similarly exacting or sensitive, this defect was diminished by the prodigious volume and richness of her tone, no less than by the rapidity with which she executed the most florid passages. Although constantly engaged as a concert-singer, Madame Catalani's *forte* was essentially dramatic, her style being both grand and imposing. Her range of characters, however, was not exclusively confined to this department of the lyric stage, since she was equally successful in lighter parts, such as Susanna in Mozart's *Nozze di Figaro*, and Aristea in *Il Fanatico per la*

Musica. The chief means by which she carried her audiences away with her were discovered in the natural volume and richness of her tone, and in the energy and force of her declamatory method. No band was sufficiently overwhelming to drown her voice, no nerves strong enough to resist its influence. Had brass instruments been as much in use in Madame Catalani's day as unhappily they are at present, she would have outsung them all, her voice ringing so as to make itself felt in every fibre. Over this magnificent organ she had absolute control. "She could vary its delivery through every degree, from the smallest perceptible sound to the loudest and most magnificent swell. She could increase or diminish the tone, either in a protracted duration of 'sweetness long drawn out,' or she could apportion the same degrees of light and shade in the most rapid alternation of diverse passages." A common saying amongst the critics of her day was, that "she could play with her voice at pleasure, and do anything with it which her flights of fancy suggested." Yet upon the stage her personification was more grand than touching. In mere ordinary concert-room singing, she fell short of these operatic qualities; and in oratorio, save in one or two individual instances, failed to make anything like a triumphant impression. In the latter, her imperfect pronunciation of English words—as is the case with so many other foreign *artistes*—told very much to her disadvantage; yet into such songs of Handel as "I know that my Redeemer liveth," and "Holy, holy, Lord God of Hosts," she threw an amount of adoration by her utterance, which concealed every defect in this particular. It was, however, in such songs as "Gratias agimus tibi," by Giuglielmi, and the "Deh parlate," from Cimarosa's *Il Sacrifizio d' Abram*, that she chiefly excelled;

showing that she was possessed of the strongest feelings of devotion, and manifested the firmest belief and the most fervent piety of any singer that had ever previously lived. When once complimented upon the manner in which she had sung Giuglielmi's above-named song, her simple reply was, "I do love to sing to my God!"—a practical comment upon the fact that "she never entered a church or a theatre to perform without solemnly offering up prayer for her success." On one occasion she is said to have produced an effect, which could never be forgotten by those who heard it, by resorting to a low and tremulous whisper. It occurred in the recitative of the *Messiah*, "And lo, the glory of the Lord shone round about them." Having poured forth the full magnificence of the prodigious volume of her voice, supported by the *arpeggio* accompaniment of the orchestra, upon the words, "the glory of the Lord shone round about them," she suddenly attenuated her astonishingly ductile tones to the least possibly audible note, and sung slowly, in a voice so slight as to be scarcely more than tremulous. The effect is said to have "congealed the very blood of her hearers, till their minds, recovering, became conscious of the simplicity, the delicacy, and the exquisite beauty of the thought, and the execution which gave expression to it."

Madame Catalani took the earliest opportunity, on her return to London from the Continent, to give a concert at the Argyle Rooms,* which was liberally patronised by the Dukes of Clarence and Cambridge, the Princess Augusta, and the Duchesses of Gloucester and Cambridge, and also by an immense number of the nobility; so much so, indeed, that "the room glittered with

* July 21, 1821.

stars and orders, notwithstanding the music for the coronation of George IV. was being rehearsed at Carlton House, and Mr. and Mrs. Coutts had a grand concert and ball at their residence on the same evening." The novelties which the great *prima donna* introduced on that occasion may seem trivial in the present day; but they were then considered marvellous specimens of talent, chiefly, as it may be supposed, on account of the manner in which they were executed. They consisted of "a new grand air," by the Marquis Sampieri, now wholly forgotten, " Della superba Roma;" Rode's air, with variations, since hackneyed to death by almost every soprano, both English and foreign, if possessed of any facility of execution; a recitative and aria by Pucetta, " Mio bene;" and Mozart's bass song, from the *Le Nozze di Figaro,* " Non piu andrai," some of the passages of which she varied, introducing a few descending notes upon the words, " Non piu avrai." With these specimens, and a verse of " God save the King," which she delivered with prodigious volume of voice and declamatory power, she once more took her hearers by storm, although it was observed that she sung with greater effort, the agitation of the muscles of her face, and the motion of the lower jaw, particularly in her shake, which had always been painful to observe, being evidently much increased.

Like many other *prime donne,* both before and since her time, Madame Catalani was exceedingly imperious, self-willed, self-sufficient, capricious, and prone to imagine that she had force enough in herself to constitute an opera—a ridiculous notion, which her husband, M. Valebreque, was at the utmost pains to foster, inasmuch as he is reported to have constantly asserted, " Ma femme, et quatre ou cinque poupées, voilà tout ce qu'il faut!" The Earl of Mount Edgcumbe, in his *Musical Reminiscences*, asserts that Madame Catalani "had come to England at this time on a journey of speculation, but was not regularly engaged, but only paid for occasional appearances (at the Opera); and as her terms were more advantageous to herself than to the manager, and her attraction not great, they were very few. She did not perform any of her fine tragic characters, but acted, five or six times only, her favourite comic opera, *Il Fanatico per la Musica*, in which she introduced some new song every night, her powers being said to be undiminished, her taste unimproved."* Although thus but little heard where her dramatic excellence could alone have had the fullest scope of development, so long as she remained in England—till 1824 —she continued to give concerts in London and in the provinces, and was engaged at several of the Musical Festivals, where she greatly distinguished herself, especially at York in 1823. After her departure from London, Madame Catalani continued to sing abroad, and finally retired from her profession at Berlin in 1827; after which she took up her residence for a time at Florence; whence she removed to Paris, where she died of cholera, June 12th, 1849, in her seventieth year. Her character is thus described by M. Fétis—"Elevée dans un couvent, elle était restée pieuse. De mœurs pures et modestes, elle a été bonne épouse et bonne mère. Généreuse, bienfaisante, elle a fait beaucoup d'aumônes, et l'on estime le produit des concerts qu'elle a donnés au profit des pauvres à plus de deux millions" (of francs).† The same character is given, and almost in the self-same words, by many of our own countrymen who had the privilege of this great

---

* See p. 41.

† F. J. Fétis, *Biographie Universelle des Musiciens*, &c., ii. 212, Paris, 1860-5.

cantatrice's friendship and acquaintance whilst she was domiciled in England.

As I had sung in public with Mrs. Salmon, so was it my good fortune to have been associated in the same manner in the following year with Madame Camporese, who was Madame Catalani's contemporary, although by no means her rival, when that *prima donna* was for the last time in England. It is, therefore, with no ordinary degree of pleasure that I turn now to record my " Recollections " of as amiable a lady, and as competent an executant, as ever adorned the musical profession. In addition, therefore, to what has been already said of her,* it is pleasurable to be able to add something even still more definite to this lady's advantage. One, whose opinion on musical subjects every one of competent knowledge will readily endorse, and who has already been quoted,† said of Madame Camporese, " that her excellence consisted chiefly in the uncommon apprehension of her sensibility, and the embodiment of her feelings in the purest language of sound ;" that whilst " her decoration was simple and powerful, she never uttered a word or a note in vain; but sung to the heart, and conveyed the power of expressiveness even into the little ornament she used. Thus elocution and execution, under her dominion, ministered to conception, as displayed in intellectual strength, and a rich but cultivated fancy. Her polished judgment could distinguish; her taste was satisfied ; and, therefore, her ambition could be content with moving the high affections. In a word, she knew, and she supported the dignity of her mind and of her art." So far as vocal power was concerned, Madame Camporese must be said to have been possessed, comparatively, of somewhat limited means. The

* See pp. 30, 31.   † See pp. 26, 41.

compass of her voice was by no means extensive, whilst it was somewhat deficient in volume and sweetness, richness and brilliancy. That compass consisted of about two octaves, reaching to B and C in alt, but the quality was only good, and by no means fine, between C and F. The command, therefore, which she unquestionably had upon her hearers arose simply from her method, the dignity of her style, and the sensibility of her expression. Whilst other *prima donnas* won their way by the sympathetic tones of voices of even more extensive range, Madame Camporesi had to depend almost exclusively upon art. In one particular, and that of the utmost importance, her intonation, she was for the most part true ; but if ever it showed a tendency to falter, neither defect of ear nor error of judgment could be accused of being its cause. Madame Camporese had also been well taught. She had not been launched into her profession before she had been half tutored, as so many singers are now-a-days. Execution, indeed, could not be said to have been her *forte*, although she was able to sing either *legato* or *staccato* passages with the utmost apparent ease, in spite of the absence of that perfect flexibility which nature had denied her. She was rather a level than a dashing singer, never taking her hearers, as Madame Catalani did, by storm ; but winning their approval by simple, quiet, and modest means. She was to all intents and purposes a thorough gentlewoman, and in everything she did, either as a singer or as an actress, she was distinguished by so much amiability of character and conduct as to have been an ornament to the profession she dignified.

At the time when Madame Camporese was in the zenith of her well-deserved popularity, and almost as highly appreciated as her elder rival, Madame Catalani, there was an English soprano before the public, who, although not to the same extent endowed with the powers possessed by either of those foreign *artistes*, or even by her countrywoman, Mrs. Salmon, was gifted with such fine natural qualities, which high cultivation had improved, that her share of popularity was quite as positive as their own—Miss Stephens. This thoroughly accomplished lady was born in London, and at an early age received the first rudiments of musical tuition from M. Lanza, a music-master of Italian extraction and considerable eminence, who had resided in England from a very early age. Miss Stephens had thus the rare advantage of her voice and style being entirely formed upon the genuine and pure Italian method, which had not then been superseded by the rough, uncouth, and hard German manner, or by the flippancy of the modern French school. It is said that the drudgery Miss Stephens had to pass through, under this master, was so severe, that it very nearly broke her spirit. She, however, still lives, as the respected and beloved Dowager Countess of Essex, to admit, that although her early progress in mastering the first elements of her art was slow, it was, to all intents and purposes, sure. Those early studies were solely confined to a preparation for concert singing ; but her vocal powers were soon discovered to be of so exceptional a character, that the principles best calculated for this purpose were speedily deviated from, that attention might be solely given to that practice which best contributes to the efforts the stage demands. M. Lanza had the privilege—indeed, I may say, the honour—of bringing out his pupil, who made her *debut* at a somewhat early age at Bath, and afterwards appeared at the Pantheon in Oxford-street, then a concert-room of considerable celebrity. In order to gain confidence—for she was of an excessively nervous temperament and easily alarmed—her master took her, in company with some other pupils, upon a short provincial tour, under an assumed name—a habit then in vogue, although not perhaps carried to the same excess which has since been adopted. From some cause or other, that has never been satisfactorily explained, and which is indeed of very little moment, Miss Stephens's father felt himself dissatisfied with M. Lanza's tuition and conduct. Mr. Welch—better known in the musical profession as Tom Welch, who taught and brought forward more vocalists, both male and female, than any other master of his day—was then applied to. He was not slow to discover what a treasure the musical profession had in store in this nervous and retiring girl. He saw at once how great was her promise of future excellence, and set to work with the earnestness and energy of his impulsive character to bring her sufficiently forward to make " her first appearance on any stage," without mention of her name, at Covent Garden Theatre, September the 23rd, 1813, in the part of Mandane in Arne's *Artaxerxes.* Her first appearance, however, although meeting with decided approbation, could be counted merely as a *succès d'estime,* it being doubted by those best qualified to judge "whether the warmth of feeling and fertility of judgment, which are indispensable to perfect dramatic performance, were inherent in her nature."

I have often heard Sir George Smart, and several of his contemporaries, say, that it was impossible to have anticipated that excellence, to which Miss Stephens gradually won her way, from any promise she gave on this occasion. It was thought that her talent was misdirected, and that she would sooner or later drift back into the position of a mere concert-room singer.

Of dramatic impulse or power Miss Stephens had not the slightest notion; and even when she had become accustomed to the stage—a result brought about by her vocal qualifications rather than by any histrionic talent—it could never be said that she had learned how to act. Her manner was cold and unimpressive. She said her "words" accurately, but evidently by rote, and added to the effect of the scenes in which she was engaged, whether in opera or comedy, in no other way than by her singing talent. So full and rich, however, was her voice, so true was her intonation, and so facile her execution, that the supposed absence of imagination, of which complaints were neither few nor far between, was altogether forgotten the moment she opened her mouth to sing. It was also speedily discovered that, although "her stage performances appeared to be subdued somewhat below the point necessary to fine expression," she was by no means destitute of true feeling. As an English and Scotch ballad-singer she has never been equalled either before or since her time. I have myself on more than one occasion witnessed the emotion she produced—by simply singing the quaint old strain, to which the well-known words of "Auld Robin Gray" are set—upon audiences, amongst whom, young and old, hard and sensitive, there was scarcely a dry eye; whilst she was evidently struggling with herself, as if she were in reality embodying the very words to which she gave such sweet and liquid utterance. In another ballad, "Donald," now wholly forgotten, she was also equally successful, although the former specimen was decidedly her *cheval de bataille.* In sacred music Miss Stephens likewise manifested neither want of feeling nor unconcern, but threw an amount of pathos into its interpretation which at once "knocked at the door of the heart," and received immediate admission. This was very apparent in Handel's then somewhat hackneyed songs, "Angels, ever bright and fair," from his now-forgotten oratorio, *Theodora,* and "Pious Orgies," from the *Judas Maccabœus.* In that most trying of all Handel's sacred songs, "I know that my Redeemer liveth" (*Messiah*), I do not believe Miss Stephens was ever excelled. If I heard her sing this aria once, I must have done so at least twenty times; but on one of those occasions—and that the last —her version of that simple yet touching exposition of the highest hopes of immortality seemed to be little else than sublime. She was in the deepest mourning for her mother's recent death, and, although "filled with sorrow," she yet sung as if she were "rapt—inspired." How her nervous system bore the strain of that severe trial has been, and always will be, a mystery to myself. The silence of one of the most crowded audiences ever gathered together was so intense, that it is no exaggeration to use the oft-repeated simile, that "a pin, had it dropped, would have been heard;" and at its close there was a stifled sob, that ran through the building, which told far more decisively than any amount of applause could have done, that in Miss Stephens —at least, on that occasion—vocal perfection had been attained. If ever there was an illustration of the old Latin adage,

" Si vis me flere, primum est flendum tibi,"

it was assuredly given on that occasion.

After " deservedly enjoying her full share of public patronage " for many years, Miss Stephens finally retired from her profession in the year 1830, after having industriously and honourably earned universal esteem and regard, her title to which was won —as it has been well said by one who knew her intimately—

" by a purity of mind and character, wholly corresponding to her professional manner." In the year 1838, Miss Stephens was married to the Right Honourable George Capel, fifth Earl of Essex, who died April 23rd, 1839.

From the most vivid " Recollections " of this period it is impossible to exclude a male singer, Thomas Vaughan, who was admitted on all hands to be one of the purest tenors that England has ever produced. Vaughan was born at Norwich, and received the rudiments of his musical education in the choir of its cathedral from the most competent musician and organist perhaps of his time, Dr. Beckwith. When Vaughan's career as a chorister had ended, his kind-hearted master and protector, in order to put him forward in life, got up a concert at Norwich in his behalf, the sad interest of which was considerably increased by the circumstance of his father dying at the very minute the first notes of that concert were performing, thus leaving him an orphan. By the advice of Dr. Beckwith, as also of a great clerical patron of music—an eccentric minor canon of the cathedral—Vaughan stood for a vacant lay-vicarship at St. George's Chapel Royal, Windsor, soon after his voice was formed; whence, coming under the immediate notice of the Court—which then invariably attended that chapel's services— he was speedily transferred to London as the legitimate successor of Harrison, a celebrated tenor of his time, both in the choir and concert-room. Vaughan, like Bartleman, was of diminutive stature; but his voice was not at all in proportion to his personal appearance, for it was round and full, and from its sympathetic quality, rather than its power, was capable of filling the vast areas of Westminster Abbey and St. Paul's with the utmost ease. It was what is called an altogether natural organ of considerable compass, and without the smallest break, or need of resorting to one solitary note of *falsetto*, the use of which is said to have been the great charm in Incledon's singing, and to which Braham owed very much of the attractive fascination of his execution.* It was principally, therefore, in English music that Vaughan excelled; although, being thoroughly acquainted with the Italian style, he "held his own" therein with no discredit to himself or imperfection of manner. As an exponent of Handel's music, Vaughan was generally said to be superior to every rival. To this opinion I must take exception. Having had the opportunity of frequently comparing him with Braham—of whom I shall next speak—I have no hesitation in saying that he never even approached that justly celebrated *artiste*. Vaughan's opening of the *Messiah*, his delivery of the recitative from *Samson*, "O, loss of sight!" and the succeeding air, "Total Eclipse;" of the song, "Why does the God of Israel sleep?" from the same oratorio; and "Thou shalt dash them," from the *Messiah*, were in manner much too unimpassioned to produce the needful effects; whilst in "Deeper and deeper still," from *Jephtha*, which I once heard him *attempt* he verily and indeed illustrated the saying, of "there being but one step from the sublime to the ridiculous." It was chiefly in such songs as Attwood's "Soldier's Dream," or Pepusch's "Alexis"—which, in conjunction with Bob Lindley's exquisite violoncello accompaniment, he sung everywhere—that he gave evidence of the chaste and elegant *cantabile* method for which he was justly celebrated. According to my own judgment—which was formed from my frequently hearing him whilst he was in the full vigour of his powers—a judgment since con-

---

* Both Rubini and Mario also used this resource with the utmost advantage.

firmed by the opinion of competent critics—Vaughan realised an image of perfection in vocal art which many had begun to think was visionary, and not to be discovered except in the hopeless contemplation of ideal possibility. His singing gave an assurance that the chastity of English taste, the manly eloquence of English elocution, and the genuine pathos of English expression may be combined with the purity and sweetness of Italian tone and the grace of Italian execution ; and although he could not be said to be in any respect equal to Braham in execution, force, extent, and variety of resources with which that accomplished *artiste* continually surprised his hearers, yet his simple grace, uniform polish, and perfect intonation will long be remembered.

Although Vaughan was no pigmy—save in stature—Braham was unquestionably a giant in his art. Whilst Vaughan was articulate and natural, dignified and forcible, Braham was swift, powerful, and impassioned in a most vehement degree. Vaughan, in fact, manifested the concentrated energy of zeal, strength, and feeling ; but Braham was ever stimulated by the force of dramatic passion, giving loose to his energetic spirit, and carrying all before him by his overwhelming *tours de force.* What the accomplished critic—to whom I have already been but too happy to refer,* in order that my own youthful impressions may be fortified—has said of the latter was perfectly true—that "he was gifted with the most extraordinary genius and aptitude for the exercise of his profession that was ever implanted in a human being. His throat was an organ of more varied power, more extensive compass, and more astonishing flexibility than was ever before possessed by any singer," whilst "his mind was

<hr>

* See pp. 26, 41.

rich with the stores of science, and his imagination bold and vivid." There was another most important point—the most important, perhaps, of all in which Braham most remarkably excelled—his intonation, which, even in his latest years, when his vigour had departed, and his force diminished, was scarcely ever untrue, but which to his prime was always perfect. Whether he sung or shouted—and he could do both—the ear was never offended by the voice being either above or below the true pitch. However much he diversified his tone, in order to give expression to any peculiar sentiment or passion, neither by forcing nor by any other jugglery did it give offence. It was only when he exhibited the bad taste of bringing down thunders of applause from the shilling galleries of Drury Lane or provincial theatres that he produced this effect, which, however, he was wise enough never to repeat, if a demonstration were made against it—as I once remember being the case at a concert at ——, when he was literally hissed off the orchestra. This took place on the first occasion of his visit to that locality, and so greatly astonished him, that he immediately inquired of an accomplished amateur what it could mean, as never before had he anywhere met with such an unwelcome reception. "Truth to tell, sir," answered the gentleman, "if you wish to be heard and esteemed here, you must *sing*." Braham's good sense immediately perceived what was intended by this reply, and, without manifesting the slightest displeasure at the honesty of its rebuke—for a rebuke to all intents and purposes it was—he said, "I understand you, sir." That he did so was apparent on the following morning, when, having to open Handel's *Messiah* he clearly enough proved that he could indeed sing.

Braham had the advantage of Storace's tuition at the opening

of his career, although he had been previously the pupil of
Rauzzini, who, having heard him on his first appearance at a
concert in Bath as a tenor singer, in the year 1794, initiated him
in the rudiments of his art. His style may be thus said to
have been entirely formed upon the pure Italian method—an
advantage he greatly improved by his having afterwards gone to
Italy to study, as also to sing in opera at Florence, where he accepted his first engagement. Thence he went to Genoa, Milan,
and Venice; and so remarkably successful was he wherever he
appeared in that "land of song," that the highest compliment
which could have been paid to him was first uttered there, as
it was afterwards constantly repeated by foreign singers engaged
in our own country: "Non c'e tenore in Italia come Braham!"

It was a singular trait in Braham's character that he had the
impression—and adhered to it—that he was much better fitted
to be a composer than a singer. Not that he was singular in
this respect, because many musicians who have been eminent in
some particular branch of their art have never been persuaded
that they did not more thoroughly excel in another direction.
Thus the incomparable violinist often thinks that he is a far
better pianist, and, *vice versâ*, the most facile of pianists sometimes believes that, after all, the flute is his instrument of
instruments. It was at Milan that the mania of becoming a
composer culminated, where he positively remained for several
months, to his pecuniary disadvantage, assiduously prosecuting
his studies under a "master" of some repute, named Isola.
Very few composers indeed of his own, or any other time, threw
off a greater number of operas, songs, duets, &c., than Braham
did, to enumerate one-half of which would be as utterly impossible
as it is needless; but of all he wrote, however popular any speci-

men might have been—and some were very much so—one only remains in public remembrance, and that merely from its having been of late resuscitated, not in the best taste, and certainly for no national cause—" The Death of Nelson "—to the character of which I have already indirectly adverted.* Of Braham's use of the *falsetto,* or head voice, I have spoken † when comparing him with Vaughan ; but so skilfully was the transition from the chest-voice managed, that it was absolutely indiscernible, even when he would, by way of experiment, for practice, or for mere whim and humour, run through the whole compass of the scales " by tones and semitones, ascending and descending with a degree of velocity and precision which can only be understood by those who have tried the experiment, and discovered how difficult it is of accomplishment."

As I shall have hereafter to speak of several occasions on which I had the opportunity of hearing this " prince of tenors," it is unnecessary to say more of him now than that at this period he may be said to have been in the very zenith of his well-earned fame.

On the 9th September, 1822—a night which I am not at all likely to forget, because the immense treat I enjoyed came most unexpectedly upon me—I had the good fortune to witness the appearance of Miss Paton at the Haymarket Theatre, in a new three-act opera by T. Dibdin, entitled *Morning, Noon, and Night ;* which had not only never been previously acted, but was spoken of at the time as " a poor piece," not good enough even for an opera. It was, in fact, one of those wretched specimens of so-called English opera, in which the music had little or no connection with the plot or any of the scenes, but was

* See p. 21. † See p. 64.

merely introduced to relieve the "words" of the tediousness which want of point and poverty of style naturally induced. Miss Paton had *débuted* before the public in the previous month (the 3rd) as Susanna, in an English version of Mozart's *Nozze di Figaro*, heralded by no announcements of particular promise, and expected, as a novice, like many a one before her, to "come like a shadow, and so depart." She had scarcely, however, on the occasion to which I refer, sung half-a-dozen bars before those of the audience who had any musical discrimination began to give her their most earnest and undivided attention. Awake to everything that was passing around me, and by no means unmoved by the beauty of Miss Paton's voice, and the purity of her style, although not then so finished and perfect as it afterwards became, I was not a little amused by a conversation which was entered into between the first and second acts by two persons seated immediately beside me. It was to this effect: "Something good *that*, don't you think?" "I should think indeed it is," was the reply. "Well, I don't understand much about music," answered the first speaker—evidently a young man from the country—"but there is something about that young woman which I mainly like." "Sir," said the other, "you will certainly hear something more of her before long, for, if I am not mistaken, she will take the place of Mrs. Salmon, and rival Miss Stephens." But then the prompter's bell rang, up again went the curtain, and the conversation ceased, not to be again renewed. The impression made by the first act was fully confirmed by the second, and the third proved to be a thorough triumph, for, to use the words of Edmund Kean, "the pit rose at her," and thereby firmly established her as a public favourite. I have never heard a single note of the music of

Morning, Noon, and Night, from that hour to the present; and I have not the slightest remembrance of any song, concerted piece, or anything else, if such there were, in it; but of Miss Paton's singing there has been no forgetfulness. Her stage presence was prepossessing, for her figure was slim and elegant, and although she had not a handsome face, yet its expression was intellectual. The largeness of her mouth, which she opened to its utmost width as she poured out a volume of rich and sonorous tone, detracted much from the possibility of her finding favour on the score of positive beauty. Her dark hair, of which she had a profusion, was greatly admired; but her eyes did her much more service, since they gave animation and contrast to a clear complexion, whilst sensibility to every change of sentiment she had to express, whether the occasion was one that required quietude of manner or vivacity of demeanour, was constantly apparent.

At the time of Miss Paton's appearance at the Haymarket she had scarcely completed her twentieth year; yet so early as her eighth year concerts had been given in her name, and she had also been recently heard at "the nobility's concerts" in London, although without giving any remarkable indication of promise or making any particular sensation. The peculiarity of Miss Paton's voice was, that it was not only sweet in tone, but also brilliant and powerful in strength, which study, practice, and growth of years thoroughly mellowed and ripened. Her compass was extensive, extending from A to D and E, of tolerably equal quality, which was somewhat marred by an imperfect method of delivering them. Her intonation was, however, even at the early age of twenty, as correct as that of the generality of singers of the highest rank. Her shake was imperfect, being too close, rapid, and hard, and given out with a jerk rather than with equal enunciation.

Owing to the imperfection of the tuition to which she had been subjected, as also most probably from her singing too early in public, she never, throughout the whole of her career, had an equal and rightly-formed scale—a defect which, although she was at the utmost pains to correct, she never conquered. She was, however, a thorough musician, and one of the best sight-singers of her time, which not one in a hundred was then, any more than they are now. Of this she gave a most remarkable instance at the sixth Philharmonic Concert of the year 1826 (May 15), when she sang Spohr's difficult *scena, ed aria,* " Si, io sento," from the *Faust,* almost at sight, the music having been sent to her only the day previously to the rehearsal. Notwithstanding this disadvantage, I remember to have heard both Sir George Smart and François Cramer, who was the leader on that occasion, say that " she executed it perfectly, doing what no other singer in London could have done." At first Miss Paton seemed to be desirous of copying Madame Catalani, and selected many of that *prima donna's* most celebrated songs for public performance ; but learning by experience that it is better to be an originator than an imitator, she laid aside the habit, and wisely trusted to her own natural resources of talent, sensibility, and execution.

As I proceed I shall have to speak at some length of Miss Paton's career, especially during the celebrated Weber period, which formed a starting-point in England in the direction of operatic performances, from which nearly all the excellence that has since been obtained may be said to have originated. Although the so-called opera in which Miss Paton " made her public " was speedily withdrawn, she still retained her engagement at the Haymarket, from time to time appearing as Susanna in an English Version of Mozart's *Nozze di Figaro* and as Rosina in Rossini's *Barbiere*, as well as in the part of Polly in the *Beggar's Opera.* From the Haymarket she transferred her engagement to Covent Garden, where, in spite of "some doubts being entertained of her voice being sufficiently powerful to fill that theatre," she instantly removed all fears on that account, and not only repeated the latter character triumphantly, "but played it" several times with considerably increasing applause.

Hitherto I have dealt exclusively with the most celebrated vocalists who sung between the years 1820 and 1823, and held the highest position it was possible to attain in the musical profession. It would, however, be a positive act of injustice were several instrumentalists of unqualified excellence, who within that period were before the public, to be passed over without notice or consideration. Amongst these—*facile princeps*—John Baptiste Cramer merits the warmest recognition. Than this gentleman—the eldest son of William Cramer, a violinist, and native of Mannheim, who took up his residence in England on being nominated chamber-musician to the sovereign, and leader of the band of the King's theatre and the Ancient concerts—no one of greater celebrity in his peculiar vocation, that of a pianist, can possibly be named. Brought over to this country at a very early age by his father, he may truly be said to have become, in every sense of the word, an English musician. The elder Cramer, being passionately attached to his own instrument, had resolved that his elder as well as his younger son (François) should excel in the same direction as he himself had done. As soon, therefore, as the youthful John Baptiste's hand could grasp the finger-board of a violin, he was put to the practice of that instrument. That the violin was, however, by no means to the boy's taste, may be inferred from the fact that he shirked practice whenever he found an opportunity of doing so, and was invariably found, at the early age even of six years, secretly playing upon an old harpsichord. Although his father—like many other self-willed parents—was most unwilling to give his consent to his son's adoption of that instrument, as the means of his future livelihood, he was at last prevailed upon by numerous friends and acquaintances to permit this mere child to follow the bent of his own inclination. Making the best of the matter, he forthwith apprenticed him to a German professor, named Benser, from whom he was not long afterwards transferred to Schröter, a celebrated Polish pianist and composer, who, having been brought over from Warsaw, obtained the favour and enjoyed the patronage of the Prince of Wales. With this master the young John Baptiste remained but a single year, being next placed with the justly celebrated Muzio Clementi, who was so great a proficient on the harpsichord that Schröter himself, when asked on his arrival in England whether he could play his (Clementi's) compositions, replied that "they were only to be performed by the author himself, or the devil!" Under this master, John Baptiste Cramer studied with the utmost perseverance till he was thirteen years of age, when, after another year's assiduous study, he began, for the first time, to play in public. Although somewhat jealous of the growing reputation of his pupil, Clementi was clever enough to perceive that he would not only eclipse himself, but every other competitor—an opinion he, it is said, was at the utmost pains to disseminate. After a brief exercise of his profession in England, the young pianist proceeded to the

Continent, where, being only seventeen years of age, he was looked upon and received as a prodigy. In 1791 he came back to England, his reputation having been largely increased by his publication in Paris of several sonatas for his favourite instrument—the pianoforte. There is no reliable information extant to tell us that he now made any great way amongst his own countrymen, the information with reference to that period of his career being so scanty as to make it to be naturally inferred that he had to submit to the mortification of discovering that "a musician" had no more reason than "a prophet" to expect that he would find honour "in his own country, or in his father's house." He therefore again started speedily for the Continent, and visited Italy, as well as Vienna. At the latter capital he renewed the friendship he had formed with Haydn, during that master's visit to London, to write the most celebrated series of his symphonies for Salomon—a circumstance which tended very considerably to his (Cramer's) ultimate professional advantage. On his return home, he married, and at once settled in London as a professional pianist, composer, and pianoforte teacher, where his fame continued to increase year by year with undiminished rapidity. With respect to his peculiar qualifications as a pianist, brilliancy of touch, genuine taste, and exquisite sensibility may be said to have been marvellously prominent.

Early impressions are invariably the most permanent, and doubtless, from the circumstance of John Baptiste Cramer being the first eminent pianoforte player to whom I was privileged to listen, my "Recollections" of him are the more vivid. At the time I first heard him I had myself become acquainted with his "Exercises," which I still believe to be the very best extant, and by many degrees superior to those of Kalkbrenner or

Czerny, by whose "Studies" those of Cramer have now been wholly superseded. I was not, however, prepared for such effects as he produced, the charm of which was not so much derived from his brilliant manipulation as from the feeling his exquisitely pure *cantabile* playing produced. In point of taste, expression, and sensibility, I believe John Baptiste Cramer to have been un-rivalled; for he possessed the power of making the pianoforte "sing," as if it were a human voice, perfectly under control.

At a later period than that to which I am referring, when Hummel was in England, the four greatest pianists of the day met at the house of a mutual friend—an amateur of universally acknowledged celebrity, Mr. Alsager, as I believe—Hummel, Kalkbrenner, Moscheles, and Cramer. The first, having been asked to play, improvised at some length, but by no means with his usual facility of invention or execution. When he had finished, Kalkbrenner and Moscheles were requested to give some "touch of their quality." Each having absolutely refused to do so, Cramer was asked to contribute to the gratification of the company. For some time he also declined, but being earnestly pressed by Hummel that he would let him hear what he could do, because of what had been told him as to his repu-tation, he at length consented. Sitting down to the pianoforte after his usual unpretending manner, he began one of Beetho-ven's sonatas, then almost entirely new to English—although by no means so to German—ears. In a few minutes his whole audience were literally entranced, and sat breathlessly listening to every note and phrase of the several *motivos*, which seemed to reveal some new inspiration at every turn. When he had concluded, Hummel rushed up to him, seized him in his arms, and kissed him on each cheek, exclaiming, "Never till now have

I heard Beethoven!" To their credit be it said, both Kalk-brenner and Moscheles, although not after quite so demonstrative a manner, echoed Hummel's praise; for, to all intents and purposes, they too had been made to understand—perhaps for the first time—the intention of "the giant of harmony," which they had hitherto failed to comprehend or appreciate to its full extent.

Of Kalkbrenner there is no need that I should speak at any length. Although he obtained a prominent position about this period, and was much fêted and followed, he never by any chance touched the feelings, or gave an indication of being anything else than a mere brilliant mechanist. His execution was indeed prodigious; but he could play scarcely any other compositions than his own with anything like taste or proficiency, and the almost total absence of genuine method or phrasing therein caused a repetition to be both tedious and wearisome. Most of Kalkbrenner's compositions were little else than frivolous *fantasias*, consisting of five or six variations upon some popular Italian (operatic) air, an English ballad, or a vulgar Scotch song, which, being anything but agreeable when even performed by himself, were absolutely intolerable whenever they were attempted either by inferior performers or mere commonplace amateurs.

Incomparably superior to Kalkbrenner in every respect was Cipriani Potter—a really sound musician and a genuine *artiste*, who must always be remembered with gratitude for having at a very early period of his career manifested a decided preference for Beethoven's works, as he in later years manfully stood up against unmitigated opposition to those of Schumann. As, in the former instance, he was somewhat ridiculed by older members of the musical profession for his devotion to Beethoven, on the presumption that he was too young to appreciate that composer's peculiar merits, so he was in later years sneered at for his admiration of Schumann, on the ground that he had become old and infatuated. As, however, Cipriani Potter lived to witness his own enthusiasm for the older " master " equalled by the whole profession, so was he spared to ascertain that his judgment had been quite as sound with regard to the latter. I had the great privilege of hearing Mr. Potter play on numerous occasions, as well as of enjoying the honour of his friendship during many years, and I have no hesitation in saying that, after John Baptiste Cramer, he must be reputed to have been, between the years 1810—22, *nulli secundus.*

Another pianist, of foreign extraction, Pio Cianchettini, made an ephemeral sensation about this time, but failed to secure a permanent position. But for his having come to England in 1809, to act for Madame Catalani as her pianist and accompanyist, and returning with her for the same purpose in 1822, it is doubtful whether he would ever have obtained the slightest consideration. So far as my memory serves, I should say that he was the flimsiest player I ever heard during this or any other time ; for both his execution and his compositions were of the most mediocre quality. It was, however, far different with respect to Moscheles, whose command over the keyboard of the piano was truly extraordinary, whether considered in relation to force, delicacy, or rapidity of execution. As Madame Catalani burst through all the fetters commonly imposed upon other singers, so Moscheles seemed to disdain all technical rules, because of his having been thoroughly acquainted with them. As the opinion of a well-instructed critic—whose opinion had great influence about this time—thoroughly coincides with my own, I have the less hesitation in quoting it respecting the talent of this eminent German professor, to whom the Leipsic Conservatoire, in later times, owed so much of its excellence and pre-eminence as the very best modern training school of the Fatherland. That critic says: "Moscheles' wrist, hand, and finger-joints exhibited a variety of position and a pliability that were truly wonderful; yet so nicely did he control his touch that when, from the elevation of his hand, the spectator might have expected its descent in thunder, as it were, the ear was never shocked by the slightest harshness. There was a spring and an elasticity in his fingers when applied to quick *arpeggio* passages, that brought out the most brilliant tones, whilst in those touching movements that constitute generally what is termed expression, his manner was no less effective. But the most extraordinary part of Moscheles' playing was perhaps the velocity and certainty with which he passed from one distant interval to another. His thumbs"—they were very large and thick—"seemed to act as intermediate points, from which his fingers were directed to almost the remote parts of the instrument, over which they flew with a rapidity wholly inconceivable; yet the uniformity of his touch and tone were so strictly preserved, that an imperfect note was never, and an unfinished note seldom, heard. Every great player has his *forte;* but in this species of execution Moscheles was unrivalled." With respect to expression Moscheles was, however, considerably inferior to John Baptiste Cramer. Had he possessed this quality in proportion to his other excellences, I should have pronounced him to have been one of the greatest pianists I ever heard. Failing, however, in this most important feature, it could scarcely be said of him, as of his truly eminent contemporary, that although he

> "Could swell the soul to rage,"

it was within his means to

> "Kindle soft desire."

CHAPTER III.

1824.

In the course of this year the good fortune befell me of making the acquaintance of Sir George Smart. It was at the —— Festival, when it happened that, from twenty other "boy choristers," I was selected to attend upon him as a sort of musical aide-de-camp. Not only did this occurrence lay the foundation of a lasting friendship between that good old man and myself, but it helped me to make the acquaintance of a considerable number of the most eminent musicians of that time, of whom I have to speak. As no man of his day had a greater influence upon the progress of music in England than Sir George Smart, it will not, I think, be considered out of place or irrelevant if some particulars of his career be recorded.

George Thomas Smart, one of the few links between the musical celebrities of the past and present times, was born in London on the 10th of May, 1776. Manifesting at a very early age a taste for music, and giving a most promising indication of correctness of ear, his father, himself connected with the musical profession, unlike other parents, such as those of Handel and J. B. Cramer, determined to encourage his inclination. Of the three chief metropolitan schools of music then existing—St.

Paul's, Westminster Abbey, and the Chapel Royal, St. James's—the last was selected as the best for the training of its future composer and organist; and it soon became apparent, from the assiduity with which he prosecuted his studies—under the tuition of Dr. Ayrton—and the aptitude he evinced in mastering the technicalities of the art of composition, that a brilliant career was before him.

Although the tendency of a cathedral training, under which the musical tuition of the Chapel Royal wholly ranges, is much more conducive to promote the cultivation than to facilitate the development of the more serious styles of progressive harmony, yet the youthful aspirant did not permit himself to be trammelled by its heavier rules and severer proportions. Handel had only been dead seventeen years when George Thomas Smart was born; and the influence of that master's majestic compositions, better appreciated afterwards than previously to his decease, was even then rapidly increasing. The attention of the juvenile student was naturally drawn to Handel's larger and broader compositions. Nevertheless he did not, on this account, neglect that master's lighter specimens, which had been written during his earlier career for the Italian opera, and which, it may be said, he had introduced into England. These, indeed, he carefully noted and studied, no less than the more stupendous passages of the great German's massive oratorios. Intuitively of a lively and versatile temperament, as he continued to be throughout a long and highly successful career, George Thomas Smart, upon leaving the Chapel Royal, was attracted to the great metropolitan theatres, where Dr. Arne had made " the power of music" to be so much felt as to have caused English opera to become a rival of the drama. Into the progress of musical dramatic art he at once threw himself with the greatest energy ; and by the skill with which he arranged and directed the performances at the houses in which he was engaged, he elevated the tone and increased the popularity of this comparatively novel means of public entertainment. During the years, however, in which his more arduous services were demanded by professional and theatrical engagements he did not cease to pay attention to the cathedral services of the Church ; but becoming, at the Chapel Royal, the deputy of Dr. Dupuis, who had given him lessons on the organ, whilst John Baptiste Cramer was his master for the pianoforte, and at Westminster Abbey of Dr Arnold when he had scarcely reached manhood, he prosecuted his studies with the utmost perseverance, being determined to rise in his profession rather by the legitimate means of scholarship and talent than by mere favouritism or patronage.*

The activity of George Thomas Smart's early career was, indeed, a source of constant remark amongst those who were aware of the numerous duties he punctually and assiduously fulfilled ; whilst his singular aptitude for meeting and overcoming difficulties, and his invariable kindness of disposition and happy tact in allaying the differences of contending musicians —always, like poets and authors, an *irritable genus*—endeared him to all classes with whom he came in contact.

In the year 1811, being called to Dublin to conduct a series of musical performances, the Duke of Richmond, at that time Lord Lieutenant, conferred upon him the honour of knighthood,

---

* Whilst Sir George Smart was a chorister of the Chapel Royal, he obtained the favour of Queen Charlotte, who was so delighted with his manners, as also with his singing, that she promised him her patronage and support in after life—a promise she faithfully kept, although her *protégé* drew very sparingly upon it, preferring to make his way by his own perseverance and industry.

as a mark of consideration for the efficiency of his arrangements, and especially for the manifestation of his musical talents. From that time the name of Thomas sank into oblivion, and ever afterwards he was invariably known in his profession only as " Sir George Smart," as I shall now continue to designate him.

Having permanently established his reputation, Sir George Smart, on his return to London, assumed the highest grade in the musical profession—that of an orchestral conductor. The advance of music in popular favour had not then attained to anything approaching the dimensions it has now assumed. The patronage bestowed upon it was, in a measure, merely partial, and emanated rather from the rich and prosperous than from the multitude. The performance of Handel's oratorios during the season of Lent attracted some attention; but until Sir George Smart was entrusted with the direction, they met with little consideration, and were shorn of more than half their importance. During the thirteen years that he filled the arduous post of conductor at Drury Lane and Covent Garden, contending against the frivolities of one set of patrons and the requirements of another, as well as against a large amount of public indifference, he yet managed to assert the claims of the higher works of musical science; and however much he was pained and annoyed at the necessity for interspersing with lighter and more frivolous compositions one part at least of those Lenten entertainments, designated by the name of oratorios, he permitted no season to pass without having done something to insure progress. Even so early as the year 1814—the second season of his oratorio administration at Drury Lane theatre— he contrived to introduce, on the 25th of February, Beethoven's

Christus am Œlberge, better known in England as the *Mount of Olives*. He also brought out at the same theatre, on the 10th of February, 1815, that master's celebrated *Battle Symphony*. Although the former work failed to obtain the general appreciation to which the genius of Beethoven was entitled, it yet marked a period in the advancement of musical taste, which led up to that appreciation of the great master which is now quite as extensive in Great Britain as it is even in Germany, the birthplace of that "mighty giant of harmony" —as grand a "tone-poet" as the world has yet produced. Of the capability Sir George Smart manifested at this period of his career as a conductor, it was well said by a severe but honest critic, " that no man in the profession possessed so large an experience, so acute and so sound a tact, so profound a judgment in apprehending what would take most surely with the public, such unwearied energy and steadiness in the prosecution of a plan, and such promptitude in seizing an advantage or repairing an unexpected evil."

In 1816 Sir George Smart was selected, as one of the most eminent musicians of the time, to take part in conducting the concerts of the Philharmonic Society, which had been instituted three years previously for the performance of the works of the more celebrated modern masters. During his membership of this Society Sir George Smart invariably evinced the spirit of a true *artiste*; for not only did he occupy the post of conductor at forty-nine concerts between the years 1816 and 1844—when he resigned his appointment—but he never hesitated to undertake a minor duty, if the perfection or success of a performance could thereby be insured. Thus, when Haydn visited London in 1791, to produce the first six of those great masterpieces—

his twelve Symphonies written to Salomon's order—he undertook on one occasion to beat the drums, and faithfully observed and diligently carried out that learned *maestro's* wishes and directions. He did not, however, cease to be a member of the Philharmonic Society on account of his retirement from his share in the musical direction; but having been one amongst the original founders of that Society in 1813, he continued to take an active interest in its affairs, and eagerly exerted himself to increase its musical efficiency and financial prosperity until a very short period before his death.

Whilst thus actively engaged as the conductor of oratorios and secular concerts, Sir George Smart still retained his attachment for the cathedral school, in which he had been originally trained; and having been appointed in 1822 one of the organists, and in 1838 one of the composers, of the Chapel Royal, St. James's, notwithstanding his numerous avocations, and the heavy demands they made upon his time, he not only fulfilled the duties of those positions, but added to the roll of classical productions which a long succession of eminent musicians, from the time of the Reformation, had provided for the services of the Church.

In the discharge of his duties as one of the organists of the Chapel Royal, Sir George Smart presided at the organ at the funeral of George IV.; at the coronation and funeral of William IV.; at the coronation and marriage of Her Majesty; and at many other royal and public ceremonies of importance.

In 1834 it was determined to celebrate in Westminster Abbey the seventy-fifth anniversary of Handel's death, and on that occasion the entire musical arrangements were placed in Sir George Smart's hands. The successful issue to which he brought that great and arduous undertaking may be inferred from the testimony borne to the efficiency of the entire proceedings by the performers, who presented him with a costly and massive silver inkstand, "to mark their esteem for his character as a man, and his talent as a musician; and also as a token of their approbation of the able manner in which he had conducted the performances."

The metropolitan reputation of Sir George Smart naturally insured for him many provincial engagements, where his talents were as fully appreciated as his character was respected. In the course of his lengthened career he conducted musical Festivals and concerts in no less than twenty-three provincial cities and towns—viz., Bath, Bristol, Edinburgh, Reading, Liverpool, Manchester, Birmingham, Norwich, Newcastle-on-Tyne, Bury St. Edmund's, Dublin, Derby, Cambridge, Hull, Greenwich, Woolwich, Colchester, Brighton, Coventry, Cheltenham, Nottingham, Clifton, and Hereford. The most remarkable, perhaps, of all these provincial engagements was that which he undertook at —— in the autumn of 1824, at which our acquaintance commenced. So successful, indeed, was the well-remembered Festival of that year, and so entirely was its musical efficiency attributable to his exertions, that the committee of management voted him a gold snuff-box of the value of thirty guineas; whilst the corporation—as that of Dublin had previously done —conferred the freedom of the city upon him, "for the zeal, energy, and ability he had exerted."

In the year 1825, Sir George Smart was induced to pay a visit to Vienna, where he was most cordially received and welcomed by Beethoven, whose genius—as I have already said— he was one of the first musicians of this country to acknowledge. His chief object in undertaking so long and tedious a journey as was the transit from the English to the Austrian capital at that period, was to ascertain the *times* of his *Sinfonias* and other compositions from Beethoven himself, in order that they might be rendered in England according to his own express wish and intention. In this respect Sir George Smart was as greatly interested as he had always been in preserving and maintaining the traditions of Handel. As to the method which that great master of oratorio adopted in giving the accurate time of his various works according to his own will and purpose, and also as to the manner in which his songs were rendered by Madame Mara, Mrs. Billington, Mrs. Salmon, and Miss Stephens, and by Harrison, Bartleman, Braham, and Vaughan, no one could have had more accurate information than Sir George Smart himself. Not only had he been taught by Joah Bates, the friend whom Handel himself had directed, but he had heard all the older, and instructed most of the younger, of the above-named singers in the very method originally intended. It may, therefore, be a source of congratulation to the musical world to learn that " those traditions " are not lost, Sir George Smart having, with the utmost care and pains, prepared a work —which it is to be hoped may soon be published—in which they are in every particular preserved.

On returning from his visit to Beethoven at Vienna, Sir George Smart made the acquaintance of Mendelssohn at Berlin, and induced him to visit England ; and it is not amongst the least of the honours which, in the course of his eminent career, he attained, that he may be said to have introduced that master's great specimen of pure oratorio composition, *St. Paul*, to an English public, he having himself conducted its first performance at Liverpool in the autumn of 1836. Between Mendels-

sohn and Sir George Smart esteem and affection were indeed as
mutual as the same sentiments had been between Weber and
himself. He was, indeed, the first amongst the musicians of
this country to recognize the talents of the composer of *Der
Freischütz*—as he had been of the author of the *Mount of
Olives*—and to make him known by the introduction of his
overture to that weird opera at those Festivals and concerts
which he conducted. It was at the —— Festival of 1824 that
I first heard that grand orchestral prelude, the melodious singu-
larity of which, as well as the novelty of its brilliant orchestration, riveted my attention. The frequent performance of the
overture to *Der Freischütz*, both in London and the provinces,
speedily led to the production of one or more versions of the
entire opera at several of the great London theatres—not without protest from Sir George Smart against the mutilations and
additions which were chiefly made—to his discredit, must it be
spoken—by Sir Henry Bishop. Its success, although it was
presented in such an ineffective form, made the author so popular in England, that nothing appeared to promise greater *éclat*
than to engage him to compose, and bring him over to conduct
the music of another opera. For this purpose Sir George Smart
proceeded to Germany in company with Mr. C. Kemble, the
result being the engagement of Weber to write his *Oberon*, and
to support by his presence the reputation he had already gained
in England. On reaching London, Weber became the inmate
of Sir George Smart's house, then No. 91, now No. 103, Great
Portland Street, and there completed the entire score of that
opera, the libretto of which was supplied by Mr. Planché.*

* It cannot but be a source of satisfaction to know that this venerable
dramatist has recently published his own personal " Reminiscences," a portion

When this celebrated musician arrived in this country, in the month of March, 1826, he was in the last stage of consumption; he, however, brought out his opera, and continued to fulfil his public engagements and prosecute his private studies with the utmost assiduity and cheerfulness. He had even fixed to leave England on his return to Germany on the 7th of June; but on the morning of the 5th he was found dead in his bed in Sir George Smart's house, which he had never left as a place of residence from the day of his arrival.

From the position Sir George Smart occupied as organist and composer of the Chapel Royal, and from the skill and tact he invariably manifested in the direction both of sacred and secular music, he obtained the patronage and encouragement of several members of the Royal family, nearly all of whom, especially the Prince Regent (afterwards George IV.) and the Duke of Sussex, were sound and accomplished musicians. So greatly, indeed, did he enjoy the confidence of the latter Royal duke, that he was nominated by him to the office of Grand Organist of "The United Grand Lodge of Free and Accepted Masons," of whom he (the Duke of Sussex) was for many years the Grand Master. The wisdom of this appointment was apparent at all the great Masonic festivals, since a rich musical treat was provided for the entertainment of the brethren of that ancient and mysterious order; the compositions selected for illustration being always of so classical a character as to add quite as much to the charm as to the celebrity of those popular *réunions*.

Among the many professional pupils who had the advantage of Sir George Smart's tuition, the following may be

of which had previously appeared in *London Society*, the interest of which is of a truly comprehensive character.

named as having obtained something more than a transient or ordinary celebrity—viz., Miss Paton (afterwards Mrs. Wood), Miss Louisa Pyne, the Misses Cawses; Messrs. T. Welsh, Henry Phillips, and Lockey; and more especially for sacred music and the traditions of Handel and the English masters, Mdme. Sontag, Mdme. Lind-Goldschmidt, Mdme. Rudersdorff, and Signor Belletti.

Throughout a lengthened and an arduous career, Sir George Smart rose to eminence and estimation—acknowledged quite as much upon the Continent as at home—by his general acquaintance with the details of business, by gentlemanly manners, by skill in his profession, and by honour and integrity in its exercise, no less than by a liberality which was both generous and beneficial to those towards whom it was extended. To many an unfortunate and unsuccessful *artiste* he afforded sympathy and aid, quite as much by his advice and counsel as by his purse. Beloved by his family, respected by his friends, his society was eagerly sought by those who appreciate worth. He attained a good old age, was active and cheerful, and possessed of all his faculties to the last, taking as deep an interest as he had ever shown in the progress of his art, and manifesting the same genial and versatile disposition which had endeared him to all who had the privilege of his friendship and esteem to the very hour of his decease, which took place at 12, Bedford Square, February 23rd, 1867, his mortal remains having been interred at Kensal Green on the last day of the same month.

Although I have delayed my own personal "Recollections" to give the preceding sketch of Sir George Smart's remarkable career, I cannot altogether dismiss him from consideration. He was so much mixed up with all the prominent musical proceedings of the period I have now reached, that it is impossible to refer to the one without continually mentioning the other. If Sir George Smart's biography be ever written—for which ample materials of his own providing exist—it will not only throw immense light upon the manner in which music progressed in Great Britain during the whole of his long and actively-occupied life, but it will be found to be rich in anecdotes of the most amusing character concerning Royalty, persons of distinction, and well-known celebrities, no less than of musicians of the highest name and talent as of those of smaller reputation. Sir George Smart was as ready with a repartee as he was in making arrangements for a musical Festival and conducting its performances. His tact was extraordinary. He seemed able, as if by intuition, to detect in an instant if anything were wrong amongst the several members of his orchestra, and at once set it right by a pleasantry which put everyone in good humour. He never wearied his forces by tedious repetitions at rehearsals, nor provoked them by constant fault-finding. He acted upon the good old principle, that " one pennyworth of oil is worth more than a whole pound's-worth of vinegar," and so smoothed difficulties, that they disappeared almost as soon as they started up. He could, however, be equally resolute in exacting obedience if anything like resistance to his authority were offered—a very rare thing indeed in his career—when he acted at once with the utmost decision, so as to enforce his authority, and to show that he could be as firm as he was kind-hearted and genial. Sometimes, however, he would effect this by a witticism, the point of which told with quite as much force as if he had displayed anger or given way to indignation. Well do I remember an instance of this character at the first evening performance of the ———— Festival of 1824, the year in which I made his acquaintance, because of Mrs. Salmon's inability to discharge her duties respectably. This anecdote appears to be so much to the point concerning Sir George Smart's peculiarity of which I am writing, that I have the less hesitation in giving it. The time had arrived for that lady to sing " Cease your funning," with variations, which was usually one of her most successful efforts. After keeping the audience waiting some minutes without appearing, a note was passed to me, which I handed to Sir George Smart, who at once gave me directions to " fetch the lady up." I met her struggling towards the orchestra, and her condition was at once apparent. She had unhappily given way to intemperance—a habit which was then but too frequent—and was positively so tipsy that she could scarcely stand. The audience having become impatient, of the male portion who at once perceived the poor creature's condition, some tittered, whilst others slightly hissed. She held her "part" upside down, and turning round to Sir George Smart, told him she would not sing "that variation," and should change it for another. Looking her through and through, he said at once, in an undertone of sarcasm, which, inebriated as she was, she immediately understood, "Madame, you are a large, a fine, and a handsome *fish*, but to a certainty you will *flounder* to-night." And flounder she did ; for, staggering round to the audience, at her first attempt to sing she completely broke down, and was then literally hissed off the orchestra. I, amongst others, assisted her to leave ; and when she was placed in safe hands, catching sight of my face, she hiccupped, " What, you again, boy !" evidently remembering, notwithstanding her unhappy condition, where and when we had previously met.* On the following morning Mrs. Salmon was but coldly received; but she managed to keep sober for that day and during the rest of the week, and so, in a measure, recovered the favour with which she was universally welcomed for the purity no less than the brilliancy of her vocal gifts, then rapidly on the decline.

About this time it was my good fortune to hear three other remarkable singers, who, unlike those concerning whom I have hitherto written, were of foreign instead of native growth and fame—Madame Ronzi de Begnis; her husband, Signor de Begnis; and Garcia, the father of Marie Félicité Malibran and Pauline Viardot. The first of these celebrated artistes was a Parisian by birth, having been born on the 11th January, 1800. At nine years of age she became a pupil of the Conservatoire, and in 1816 married De Begnis, who had already obtained a well-deserved reputation as a buffo actor and singer of the first class in his native country, Italy. No one could fail to be struck with the beauty of Madame Ronzi de Begnis at the moment of seeing her. In a somewhat inflated description of her it was said that " she was a model of voluptuous beauty;" and that "perhaps no performer was ever more enthusiastically admired." Although French by birth, "her features, but not her complexion, were Italian, the characteristic of the latter being a fairness so perfect as to be almost dazzling; the more so, because palpably set off by the glossy blackness of her hair. Her face was beautiful and full of intelligence, and made almost eloquent by the incessant brilliance of eyes, large, black, and expressive, and in which the

* See p. 39.

playful and the passionate by turns predominated; either expression being so natural to them, that it seemed for the time incapable of being displaced by another as suitable and as enchanting. Her mouth was so delightfully formed that she took care never to disfigure it, and whatever she sung, she did not forget this care. Her figure, if a thought more slender, would have been perfect. The exquisite outline of her swelling throat, pencilled when she sang with the blue tinge of its full veins, admitted of no parallel; it was rich and full—ineffectual terms to convey an idea of its beauty."* Boy as I was at the time I first heard this *prima donna*, I could not fail to be struck with the comeliness of her personal appearance. But I must confess that her vocalisation made a much deeper impression upon my mind, although there was a certain thinness about her voice which gave sharpness, if not shrillness, to her intonation, which, however—to use the words of a severe critic—"was respectably correct," whilst "this natural deficiency in sweetness had been little ameliorated by art." Madame Ronzi de Begnis' execution, however, in a very great measure covered this defect, as it would have done "a multitude of" other "sins." She positively revelled in the superabundantly luxuriant *roulades* which were met with in Rossini's operatic music, of which she was one of the original and most successful exponents; yet she was not merely content with singing such passages after the level manner, to which Catalani always trusted, but seemed to think that she could only accomplish her intention, as it were, with a rush, and by forcing her voice, especially in ascending the scale. To understand of what this habit consisted cannot be better explained than by the exclamation of a lady of intelligence and musical taste on

---

* Ebers' *Seven Years of the King's Theatre*, pp. 50-2.

first hearing her, "Ha! there goes a rocket!" She was not the first Rosina of Rossini's then famous and still popular *Il Barbiere;* but at least she was the first *prima donna* I ever heard in that character, as her husband was the first Figaro and Garcia the first Almaviva—a cast often since equalled but never excelled. In this part she not only sang to perfection, but she played with the utmost vivacity, indulging in all that innocent mischief in which the spoiled child but constrained ward of the imperious Dr. Bartolo might be expected to revel and delight. In the famous duet with the Barber, "Dunque io son," the point she made upon the words "Eccola qua," when giving him the note for her lover that was already written, there was an artlessness combined with an archness that few since her time have been able to excel; showing, indeed, the truth of the saying, that "upon the stage she was certainly one of the most demure, sly, lively, and arch little coquettes that one had ever learned to admire."

This will account for her having chiefly excelled in buffa opera, such as in the character of the *Barbiere* just named, and in that of Fatima in *Il Turco in Italia;* yet she was by no means deficient in the more severe parts of Agia in the *Mosè in Egitto*, and of Donna Anna in *Il Don Giovanni.* Mr. Ebers so comically expresses Madame Ronzi de Begnis' characteristics in these respective operas, that I can by no means refrain from repeating them, especially as, having seen her in all three, I can to a great extent indorse his convictions. "In the first"— Fatima in *Il Turco*—he says, " her beauty, gaiety, and that little touch of the devil so exquisite and essential in a comic actress, were almost too bewitching; but admiration was blended with astonishment when the representative of the coquettish

Fatima, changing her walk, exhibited with a life and force that spoke to the soul the wretchedness of the bereaved Donna Anna, when in thrilling accents of despair she calls on her dead father, and invokes her lover to avenge his fate."* Madame Ronzi de Begnis came to London in the year 1821, for the operatic season, with her husband, at a salary of 600*l.* each, which was raised to 1100*l.* each in 1824—a sure proof that the brilliant reputation they had previously won at "Les Italiens" (Paris), where they had both occupied positions of the first rank, was fully confirmed by the London *cognoscenti.*

It is now, however, time to describe the accomplishments of the husband, than whom "few performers had a more original conception of their parts, although he, perhaps, sometimes filled his [comic] characters to exaggeration."† In personal appearance, Signor de Begnis was "of tall stature, with strong but quick and intelligent features"—notwithstanding he was fearfully pitted with the small-pox—"and a piercing eye." Unlike his wife, he was an Italian by birth and education, having been born at Lugo, a comparatively small town in the Pontifical States, either in the year 1793 or 1795. He began his musical studies at seven years of age, under the tuition of Père Bongiovanni, a monk, by whom he was transferred to Signor Mandini, a celebrated singer, and to Signor Saraceni, a composer of no great note or celebrity, when, after seven years' drilling in the chapel of his native town, his voice broke.‡ At the carnival of the year 1813 he made his *début* at Modena in an opera by

---

* *Seven Years of the King's Theatre*, pp. 52-3.   † Ib. p. 55.

‡ See Fétis, *Biographie Universelle des Musiciens*, &c., tom. ii. 447 : Paris, 1860-5.

Pavesi, entitled *Marco Antonio*, whence he went to Forli and Rimini, and then to Sienna, for the same festival of 1814, where he made his *entrée* in the comic part of Pazzo in Paer's *Agnese.* From this time his reputation was confirmed, although neither he nor his wife reached Paris till the carnival of 1819. During the intervening five years he had, however, sung and acted in very many of the leading opera-houses of his native country, Venice and Naples excepted. It was not till after three years of Parisian success—in 1821—that either the one or the other came to London, when the opera selected for the occasion was Rossini's *Il Turco in Italia*, by means of which their popularity was immediately insured. Signor de Begnis' voice was a bass of pure and legitimate tone, and, unlike the organs of Angrisani or Zuchelli—of the latter of whom, having heard him afterwards, although he came to England in the same year as the De Begnis, I have yet to speak—was not remarkable for the roundness, weight and volume of its tone, nor more light, brilliant, or expressive. It rather possessed a peculiar distinctness, although in the tone itself there could be said to be little or nothing to raise it in any other respect above the ordinary powers of a moderately gifted bass voice. He had also by no means the peculiar rich finish which is so essential to perfect vocalisation, notwithstanding his intonation was more correct than is the general rule with Italian male singers of that class, of which he must always be named as a thorough representative.

My own "Recollections" so perfectly accord with what was said of Signor de Begnis' articulation by the same critic to whom I have had occasion once and again to refer,* that I cannot but prefer to use them, rather than to rely upon my

* See pp. 26, 41, 65.

own explanation. "Few persons," says Mr. R. M. Bacon, "who have not made the attempt, can judge of the delicate formation of the organs of speech indispensable to the rapid articulation which a singer in this style—that of buffo—must possess; and even with organs well adapted for the purpose, the difficulty is overcome only by continual and laborious practice. The Italian tongue, in the frequency of its vowels and the favourable disposition of its soft syllables, presents indeed a facility which no other language affords; and it is very doubtful whether, without such a selection and arrangement of words as imply more study than the lyric poets of our own country are disposed to bestow upon their diction, the same expedient could be employed in English with any approach to success. In this accomplishment, however, Signor de Begnis was supreme. His power of rapid pronunciation was so complete, that it was very seldom the orchestra could keep pace with his desires in this respect. He fairly outstripped the instrumentalists and the conductor, who could rarely stretch their imagination to the belief that the human voice and tongue were capable of such velocity. He was, nevertheless, as distinct as he was rapid, and cut his syllables so finely, that the hearer scarcely ever lost any of the distinctions of the character or of the language. In these particulars Signor de Begnis was supreme."* "For refined embellishment comic bass singing allows no room, and such an air as will permit the addition of polished *rifioramenti* very rarely falls to the lot of the legitimate *buffo caricato*, which we esteem Signor de Begnis exactly to be. In the very few attempts at serious music in which we heard this performer, he might fairly have pleaded with Signor Arionelli, in the *Son-in-Law*, when

* *The Quarterly Musical Magazine and Review*, vol. iv. pp. 310-11.

pressed to marriage, 'that it was entirely out of his way;' but in all that respected the mere mechanical branches—such as certainty in his distances, time, &c.—Signor de Begnis appeared to be generally accurate and informed."*

This critic was by no means an admirer of Rossini's music. Purcell and Handel in his estimation were gold; Haydn and Mozart were silver; but "the sweet swan of Pesaro" was nothing else than "tin"—the quality of that ore itself; although, in all human probability, Rossini produced more of that commodity, in the sense of £ s. d., than those greater masters who preceded him had ever managed to extract from the pockets of the public, either for their own personal advantage or by the amusement they afforded. The opinion which he expresses must, therefore, be taken "with a difference;" for although Rossini may by no means be said to be equal to the above-named composers —superior to them even his greatest admirers will never be induced to believe or say he was—yet, to all intents and purposes, he was "a great master," and founded an operatic school, in which, although he has had a host of imitators, he has by no means at present been excelled.

"Upon the execution of a bass singer," this critic continues, "Rossini certainly makes far larger demands than any preceding composer; and notwithstanding the ascent has been very much sloped and smoothed by the graceful passages with which the writers of the last fifty or sixty years† have invested this path, both in the church, the orchestra, and on the stage, a singer of this description might well be pardoned for throwing away

---

* *The Quarterly Musical Magazine and Review,* vol. iv. p. 311.

† This, be it remembered, was written in the year after the De Begnis first appeared in London.

much of what Rossini has allotted to him, in absolute despair of executing it with effect, or indeed at all. If this assertion should seem unwarranted, we refer the disputant to *La Gazza Ladra* and *Il Barbiere di Seviglia*, where he will find divisions which, from their compass, rapidity, and construction conjoined, should appear to be absolutely unattainable to a legitimate bass voice. Difficulties, however, of this nature did not dismay Signor de Begnis; and though the articulation of words combined with notes—the syllabic rather than the melismatic construction of passages—displayed him to the greatest advantage, he had yet a great facility in the execution of divisions, considering the weight of his voice, which, though not of the fullest description, could not be considered as light-toned."* " There was the same purity, precision, and delicacy both in Signor de Begnis' intellect and organ. His humour "—although by no means so unctuous as that of his gigantic successor Lablache— "was piquant and poignant, but never broad or coarse ; and thus, if he sometimes fell short of the exuberantly rich fancy and the unceasing bustle which made Ambrogetti occasionally so irresistibly comic, he avoided the extravagance which sometimes rendered that admirable performer offensively absurd, at the same time that, as a singer, he was in every respect infinitely his superior."† " On the whole, therefore, Signor de Begnis was, both as an actor and a singer, unquestionably of the first class; and if he did not rise to the excellence to which both Naldi and Ambrogetti attained, he exceeded them both infinitely in the other."‡

From some unexplained cause, Madame Ronzi de Begnis,

---

* *The Quarterly Magazine and Review*, vol. iv. p. 312.
† *The Quarterly Magazine and Review*, vol. iv. p. 312.   ‡ Ib. p. 313.

soon after the opera season of 1825, separated from her husband, and they were no more heard together. She retired to Italy, and was the leading *prima donna* of the San Carlo at Naples until the year 1843, when, after having sung in public for twenty-seven years, she retired into private life, her powers being wholly impaired, scarcely a ghost of her former excellence remaining. Signor de Begnis remained in England, chiefly at Bath, until after 1827, when he left for the United States, and established an operatic company in New York, which he carried on for a considerable time with varying fortune, and eventually died there of cholera.

I now approach the grandest foreign operatic tenor whom the past generation ever saw or heard—Manuel-del-Popolo Vincente Garcia, who possessed a voice of so great a volume and compass as to leave most others at a distance. Like by far the greater number of operatic celebrities, this extraordinary man commenced his musical career in a cathedral choir—that of Seville, where he was born, January 22, 1775—at the early age of six years; his masters being Don Antonio Ripa and Juan Almarada. At this period there was no theatre at Seville, so that he heard in his childhood nothing but church music. His talent, however, was so considerable, that not only had he become at seventeen years of age known as a singer, but he had established himself as a composer and an orchestral director; on which account the manager of the Cadiz theatre secured his services, where he *débuted*, but made no sensation whatever, histrionic genius seeming in no way whatever to have been by nature imparted to him. Returning shortly afterwards to Madrid, he appeared there in oratorio with no better success.

The innate talent, nevertheless, which existed in him was not to be crushed by such early failure. Garcia was a man of iron will, and, one way or other, either as a composer or as a singer, had resolved to win his way to fame and fortune. In this pursuit he at first adopted the profession of an operatic composer, and in the course of a few years so far succeeded, that his works were successfully represented in most of the Spanish theatres. Ambition then directed his steps to Paris; and although he had never previously sung in any other language than his own, he ventured to appear at the Opéra Bouffe on the 11th of February, 1808, in Paer's *Griselda*, where, instead of failing, he made so great a success, that in only three months afterwards he was engaged at "Les Italiens," where "he led the business," and was so much in demand that his health gave way. In 1811 he went to Italy, and was accepted with the utmost enthusiasm, as an *artiste* of the first rank, at Turin, Naples, and Rome. Not deeming his method by any means perfect, he availed himself of his residence in "the land of song" to study under Anzani—one of the most celebrated tenors of that time —the pure Italian method, in which he made such strides, that in the following year he completely carried away the Neapolitan public by his singing in his own opera, *Il Califo di Bagdad*. Whilst at Naples in 1815 Rossini wrote one of the leading parts of his *Elizabetta* for him, and in the following year that of Almaviva in the *Barbiere*, which was given at Rome, and all but failed from a variety of *contretemps* which drove both composer and *artiste* nearly frantic. In 1816 Catalani secured his services as her first tenor at "Les Italiens" in Paris; from which point of time his prosperity proceeded onwards with unabating increase. In 1817 he came to London, and sang at the King's Theatre with Madame Fodor in the *Barbiere*, as well as at various concerts. Returning to Paris in 1819, he introduced that opera for the first time to the French public, and remained their especial favourite till 1824, during which time his greatest parts were that already named, *Otello* and *Don Giovanni.* In the last of these operas he rivalled Ambrogetti by the grace and elegance of his deportment, and the marvellous efficiency of his execution of the music, although much of it had to be transposed—being written for a baritone—to suit the compass of his voice. It was remarked on all hands, that not only did he look like a Spanish Don just stepped out from the frame of one of Velasquez's grandest portraits, but that his bearing was essentially that of the noble Spanish hidalgo. Yet, in spite of his acknowledged talent, Garcia scarcely excited that degree of attention or consideration in England that the rest of Europe had accorded to his merit and acquirements—a singular coincidence, indeed, inasmuch as " a more commanding actor or a more gifted singer had previously to his day rarely appeared."

As I have already said, Garcia's voice was a tenor of great volume and compass, which he had been at the utmost pains to cultivate and form according to the methods of the best schools; but perhaps it was not so rich as those of others, before or since his time, in quality or freshness. It was, however, very brilliant and flexible, and so highly cultivated, that not only did no passage seem difficult to his facility, but he executed every conceivable combination of notes in a highly-finished manner, tempering and preparing, as it were, his utmost vehemence according " to the most rigid laws of science." He was also an admirable musician, which rendered his invention more fertile than that of any other singer, either male or female, I ever heard, not even excepting his two gifted daughters, and especially the elder of the two—the too early lost and never to be forgotten—Marie Félicité Malibran.

But what chiefly exalted his style was the sensibility with which he penetrated into the full meaning of everything he sang; for he entered heart and soul into the music, as well as the action, of the scene; and from the moment he set his foot upon the stage he devoted himself wholly to its expression, giving all his faculties and powers to the character he had to sustain and to the composition he had to sing. "He was alike forcible and tender, and hurried his audience with him wheresoever he designed to carry them. No part of his performance ever languished for an instant; and even if he had a weak passage," he always managed to strengthen or conceal it by the most appropriate and elegant embellishment. For this he encountered the objections of hypercritical judges, who pronounced his style to be much too florid, if not consisting of an unmeaning profusion of passages, that the failure and decadence of his voice might be hidden. On the first occasion of my meeting with Garcia, not having been accustomed to this kind of vocalisation, it completely bewildered me; but having the opportunity of hearing him very frequently afterwards, I became charmed by the facility with which he encountered difficulties of his own contrivance and overcame them. Acting upon a judgment which has since been matured by many opportunities of hearing the best singers from Garcia's day to the present time, I am thoroughly convinced that "his playfulness was the effect of exuberant power and facility." It might too—as has been pertinently suggested by competent persons—have been the result of his long-continued personation of the leading tenor " characters of Rossini's operas, which not only task the execution of the singer, but which, by identifying ornament with expression, stimulated him to new experiments, by relieving his judgment from those limitations which the older—and, as some think, the purer—style of writing laid upon him."

Such was Garcia—" a man, take him for all in all, whose like I ne'er shall look upon," or hear, " again." I cannot, however, yet dismiss him wholly from my " Recollections," because I am now entering upon a period when, in bringing out his eldest daughter, he was engaged in musical transactions of the greatest importance, which caused the progress of music not merely to move more rapidly in England, but gave it an impetus, the effect of which was little less than electric, and the force of which is felt in all its intensity even at the present time.

CHAPTER IV.

1824-1826.

ABOUT this period there were four remarkable violinists before the public, whom it was my privilege not only frequently to hear, but also to have been acquainted with—François Cramer and Mori, Spohr and Kiesewetter. There was a fifth, who was much esteemed and highly appreciated, Spagnioletti ; but as he was chiefly known as the leader of the King's Theatre —or Opera—band, and not as a concerto player, it is unnecessary more particularly to refer to him than to say that he was considered to be highly competent for the position he held, but to have had very little talent beyond it. It was vastly different, however, with his four contemporaries already named. François Cramer, one of the most amiable men that ever lived, was the second son of William Cramer, to whom I have already referred.* Unlike his brother, John Baptist, who had a decided aversion to the violin, and speedily gave it up for the pianoforte, François set himself with hearty goodwill at once to master the mechanical difficulties of that instrument, and to fit himself for orchestral playing. So rapidly did he advance, that his father, who was as severe a master as he was an accomplished performer himself, deemed him to be competent for a place in the opera

* See p. 71.

band, although he was scarcely seventeen years of age at the time of his appointment. Perseverance was the great characteristic of the Cramers, and by means of that invaluable faculty, a very few years elapsed before François became principal second violin, under his father, not only at the Opera, but at the Ancient concerts and the musical Festivals which were then beginning to be given in various provincial towns. In 1800 he succeeded his father as leader of the Ancient concerts, by the express wish of George III., and by the unanimous election of the directors, who consisted of noblemen, archbishops, and others of the highest distinction. He was likewise engaged as one of thè leaders of the Philharmonic Society's concerts, and had the honour of holding the same place, by immediate command, at the coronation of George IV. As an orchestral *chef d'attaque,* François Cramer was better known than as a concerto player, and it was but seldom, during a very long career, that he undertook the latter position. I had once the good fortune to hear him play one of Meyseder's concertos, which he undertook at a very short notice for a brother *artiste,* who was prevented from appearing by sudden illness ; and although there was a comparative absence of brilliancy in his execution, it was neat and facile, and thoroughly compensated for higher qualities by purity of tone. He continued, till within a very short time of his death, in 1848, to perform the duties of his profession, pursuing them quite as much for the sake of relief from severe mental trials as for that of subsistence. He had set his affections upon his second son, named after himself—a young man of the highest character and promise, who had passed through his academical career at Oxford, first as a chorister, and afterwards as a Bible clerk, at New College, with far greater success than might have been expected, considering the few advantages he derived from the education then granted to that class of students. Scarcely, however, had he proceeded to his B.A. degree, and was looking forward to his ordination—a chaplain's appointment in the same college having been offered him by the late Dr. Shuttleworth, the then warden, and afterwards, for the brief space of one year only, Bishop of Chichester—when the seeds of pulmonary consumption so rapidly developed themselves, that he did not live to be admitted into "holy orders," the hope of which had been as strong in his own breast as it had been in that of his father. The young François Cramer was a contemporary of my own, and my most intimate friend at Oxford; and out of affectionate regard to his memory, as well as respect for his father, I cannot refrain from mentioning the chief cause of the latter remaining much later in his profession than is generally usual.

It is not often that three violinists of such distinguished eminence as Mori, Spohr, and Kiesewetter—the three consummate contemporaries of François Cramer—are brought into such immediate contiguity and comparison as they individually and collectively manifested. Three more generous rivals have perhaps rarely existed; for each had a just appreciation of the other's talent, and never failed to express it. As I have often heard them do so, I can the more positively speak of a characteristic unfortunately much more rare than prevalent amongst the members, not only of the musical, but of many other professions. To determine which of the three had the precedence was impossible. Their style was essentially different, yet equally excellent. Mori was one of the most shining ornaments of the great school of Viotti,* his natural gifts being both energetic and strong. Possessed of a lively temperament, a keen sense, a just reliance on his own powers, and last, not least, an ardent love of his art, and an unrelaxing enthusiasm, stimulated by a desire to reach and maintain, and indeed only to be satisfied with, the highest rank, he backed all these qualities by industry and perseverance, bringing also to the technical part of his profession other great requisites. " His attitude had the grace of manly confidence. His bow-arm was bold, free, and commanding, and the tone he produced was eminently firm, full, and impressive. His execution was alike marked by abundant force and fire, by extraordinary precision and prodigious facility." Notwithstanding, however, that Mori had all these qualifications, so much needed " to make a consummate player, he either overlooked, or did not sufficiently appreciate, those nice points of finish, and those graces and delicacies of expression, which, like the setting of a jewel, give it a preciousness highly enhancing its original worth." Had he travelled abroad, the comparative defects, which I have been compelled to mention, might have been in a great measure remedied, " whilst, on account of the native vigour of his talent, there would have been but little apprehension of his manliness and fire being diminished by refinement."

Although of Italian parentage, Mori was born in London in the year 1793, and from this cause he seemed to set himself up " as a sort of English champion upon his instrument "—a determination which his numerous admirers were not slow to applaud— most unwisely, as I cannot but think. He therefore persisted

* Giovanni Battista Viotti, a celebrated Piedmontese violinist, born May 23rd, 1753, and died at London, March 10th, 1824. See Fétis, *Biographie Universelle des Musiciens*, &c. tom. viii. pp. 360-364.

in staying at home to hold his own against all comers. This was undoubtedly " a gallant and chivalrous determination, alike honourable to himself and the country of his birth, because it proved to what an exalted pitch that country"—in spite of continental depreciation—" can rear such talent as he possessed." But it was scarcely fair to himself; " for such talent as he enjoyed, and which shone forth so brilliantly in his style and execution, could but have received that enlargement which can only be attained by seeing cities and men abroad. Then he might have assimilated the great and the good from others, whilst softening some and exalting other features of his performance." Mori's powers, towards the termination of his career, considerably failed. He had the folly to embark in a musical publication business, which took away from him the invaluable opportunities and means for constant practice, without which no instrumentalist, however great he may be, can maintain either his position or his reputation. He also chiefly appeared, from this cause, at his own benefit concerts, one of which, just before his death—which was comparatively sudden—he had announced with the bad taste of the programme being headed with the design of a death's head and cross-bones, with the motto " *Memento mori* " underneath. His death was indeed a practical and memorable illustration of the uncertainty of human life, as also a proof of something even more objectionable than vanity and folly. This happened in the year 1842.

If Mori's idiosyncrasy " disposed him towards all that was energetic, there were traces in his great contemporary Spohr's execution of a mind continually turning towards refinement, and deserting strength for polish." This celebrated violinist's tone was pure and delicate rather than remarkable for volume or richness. His taste was cultivated to the highest degree, and his execution was so finished that it appeared to encroach in a measure upon the vigour of his performance. But he was very far from being deficient in the necessary execution that constitutes a great violinist. The fact seemed to be, that this quality, which from its inherent pre-eminence is usually distinguishable in most violin-players, was considered by Spohr to be of secondary importance, and was, on that account, rendered less discernible by the predominating influence of superior refinement. His delicacy was so exquisite that his force was diminished in comparison. Although his bow-arm had not the nerve and command which were so exceedingly striking in Mori, he could yet sustain and protract his tone to a most extraordinary duration. His method of playing *staccato* passages was peculiar, and for the most part original, but the distances he frequently took—as if for the purpose of astonishing rather than gratifying his hearers—in passages of extremely difficult execution, could not be said to be altogether consistent with the general character of his method.

It was doubtless for this cause that Spohr was by far the least popular of the three violinists at this time before the public; for although he was undoubtedly in the very first rank of his profession and talent, especially as the founder of a purely legitimate school, the interest he excited was lower in degree than that which, both before and since, has frequently attended the performance of players considerably below the standard he himself reached. Except in the instances already alluded to, Spohr did not condescend to astonish "the ears of the groundlings," and so lost the approbation which extreme cultivation and polish will never create, simply because they transcend the judgment of "the million." When Spohr was heard in Italy, the critics there—no mean or incompetent authorities—were loud in their praise, because his playing was enriched by a strict imitation of the effects of the human voice. " They said he was the first singer on the violin that had ever appeared ;" and they were right in thus according the highest praise that could be bestowed ; for, as it has been well said, " although instrumental music certainly raises emotions and passions, yet they are very faint and vague when compared with the full, deep, and definite affections awakened by the human voice. The nearer an instrument approaches the voice, the nearer is art to the attainment of its object ; and the reverse of the proposition equally applies to singers. The more they wander through the mazes of execution towards instrumental effect, the farther they stray from the seat of their own dominion—the heart." *

Spohr, after many years of active occupation as a violin teacher and player, turned his attention almost exclusively to composition, and in this higher walk of his profession produced works of a class so excellent in oratorio, operatic, and symphonic details, that they entitle him to be placed amongst the most illustrious " masters," both of his own and other countries. It has been the fashion to decry Spohr in England, and to treat his works with something closely akin to contempt, because of Mendelssohn having caught the English taste in a higher degree, and in a great measure overborne many others of his contemporaries. It is not, however, in this portion of my " Recollections " that I shall speak of this eminent violinist as a composer, inasmuch as the time is approaching when reference at some length will have to be made to those sacred composi-

---

* *The Quarterly Magazine and Review*, vol. iii. p. 325.

tions which, being heard before those of Mendelssohn were produced, stamped him as a proficient in this department of his art. Spohr was a German by birth and education, and essentially so in manners. His character was as simple-minded as that of a child, and in such a nature as he was blessed with, jealousy of a rival found no place for existence. Whilst he could appreciate, he could also allow that there is "ample room and verge enough" for the development of talent, by whomsoever possessed, or wherever manifested.

I now come to the last of the three great violinists brought prominently before the English public at the time about which I am recording my "reminiscences"—Kiesewetter,* to whose violin-playing, if allowed to express any preference, I must confer the palm of superiority above that of Mori and Spohr. Although this truly celebrated and accomplished Bavarian appeared in London in the year 1821, at a Philharmonic concert, and at once established himself in the good opinion of those who truly understood in what musical preeminence consists, it was not my good fortune to hear him till about the end of 1824, when it was only too apparent to my ears that it could have been no wonder that his first performance was greeted "with the very extravagance of approbation and applause," before an audience the major part of whom, then as now, consisted of professors, or persons most immediately connected with music. Kiesewetter's command of his instrument was so great that no single difficulty

---

* Christopher Godfrey Kiesewetter, born at Anspach in Bavaria, September 24th, 1777, died in London, September 24th, 1827, of pulmonary consumption in great distress, occasioned, M. Fétis says, by the neglect which a denial of his talent had caused. This is not the least, assuredly, of the many blunders that author has stereotyped in his otherwise very useful Biographical Dictionary. See Fétis, *Biographie Universelle des Musiciens,* tom. v. p. 28.

seemed to be beyond his accomplishment. On account of this facility of execution, he certainly was not unfrequently induced to carry his interpretation of intricate passages somewhat to excess.

As an illustration of my meaning, I may relate an anecdote connected with the first occasion of my hearing him, at a rehearsal for the —— Festival of 1824. The chorus, not being required at the time he was playing, were dispersed in all parts of the room. Near to the place where I had taken up my position sat an old and peculiarly narrow-minded specimen of the *laudator temporis acti* school. That old gentleman sat without giving any indication of emotion or pleasure during the earlier parts of the *motivo,* which the player was more calmly executing ; but the moment he entered upon the development of a passage to which the legitimists of that day had applied the term of trickery, that was too much for the hearer. With an expression of contempt, not easily to be forgotten, he literally jumped from his seat, and exclaiming, " I don't want to have another shilling's worth of such nonsense cut off!" abruptly left the room, and could not be induced again, either at rehearsal or at the concerts, to sit out Kiesewetter's performance !

Notwithstanding the too frequent resort on Kiesewetter's part to superabundant and superfluous exaggeration, his tone was good, although a trifle thinner than that of either Mori or Spohr, for which his energy scarcely compensated. Indeed, that energy seemed at times to be scarcely within his control, whilst, owing chiefly to ill-health, he at times manifested so much irritability that his intonation suffered in consequence. Nothing, however, prevented or incapacitated him from mastering the most intricate and embarrassing difficulties of execution. The rapidity and distinctness of his *staccato* playing were truly wonderful, and had he executed anything worthy of consideration, and refrained from the extravagant and often incongruous conceits of his own compositions, and presented anything that did not detract from his claims to genuine taste, or even derogate from the intense feeling of which he was possessed, and which were amongst the attributes of his musical character, he would have been entitled to the highest commendation that could have been accorded to him. Kiesewetter, however, showed his real power when he undertook to lead a concert instead of playing a concerto. Unlike Mori, who was continually so full of boldness and impetuosity as almost entirely to overlook those *nuances* which the composer had distinctly marked in his score, and Spohr, who seemed to be wholly impassive, and content that he himself and those under his direction should simply play the passages intrusted to them, with no particular evidence of anything beyond mechanism, Kiesewetter seemed to be always on the alert to bring out intended effects, and to be absorbed in the work he had in hand, without being at all occupied with a consciousness of the part he himself had to perform. The complaint of him, both amongst players and audiences, was indeed that he was too energetic, and that it required no little effort on his own part to restrain that impetuosity to which he gave such free course, whenever he was in the position of a soloist rather than in that of the leader of an orchestra.

It is time, however, to pass from the "Recollections" of these eminent instrumentalists, and to take notice of certain vocalists, male and female, who were in the zenith of their well-established reputation between the years about which I am now writing. Foremost amongst these was the truly accomplished and amiable Madame Caradori-Allan, whom to know was a privilege indeed, not merely during the period in which she so consistently and satisfactorily discharged the onerous duties of her profession, but in after-life also, when in retirement she manifested all the kindly feelings and polished taste of a truly well-born and perfectly educated gentlewoman. I say this of Madame Caradori-Allan once for all, because I had the privilege of her friendship from the year about which I am writing to the day of her decease, when she fell a victim to one of the most cruel diseases which can befall a human being—cancer in the tongue—with no relative near her to soothe her dying hours. Her husband, also one of the most amiable and kind-hearted of men, had died a year or two previously, and her son—an only child, unhappily estranged from both his parents for many years—was not within reach of England to be present at that

> " Last scene of all,
> That ends this life's eventful history."

She had, however, the satisfaction of constantly seeing her old, tried, and truly valued friend, Sir George Smart, who ministered with his usual kindness, not to her necessities—for both she and her husband had been frugal and careful for the future during her deservedly popular career—but to her personal comfort, cheering her with reminiscences of the past, and also affording her those consolations which his own firmly established religious faith so well fitted him to offer.*

Madame Caradori-Allan was not originally educated with a view to the adoption of the musical profession as a means of livelihood. She was the daughter of Baron de Munck, a native

---

* Madame Caradori-Allan died at Surbiton, October 15th, 1865.

of Alsace, and a colonel in the French army. To her mother, who was an excellent musician, and of Russian extraction, she entirely owed her education, without the aid of masters or any other auxiliaries. At the death of her father, owing to the total failure of every pecuniary resource, she found herself compelled to turn her musical acquirements to the improvement of her own means, and assisting those of her mother, whose maiden name—Caradori—she assumed. She herself was born in the Casa Patalini, Milan, in the year 1800. That she entered very early upon the duties of her adopted profession may be clearly ascertained from the fact that she made her first appearance at the King's Theatre in London—and indeed on any stage—January 12th, 1822, as Cherubino in Mozart's *Nozze di Figaro*, at three days' notice ; and, notwithstanding this part is amongst the most hazardous an actress can encounter, she succeeded perfectly, and at once obtained a popularity which never for an instant declined throughout her whole career. Of her *début* it was said, that " Madame Caradori possessed so perfectly every qualification of a singer, considered without reference to the place in which she had to appear, that in a theatre requiring less physical power she would probably have been found faultless." This deficiency, however, did not prevent her from being correctly estimated as a valuable acquisition to the theatre ; and with those whose object it was to be pleased rather than astonished, Caradori became a leading favourite. " The mellow sweetness of her voice, so soft, so touching, was united with the truest expression of the feeling of what she sang, nor did she ever sing without calling forth emotions at once tender and powerful in all who heard her. If Caradori's singing possessed thus much interest, her acting had no less, perhaps rather

from its unassuming grace and elegance than from more
decided characteristics. Her conception of character was just,
and her performance always in keeping. She never offended,
and very rarely failed to please. Her natural talents were
aided by a knowledge derived from the careful study of her
art, which appeared in the judicious conduct of her voice, and
her choice and elegant style of execution. Caradori, independently of her musical knowledge, was a very accomplished
woman; she spoke and wrote German, French, Italian, and
English perfectly well, and drew most beautifully. It is com-
prising a great deal in a few words to say, that Caradori's public
excellences were only exceeded by the virtues of her private life."*

My own impressions of this irreproachable *prima donna* are
exactly in accord with the above warmly expressed opinions.
Her " voice was not one of those of such extensive volume that
it filled the ear with its tone, and commanded admiration, as it
were, by its force; neither could it be called thin; but it had a
sort of middle power, whilst its quality was sweet, pure, and
delicate. It was probably owing to this, that she pleased even
more in the orchestra than on the operatic stage: for it was in
the nearer approximation of the chamber that her perfections
were all to be apprehended—extreme delicacy both in conception and execution being the peculiar and capital property of
Madame Caradori's singing. Her intonation was far more
correct than usually appertained to the performers of the King's
Theatre. In point of conception Madame Caradori tempered
the warmth of Italian sensibility with a chastity that was all but
English, and whilst her own countrymen esteemed her more
cold than comports with their fiery temperament, the English

* See Ebers' *Seven Years of the King's Theatre*, pp. 144—5.

were delighted with the sweet and elegant, but obviously restricted, manner to which she at all times adhered. It was this quality perhaps that rendered her English singing more like that of a native than the execution of most foreigners. She had married," soon after the establishment of her successful position had been obtained, Mr. Allan, the secretary of the King's Theatre,* and "thus her acquaintance with the English language, which she wrote and spoke like a native, was probably facilitated."

But to return to Madame Caradori's musical and professional qualifications, than which scarcely one that I have ever met with possessed higher. "Her execution was facile, neat, and polished in a very high degree. Indeed this was reckoned amongst the chief of her vocal accomplishments. The same chaste elegance that pervaded the rest of her performances was found to govern her display of ornament. If she never astonished, she was always gracefully pleasing. The embellishments she appended never seemed to be extravagant. If they seldom surprised, they were never without their effect, because they were never common. They were, in fact, the offspring of the delicate fancy and calm judgment which cast so polished an air over all the demeanours of this elegant and accomplished lady."† As a musician Madame Caradori-Allan could but be classed in the highest rank. Not only could she sing and play any music with the utmost ease and accuracy "at first sight," but she could read a full orchestral score with the utmost facility—no very easy task to perform—and farther, whenever needful, could herself supply the orchestration of any composition she was

* In August 1823.
† *The Quarterly Musical Magazine and Review*, vol. vii. pp. 348—9.

desirous of having thus accompanied. She could also transpose into any key, at a moment's notice, any music that she had to sing, and accommodate herself to difficulties, whether unforeseen or otherwise, that might suddenly or unexpectedly turn up. Her manner of making herself acquainted with the music she had to perform was not to rely upon a pianist, who drilled into her ear, note by note, the passages she had to sing—which was the case with Pasta, Grisi, and a host of other *prime donne*, who rose to celebrity—but she took the score at once in hand, and read off from it not only her own immediate line, but every point of the accompaniment, so that she was at once *au fait*, whatever demands might be made upon her powers. In some measure this faculty might have been a gift, but it never could have reached the excellence which Madame Caradori-Allan obtained and matured, unless she had been thoroughly trained according to the strictest rules of musical science and theory.

But with all these qualities, as is invariably the case with every really gifted genius, Madame Caradori-Allan was always simple and unaffected, never pretending to the possession of resources which, she was well aware, she did not possess. No one, indeed, was more ready than she herself to admit that " the grand style," which depends almost wholly upon energy—or rather impulse—of character, was not her forte. To be lost in the passion of the character of the song, and to "think of nothing else "—to be the creature for the time and not a mere representative thereof—" to deliver up all the feelings and all the faculties "—to be absorbed and, as it were, to be transmuted into the very being—as Malibran and Viardot afterwards were —requires a temperament as fearless as it is commanding—a mind which, if not absolutely conscious of its own force, is yet so free from all selfish considerations, so wholly possessed and inflamed with the love of art, as belongs only to the enthusiasm of high feeling. Such a creature assuredly Madame Caradori-Allan was not. She was rather of that nature which charms by simplicity and elegance, and seldom fails to accompany a truly feminine disposition. Madame Caradori-Allan was, indeed, one of those pure and bright characters who frequently rise to dignify a profession which is much too often—most untruthfully and cruelly—stigmatised by accusations of exceptions to virtuous conduct than by such qualities as necessarily pertain to its exercise, and concerning which, even if open to proof, it would be well to remember the admonition, "He that is without sin, let him cast the first stone." Her manners were most amiable in private life, and she had her reward in the estimation that awaited her wherever she appeared, and in the friendship of persons in the first condition of society. In the discharge of her professional duties, Madame Caradori-Allan invariably showed her willingness to aid the interests of the theatre, or of the *bénéficiaires* for whom she had to sing, by readily undertaking any part inferior to her professional claims, which she might well have refused; and her not doing so afforded a striking contrast to the conduct of others, not only during the period of her own immediate career, but, in not a few instances, even up to the present time.

In introducing the subject of Velluti's appearance, I may adopt indeed the language of the Earl of Mount Edgcumbe, and say, "I have now to record an event which excited great curiosity in the musical world, and for a time was of considerable advantage to the theatre" (the Opera House), "closing its season with great *éclat*—the arrival of a male soprano singer, the only one left on the Italian stage, who had for many years, perhaps only from having no rival in his line, been looked upon as the best singer in his country."* This remarkable man was born at Monterone, in the marshes of Ancona, in 1781, and commenced his dramatic career at Rome in 1805, and ever afterwards excited the highest enthusiasm wherever he appeared in various continental cities, and especially in those of his native country. From Rome he went to Naples, where he remained five years at the San Carlo Theatre, and then proceeded to the Scala at Milan, where he became acquainted with Rossini. Upon the manner in which he sang a cavatina in that "master's" *Aureliano in Palmira*, it was said his future style was determined.† An anecdote from Stendthall's *Life of Rossini* concerning this acquaintanceship is, I think, worth recording. "Velluti, then in the flower of his youth and talents, and one of the handsomest men of his time, had no small share of vanity, and was fond of displaying and abusing the powers of voice with which nature had gifted him. Before Rossini had an opportunity of hearing this great singer he had written a cavatina" (the one above named) "for the character he was to perform. At the first rehearsal, Velluti began to sing, and Rossini was struck with admiration. At the second rehearsal, Velluti began to show his powers in gracing (*fiorire*). Rossini found the effect produced just and admirable, and highly applauded the performance. At the third rehearsal the simplicity of the 'cantilena' was entirely lost amongst the luxuriancy of the ornaments.

"At last the great day of the first performance arrived. The cavatina and the whole character sustained by Velluti were

* The Earl of Mount Edgcumbe's *Musical Reminiscences*, &c., pp. 150—1.
† See Ebers' *Seven Years of the King's Theatre*, p. 262.

received with *furore;* but scarcely did Rossini know what Velluti was singing. It was no longer the music he had composed. Still the song was full of beauty, and succeeded with the public to admiration. The pride of the young composer was not a little wounded. His opera fell, and it was the soprano alone who had any success. The ardent mind of Rossini at once perceived all the advantage that might be taken of such an event. Not a single suggestion was lost upon him. 'It was by a lucky chance,' we may suppose him to have said to himself, 'that Velluti discovered he had a taste of his own; but who will say that in the next theatre for which I compose I may not find some other singer who, with as great a flexibility of voice and an equal rage for ornaments, may so spoil my music, as not only to render it contemptible to myself, but tiresome to the public? The danger to which my poor music is exposed is still more imminent when I reflect upon the great number of different schools for song that exist in Italy. The theatres are filled with performers who have learned music from some poor provincial professor. This mode of singing violin concertos and variations without end tends to destroy not only the talent of the singer, but also to vitiate the taste of the public. Every singer will make a point of imitating Velluti, without calculating upon the relative compass of his voice. We shall see no more simple " cantilenas ;" they would appear cold and tasteless.* Every-

---

* Was not this imaginary reasoning of Rossini little less than prophetic ? Certainly the time anticipated has arrived, so that it would be indeed a real blessing to hear a true specimen of pure and sustained " cantilena." If Rossini did determine to write all the embellishments that he deemed to be needful in the interpretation of his music, he lived to see the day when scarcely a passage was delivered as he had written it, and had to lament the progress of that bad taste which he undoubtedly did all in his power to prevent.

thing is about to undergo a change, even to the nature of the voice. Once accustomed to embellish, to overload the " cantilena " with high-wrought ornaments, and to stifle the works of the composer, they will soon discover that they have lost the habit of sustaining the voice and expanding the tones, and consequently the power of executing large movements. I must, therefore, lose no time in changing the system I have followed heretofore. I am not myself ignorant of singing—all the world allows me a talent this way. My embellishments shall be in good taste; for I shall at once be able to discover where my singers are strong, and where defective ; and I will write nothing for them but what they can execute. My mind is made up. I will not leave them room for a single appoggiatura. These ornaments, this method of charming every ear, shall form an integral part of my song, and shall be all written down in my score.' "*

At Milan, Velluti was the idol of the people. So great, indeed, was his popularity, that it was reported that " a Milanese gentleman, who had a rich uncle who was ill, met a friend in the street, and being asked where he was going, answered, ' To the Scala, to be sure.' ' How !' said his friend ; ' your uncle is dying.' ' Yes, indeed,' was the reply ; ' but Velluti sings to-night !' "† At Vienna, the place of his next engagement, he was crowned, medallised, and recorded in immortal verse.‡

---

* Stendthall's *Life of Rossini,* quoted in *The Quarterly Musical Magazine and Review,* vol. vi. pp. 5, 6.

† Ebers' *Seven Years of the King's Theatre,* p. 263.

‡ A medal struck about this time, in Velluti's honour, bore the following inscription :—

> " Grande se il Duce simuli
> Che Roma insulta e freme

Having remained two years in the Austrian capital, he went to Venice, where he sang in the Theatro San Benedetto with Catalani.

After making the tour of all the principal Italian and German theatres, Velluti arrived at Paris, where the musical taste was not prepared for him. Rossini being at this time (A.D. 1825) engaged at "Les Italiens," Velluti did not enter into his plans; and having made no engagement there, he came over to England, without any invitation, but strongly recommended by Lord Burghersh* and other people of distinction abroad. He brought letters to many persons of rank, by all of whom he was noticed in the most handsome and flattering manner, and received most decided support from them on his *début*.†

Velluti's first reception at concerts is reported by the Earl of Mount Edgcumbe to have been "far from favourable; and the scurrilous abuse lavished on him before he was heard, cruel and illiberal. It was not till after long deliberation, much persuasion, and assurances of support, that the manager "—Mr. Ebers, of the King's Theatre—"ventured to engage him for the remainder of the season. Even then, such was the popular prejudice and general cry raised against him, that unusual precautions were deemed necessary to secure a somewhat partial audience, and prevent his being driven from the stage on his

> Dolce se imiti i palpiti
> D' un tristo cor che geme,
> Adria de schietta laude
> Sommo cantor ! t' applaude."

—*The Quarterly Magazine and Review*, vol. vii. p. 268.

* Afterwards Earl of Westmoreland. He had been British ambassador at Vienna, where he was well known as a *Fanatico per la musica*.

† Ebers' *Seven Years of the King's Theatre*, p. 264.

very first entry upon it, which seemed to be a predetermined
measure. At length the first appearance of Signor Velluti was
announced to take place on an unusual night, *for his own
benefit,* granted him, it was said, on account of the great trouble
he had taken (to use a theatrical phrase) in getting up the new
opera ; which, indeed, was true. As he had a perfect knowledge
of the stage, he entirely directed all the performances in which
he took a part. At the moment when he was expected to appear, the most profound silence reigned in one of the most
crowded audiences I ever saw, broken on his advancing by loud
applauses of encouragement. The first note he uttered gave a
shock of surprise, almost of disgust, to inexperienced ears ;
but his performance was listened to with attention and great
applause throughout, with but few audible expressions of disap-
probation, speedily suppressed. The opera he had chosen for
his *début* was *Il Crociato in Egitto,* by a German composer
named Meyerbeer, till then totally unknown in this country.
The music was quite of the new school,* but not copied from
its founder Rossini. It was original, odd, flighty, and might
even be termed fantastic, but at times beautiful. Here and
there most delightful melodies and harmonies occurred ; but it
was unequal. Solos were as rare as in all the modern operas ;
but the numerous concerted pieces much shorter and far less
noisy than Rossini's, consisting chiefly of duets and terzettos,
with but few choruses, and no overwhelming accompaniment.
Indeed, Meyerbeer has rather gone into the contrary extreme,
the instrumental part being frequently so slight as to be almost

---

* What would the Earl of Mount Edgcumbe have said had he lived to have
heard Meyerbeer's improvement upon this school, as afterwards more fully
developed in the *Roberto,* the *Huguenots,* &c. ?

meagre, while he has sought to produce new and striking effects from the voices alone."*

It did not fall to my lot to be present on the occasion of Velluti's *début* at the King's Theatre; but I had the pleasure of hearing and seeing him once during the season, and I well remember that he was of a tall and slender figure; that his face was handsome, and his eyes dark and brilliant; and that the moment he began to sing his features lighted up, so as clearly to indicate the sentiments to which he was about to give expression. The delicacy and finish of his method were indeed

---

* The Earl of Mount Edgcumbe's *Musical Reminiscences*, pp. 150-154. It may not be uninteresting to record here a few observations contained in an elaborate criticism in the *Quarterly Musical Magazine and Review*, of the same year (1825), vol. vii. pp. 373, 374, and 369, concerning this great "master:"—"The name of Giacomo Meyerbeer has risen upon the English public even more suddenly than that of Carl Maria von Weber, his contemporary and fellow-student. The son of a rich banker, of the Jewish religion, and an amateur, his success is perhaps not so surprising as the devotion of his time to the study and practice of composition. But his impulse is that forcible attraction which men call genius, and whether the organ of music be considerably developed—as we are led to conclude from the portrait of his handsome and intelligent countenance prefixed to the score—or whether any early and accidental cause, such as directed Sir Joshua Reynolds to painting, determined his course towards music, it is clear both that his faculties were capable and his attention drawn to the exercise of the art at that almost infantine period of existence, which has very commonly marked the dawn of great musical talent. Little was known of his fame or his merit when *Il Crociato in Egitto* was performed at the King's Theatre. The foreign journals had indeed rung forth his praises, and a particular account of his reception at Trieste, where he was attended from the theatre, on the night of the first representation of his opera, by a vast concourse of people, invited to the casino, and crowned, had been printed. Meyerbeer must be classed with florid writers; but at the same time he has mingled the portion of ornament with so much of what is much more sound, that one of the strongest reasons for which we commend him is, that he obviously aims at moderating the rage for execution, and shows a taste for purer means of expression, without a particle of affectation or extravagance."

exquisite, resulting unquestionably from a truly intelligent apprehension, most skilful management, and intense practice. The quality of his tone was that of the male counter-tenor, and was somewhat unequal in a portion—particularly in the middle —of his register, which extended from A on the upper line of the bass clef to A above the treble staff—just two octaves; the upper part of the compass, from C to G, when I heard him, being most clear and resonant. Upon a lengthened note he would hold for a considerable time without taking breath, ringing it, so to speak, with increasing and diminishing power, so as to resemble the tone of a bell, which, in all probability, accounted for the term used by the Italians, that he had a *bel metallo di voce.* His lower tones, which resembled those of the female contralto, were well cultivated, and would have been equal to his upper notes, had they not wanted the power which, by contrast with tenors and basses, is always strongly anticipated by the hearer. Of his acting, the same judicious critic, to whom I have already had the privilege of referring,* most truly observed, " As an actor, Velluti is scarcely less to be admired than as a singer. His entrata in *Il Crociato* was magnificent.† His movements were as measured as those of John Kemble, for instance, or of Young. He had the expressive turn of the hand and elevation of the arm which are peculiar to the opera stage, and the carriage of his head was extremely dignified. It was only when muscular force was required that his physical powers did not second his conceptions. Here his action

* See pp. 26, 41, and 98.

† Mr. Ebers (*Seven Years of the King's Theatre*, p. 267) also says, " Velluti's demeanour on entering the stage was at once graceful and dignified ; he was in look and action the son of chivalry he represented."

was often too graceful to consist with vigour; but all he did was stamped with the impress of mind." So thoroughly do my own " Recollections " accord with this tribute to Velluti's acting powers, that I readily and gratefully adopt it.

It is pleasant to be able to record that " the favourable reception of Velluti on his first night completely put an end to any effective opposition; and the uneasiness he had sustained in consequence of the attacks made upon him, and to which his susceptible temperament rendered him peculiarly open, was compensated by the numerous testimonies he received of support and regard. He received many handsome presents, not a few of which came anonymously or under evidently assumed names. These marks of attention were encouraging to a man who had suffered no little from the exertions made to prevent his appearance. It is agreeable to be able to say that, high as Velluti stood with the public, his professional excellence fell short of the goodness of his private character. As a man of kind and benevolent disposition, and equally gentlemanly feeling and deportment, he was known to many, who duly appreciated and respected him. His private habits were of the most simple and inoffensive kind. He never failed to interest those with whom he associated, amongst whom the apparent melancholy of his disposition was exchanged for a lively and almost playful exuberance of good humour—a feature of character not unusual with persons of much sensibility."*

Velluti was re-engaged for the season of 1826 at a salary of £2,300; but the favour towards him had sensibly declined, and in his second opera, *Tebaldo e Isolina*, by Morlacchi, which he considered his *chef-d'œuvre*, he was much less admired than in

* See Ebers' *Seven Years of the King's Theatre*, pp. 270-1.

Meyerbeer's *Il Crociato*. For his last benefit he brought out Rossini's *Aureliano in Palmira*; the only opera of that composer he would ever sing,* but he made scarcely any impression in it. At the end of the season of 1826 he returned to the Continent, but little or nothing was heard of him afterwards, although he was induced to reappear in London in 1829, where, his voice having materially decayed, he obtained no engagement of any kind. After this failure he settled in Italy, and died on the 1st of February, 1861, at the age of eighty years.† He was the last male soprano heard in this country, or likely ever again to be heard; but, to all intents and purposes, the Earl of Mount Edgcumbe was not far wrong when he asserted that "to the old he brought back some pleasing recollections; others, to whom his voice was new, became reconciled to it and sensible of its merits; whilst many declared that to the last his tones gave them more pain than pleasure." ‡

---

* See the Earl of Mount Edgcumbe's *Musical Reminiscences*, pp. 157-8.

† Fétis, *Biographie Universelle des Musiciens*, &c. tom viii. p. 316.

‡ *Musical Reminiscences*, p. 156.

CHAPTER V

IT is absolutely impossible to pass away from this period without referring to a most important event, which made an indelible impression upon the English musical public, the influence of which none but those who were privileged to witness it can in the slightest degree understand. I have already alluded to the visit of Sir George Smart and Mr. Charles Kemble to Germany* for the purpose of bringing over to London Carl Maria von Weber, not merely to conduct the great opera *Der Freischütz*, by which that "master" had made his reputation, but to write another, the *Oberon*, which became his last. Amongst the "Recollections" most vividly impressed upon my mind is my introduction to that most remarkable man by Sir George Smart, at whose house, in Great Portland Street, he took up his abode, and remained a welcome guest to the day of his decease. It was evident at once that "death had marked him for his own." Buoyant as my spirits were at this period, and excited as I was by the permission to visit the house of my friend, no less than to attend both rehearsals and performances at Covent Garden whilst *Der Freischütz* was in the course of preparation and the *Oberon* was being written—a

* See p. 88.

privilege I even then prized most highly, and which I have since learned to estimate, I trust, at its full value—I was again and again depressed, as I could but perceive that he was wasting away, and that every exertion he made was but the means for bringing him to his end more speedily. I had seen him, whilst conducting his music, throwing his whole heart and soul into the work, imparting a stimulus to principals, band, and chorus such as they had never experienced before, and manifesting an energy that would have wearied a man in rude health; and I had caught the infection, as it were, of his influence, so as to enjoy all I heard without being able to give expression by words to the feelings it engendered. But on passing to his private room—where the *entrée* had been most kindly accorded to me both by Sir George Smart and himself—as I then saw him panting for breath, torn to pieces by a hacking consumptive cough, and reeking with cold perspiration, all the delight I had experienced vanished. How gratefully would he recognise with a weary smile any slight attempt to minister some small relief to the excruciating agony of the half-suffocation against which he struggled with all the determination of his energetic spirit! How kindly, too, would he press my shoulder as he leaned upon it whilst tottering to the stage-door to be driven to his home! How, with all the good-breeding of a thorough gentleman, he tried to keep up a conversation with numerous indiscriminating persons who, without apparently the slightest cognisance of the pain they were inflicting, crowded upon and about him ; and how wearily he sank back in his carriage, and sighed as if his spirit would escape thereby, when he had got quit of them,—are incidents that could not fail to make an indelible impression upon a mind which, young and inexperienced as it was, even then understood how mighty a genius it was contemplating. I would also occasionally call upon him whilst he was writing in the early morning, and working, as it were, against time to finish the scoring of his *Oberon*—the last notes to the overture of which I saw written upon the table which is to remain, by Sir George Smart's will, an honoured heirloom in his family—always to be welcomed with a kindly glance, or some more marked means of friendly recognition. When the rehearsals of this opera were going on, I followed him again and again to the theatre, to witness the annoyances he had to struggle against, and the perseverance with which, ill as he was, he fought against and overcame them. With Miss Paton on the one hand, and Fawcett, the stage-manager, on the other, poor Weber was constantly at issue ; for the former would interlard her part with embellishments of her own invention wholly unsuited to the character of the music ; and the latter was constantly vociferating, " Cut *that* out !" whenever a hitch took place in any one of the scenes, which he, without a particle of music in his composition, attributed wholly to the composer's supposed ignorance of stage management. The rebuke offered to Miss Paton on one occasion for this display of bad taste I can vouch for, since I heard it. It was to this effect : " My dear lady, why give yourself so much trouble ?" Upon her assuring him that anything she could do was no trouble to her, and that she was only too happy to oblige him, his ready answer was : " But I not wish you to sing so much more notes than I have written ;" at which that somewhat imperious lady was evidently greatly chagrined, especially as it raised a hearty laugh at her expense.

As to Fawcett, my old friend Planché* has related so charac-

* Mr. Planché furnished the libretto of the *Oberon*, the subject having been

teristic an anecdote in his interesting " Recollections," that it is preferable to record it in his own way.* " A young lady," he says, " who subsequently became one of the most popular actresses in my recollection, was certainly included in the cast; but she had not a line to speak, and was pressed into the service in consequence of the paucity of vocalists, as she had a sweet, though not very powerful, voice, and was even then artist enough to be entrusted with anything. That young lady was Miss Goward, now Mrs. Keeley,† and to her was assigned the exquisite Mermaid's song, in the *finale* to the second act. At the first general rehearsal, with full band, scenery, &c., the effect was not satisfactory; and Fawcett, in his usual brusque manner, exclaimed, 'That must come out! It won't go !' Weber, who was standing in the pit, leaning on the back of the orchestra, so feeble that he could scarcely stand without such support, shouted, 'Wherefore shall it not go ?' And leaping over the partition like a boy, snatched the baton from the conductor, and saved from excision one of the most delicious *morceaux* in the opera." The cause of the *Oberon* falling somewhat flat upon its production doubtless arose from the comparatively uninteresting character of the story, the working out of which had given Mr. Planché considerable trouble ; but, according to his recently recorded opinion, inasmuch as "justice was fairly done to Weber" by the vocalists "who created" his music, "any shortcomings, as far as the

chosen by Weber himself. See *Recollections and Reflections,* vol. i. pp. 74-86. Tinsley.

* See p. 88.

† With Mrs. Keeley, when Miss Goward, and before she came to London, I had the pleasure to be acquainted, and often to accompany upon the pianoforte at the houses of mutual friends, where her genial manners, good taste, and irreproachable character, always rendered her a welcome guest.

drama was concerned, were of secondary importance. My great object," he states, "was to land Weber safe amidst an unmusical public; and I, therefore, wrote a melodrama with songs, instead of an opera such as would be required at the present day. I am happy to say," he proceeds, "that I succeeded in that object, and had the great gratification of feeling that he fully appreciated my motives and approved of my labours;" as a proof of which he goes on to state, that "on the morning after the production of the opera (April 12, 1826) I met him on the stage. He embraced me most affectionately, and exultingly exclaimed, 'Now we will go to work and write another opera together; and *then* they shall see what we can do!' 'Man proposes, and Heaven disposes.' In a few weeks after, I followed him to his grave! *Oberon* was the song of the dying swan. The hand of death was upon him before he commenced it, and the increasing weight upon his spirit is unmistakably evident in the latter portion of his work."* Weber continued to direct the performances of the *Oberon* for a few nights afterwards, although continually exposed to the suffering occasioned by the distressing languor and difficulty of breathing which attended the fatal disorder that brought him to a too early grave.

Although completely prostrated and wholly unequal to attend the theatre, Weber had fixed to leave England, on his return to Germany, on the 7th of June; but on the morning of the 5th he was found dead in his bed. Sir George Smart has often told me that he had no apprehension of Weber's death being so sudden. When he parted from him on the previous night, after having seen him in bed, he really thought he might rally for a short time. He had retired to rest in better spirits than usual,

* Planché's *Recollections and Reflections,* vol. i. pp. 82-3.

which were raised by the expectation of speedily seeing his wife and children, to whom he was most devotedly attached, and by having overcome the anxious solicitations of his friends that he would defer his journey in the hope of better health returning, which they could have had little expectation would be realised.

At 7 A.M., June 5th, 1826, when Sir George Smart, after his usual custom, went to call him, he found him lying upon his right side, as for an instant, he thought, sweetly sleeping; but it was "the sleep of a corpse, the sad cold stillness of death." I had left London for the country a few days previously to Weber's death, and, therefore, was not present at his funeral, which took place at the Roman Catholic chapel in Moorfields, on Wednesday, the 21st of June, when a large number of the musical profession paid the last tribute of respect to his memory. Mozart's "Requiem" was sung, at the conclusion of which his body was deposited in a vault under the chapel, whence it was removed a short time afterwards, and conveyed to Dresden, where it now rests.*

In the course of the opera season of 1826, Pasta, the greatest operatic *tragédienne* of her day, came under my notice. She had returned to London two years previously with a reputation

---

* It may not be uninteresting to record who were the principal vocalists and members of the band who took part in the funeral service at Moorfields : the vocalists were Mesdames Cubitt, Betts, Povey, Andrews, and Farrar ; Messrs. Braham, Pyne, C. Evans, Pinto, and Phillips, assisted by the ladies and gentlemen of the chapel, and a chorus consisting of thirty-six persons. The band consisted of : (violins) Messrs. François Cramer (leader), Mori, Ella, and Thomas ; (second violins) Messrs. Betts, Kemis, Pigot, and Davis ; (violas) Messrs. Moralt and Daniels ; (violoncellos) Messrs. Hatton and Hagart ; (double basses) Messrs. Woodham and C. Smart ; (flutes) Messrs. Birch ; (clarionets) Messrs. Wilman and Powell ; (bassoons) Messrs. Godfrey and Mancon ; (trumpets) Messrs. Harper ; (trombones) Messrs. Mariotti, Smithies, and Shöngen ; (drums) Mr. Chipp. Mr. Attwood, the eminent composer and

largely increased since 1817, when she made " her first appearance on any stage" at the King's Theatre, "in company with
Mdmes. Fodor and Camporese. So little, however, was then
thought of her talent, that, if not condemned, she was at least
neglected, and suffered to depart at the end of the season without having met with the slightest encouragement." * Pasta was
not a person, however, to give way before disappointment. She
understood what her deficiencies really were, and determined to
master them. She therefore retired to Italy, and devoted herself
unremittingly to study and the improvement of her voice. She
knew that the means of greatness were within her reach, and
great she determined to become. Originally her voice is said to
have been coarse in its tone, limited in its compass, and probably untractable with respect to execution. If this were so,
the greater praise was due to her judgment, perseverance, and
industry, by which means she increased the compass of a *mezzo-
soprano* organ, so as to sing from A on the bass staff to C or D
in alt—about eighteen notes. These upper notes, though taken
with comparative ease, were sometimes a trifle crude, and not

organist of St. Paul's, presided at the organ as conductor, which Mr. Terrail
relinquished on the occasion. The following inscription was placed on the
coffin-lid :

" Carolus Maria Freyherr von Weber,

nuper

Præfectus musicorum Sacelli regii

apud Regem Saxonum.

Natus urbe Eutin, inter Saxones,

Die 16 Decembris, 1786.

Mortuus Londini

Die 5 Junii 1826.

Anno quadragesimo

Ætatis suæ."

See *Quarterly Musical Magazine and Review*, vol. viii. pp. 121-128.
  * Ebers' *Seven Years of the King's Theatre*, p. 218.

unfrequently, especially in rapid passages, false in intonation. The lower notes were positively harsh, and what the French designated as "veiled."

The execution of passages and ornaments *sotto voce* was the best part of Pasta's vocalisation, whilst the good taste she displayed in adhering to a comparative simplicity of style obtained for her general approbation. Had she been, however, by many degrees a worse singer than she was, even that defect would have been tolerated, on account of the magnificence of her histrionic talent. Pasta was, to all intents and purposes, the Siddons of the Italian Opera stage. She could awe her audience by the grandeur of her declamation, by the intensity of the passion she imparted to every character she assumed, and by the majesty of her deportment, notwithstanding as to personal appearance she was short in stature, and inclined to *embonpoint*. Her *recitativo parlante* was the most perfect I have ever heard, every word being as distinctly enunciated as if it had been actually spoken. The characters in which I most distinctly remember her were Desdemona, in Rossini's *Otello ;* Tancredi, in that composer's opera of the same title ; Romeo, by Zingarelli ; Norma, by Bellini ; Semiramide, by Rossini ; and, although last, by no means least, Medea, by Meyer. The last time I ever witnessed her performance was at the King's Theatre, on Easter Tuesday, 1833, when she sang, for her benefit, the Norma of Bellini's always popular opera. A more grand performance than this it would be wholly impossible ever to witness. Great as Grisi was in this character, and extensive as was her *répertoire*, she was not to be compared for a moment with her gifted predecessor, from whom alone, it may in truth be said, she copied most of those excellencies which caused her

to be pre-eminent in her profession. On the occasion to which
I refer, Pasta's voice was all but gone. So defective, indeed,
was her intonation, that in the celebrated duet, "Deh! con te,"
she had gradually got down a whole tone, to which the stringed
instrument players were cleverly accommodating themselves;
whilst those who had to deal with the wind instrumentation
gave up playing altogether, as a hopeless affair. Expecting
the whole thing to come to grief, I listened in agony for the
result which might be expected on the instant of her having
finished her line. When she had so done the band altogether
ceased to play; but then Mdme. de Meric—who undertook the
part of Adalgisa, and of whom I shall have by-and-by to
speak—manifested on the instant how clever and well-instructed a musician she was by taking up her line in such
perfect tune that it could only be compared to the clearness of
a bell. No similar *contretemps* afterwards happened, although
Pasta's tone still continued to ebb and flow to the end of the
opera. Yet, in spite of this deficiency, her acting so covered it,
that I would willingly undergo the same torture again, were it
possible. On her reappearance in 1824, Garcia played Otello
to her Desdemona. Rossini had written this opera specially for
that great tenor; but the lady carried away the palm; for not
only were his earlier powers failing, but he was ill at ease
on finding himself of merely secondary consideration with the
audience.

After the performance of *Norma* in 1833, Pasta retired,
and appeared no more in London till some years later, when she
was unwise enough to accept an invitation to sing both at Her
Majesty's Theatre and at the Princess's Theatre under the direction of the late Mr. Maddox, the only effect of which was to

inform those, professionals and amateurs, who then heard her for the first and last time, whence Grisi derived that instruction which made her—as from the first she desired to be—the legitimate successor of so accomplished a predecessor.

I have spoken of Pasta's representation of the chief *rôle* in Meyer's *Medea* as assuredly her greatest effort. To describe the impression she left upon my mind might be tedious ; but inasmuch as the opinion recorded by the eccentric amateur I have so frequently quoted may not be so, I will—most unwillingly, I must confess—part with this great *prima donna* (with whom I twice sang in public, and who treated me with unvarying kindness), after giving it as he so explicitly stated it. After speaking of the causes which induced Velluti to shrink from appearing with Pasta in the same opera, he thus proceeds :—" I was enabled to form this judgment and comparison by having, at an earlier period of the season, been present at Pasta's benefit, and witnessed her performance of Meyer's celebrated opera of *Medea*. Having heard her once before at a private concert with, I own, less pleasure than I had anticipated, I had much curiosity to see her on the stage, and there she fully answered my highest expectations. In a small room her voice was too loud, and sometimes harsh, her manner too forcible and vehement ; but in the theatre all blemishes disappeared. She is really a first-rate performer, both as singer and actress, and that by mere dint of talent, without any very pre-eminent natural qualifications ; for, though a pretty woman, her figure is short, and not graceful ; and her voice, though powerful and extensive, is not of the very finest quality, nor free from defects. No part could be more calculated to display her powers than that of Medea, which affords opportunities for the deepest pathos and the most energetic passion. In both she was eminently successful; and her performance both surprised and delighted me. None since Banti had equalled it; and perhaps she even excelled her great predecessor as an actress, though in quality and sweetness of voice she infinitely falls short of her."—"Pasta's other principal characters are that of Romeo of Zingarelli, Semiramide of Rossini, and Tancredi, all of which she is said to perform admirably. In the last her manner of singing 'Di tanti palpiti'* is much better than that of any other performer of the part. She sings it much slower, thereby doing away in a great degree with its *country-dance-like* character."† After retiring from her profession, Pasta resided in a handsome villa upon the Lake of Como, where, on passing by the steamboat plying between Colico and that town, I saw her for the last time, late one evening in August, 1861, driving a string of twelve or more turkeys with a long stick towards their roosting-place, and could but mentally exclaim, "Quantum mutata ab illâ!" A few years afterwards I heard with deep regret of her death.

In 1825, Marie Félicité Garcia, elder daughter of Garcia,‡ made her *début* as Rosina in Rossini's *Il Barbiere*, and exhibited " a degree of talent and of stage-tact rarely witnessed in so young a *débutante*; for her age did not exceed seventeen. Her voice was a contralto, and managed with great taste."§ Her father, the most stern and severe of masters towards all his other pupils, was really cruel towards his own child. He

---

* This opinion I most thoroughly indorse.
† Earl of Mount Edgcumbe's *Musical Reminiscences*, pp. 159-62.
‡ See p. 103.
§ Ebers' *Seven Years of the King's Theatre*, pp. 259-60.

had the perception which prognosticated her future greatness, and he spared no pains to prepare her for that career, which was the most distinguished above every other *prima donna* of her time. The young Marie was but fifteen years of age when her studies, under the tuition of her obdurate father, commenced in good earnest ; and but for her inheritance of a considerable portion of his temper and spirit, she must have broken down under the fear his violence produced in each of his children. Often has Marie Malibran—by which name she was best known—told me that at times she was almost driven to fly from her father's house, and take any employment she could meet with, to escape the terrible infliction of his lessons. Yet, in spite of all she had to endure, she resolved to bear up, and so to persevere that eventually she would do more than he expected of her. It was not till after two years' incessant study that Garcia would permit his promising daughter to be heard even by his private friends ; and in all probability he would have delayed her *début* for at least another year, had not an unexpected circumstance arisen which offered a chance for the establishment of her position that was not to be overlooked. Pasta having become indisposed, the manager of the King's Theatre was at his wits' end how to supply her place, when Garcia, his interest prompting him to manifest an unwonted generosity, offered his daughter as the leading *prima donna's* substitute. She was well acquainted with all the "numbers" of the score in which Rosina had to take part, but by no means equally perfect with the recitatives. Two days under her father's direction sufficed to make her cognizant of these ; and on the 7th June, 1825, she "made a hit," which enabled her father to demand and insist upon a salary of

£500 for the remainder of the season. On the production of Meyerbeer's *Il Crociato in Egitto* for Velluti, she reappeared in the part of Felicia; and so improved her primary success, that engagements were accepted for her at the Manchester, York, and Liverpool festivals. Here, however, her reception was much less warm and complimentary. Wearied with incessant study—for Garcia, notwithstanding her appearance in public, did not permit a minute of her time to be given to recreation—and the excitement of her operatic progress, her health began so to fail, that it was impossible for her to bear the wear and tear of travelling from place to place—there were no railroads then—and singing night after night, without breaking down. The consequence of this was, that she was said to have " failed."—in singing " Una voce," the *aria d' intrata* of Rosina in *Il Barbiere,* at York—"from attempting more than the song or her powers would allow," although " she sang the *rondo* excellently," * whilst her version of " Rejoice greatly," in the *Messiah,* was so complete a failure, that the English singers not only felt, but expressed, the injustice done them by the enormous sum † given to this young, unformed, and incompetent *prima donna,* however clever—which she certainly was— she might be upon the Italian stage. ‡   As I only heard her in

---

* *Quarterly Musical Magazine and Review,* vol. vii. p. 436.

† Three hundred and twenty guineas, whilst Miss Stephens received only two hundred pounds, Braham two hundred and fifty guineas, and Vaughan one hundred pounds.

‡ *Quarterly Musical Magazine and Review,* vol. vii. pp. 417, 437. Malibran never willingly sang the " Rejoice greatly," even in the days of her greatest celebrity. On one occasion, just previously to her having to do so at the —— Festival of 1833, she whispered to me, whilst at the same time pointing to her part, " That is for Charles to play, not for me to sing ! "—referring to De Beriot, the celebrated violinist, who married her in 1830. She had been previously

Meyerbeer's *Il Crociato in Egitto* in 1825, and she then made but very little impression upon my mind, I shall defer my " Recollections " until her return to England in 1829, and upon my becoming personally acquainted with her in the autumn of the following year. How little it was expected at the time of her departure for America in 1825 that she would ever make a mark upon her time may be ascertained from the criticism of the Earl of Mount Edgcumbe, who—after declaring her to have been " as yet but a mere girl, who had never appeared on any public stage " until 1825, and although compelled to confess that " from the first moment of her appearance she showed talents for it [the stage] both as a singer and an actress "— after his usual manner most assuredly " damned her with faint praise ; " for he immediately added :—" Her extreme youth, her prettiness, her pleasing voice, and sprightly, easy action as Rosina in the *Barbiere di Siviglia*, in which part she made her *début*, gained her general favour; but she was too highly extolled, and injudiciously put forward as a *prima donna*, when she was only a very promising *débutante*, who, in time, by study and practice, would in all probability, under the tuition of her father—a good musician, but (to my ears at least) a most disagreeable singer—rise to eminence in her profession." That the noble lord had no idea she ever would " achieve greatness " may be inferred from his prognostication ; for he adds :—" But in the following year she went with her

married (March 25, 1826) to M. Malibran, a French merchant resident at New York, a man much older than herself—whose offer her father compelled her to accept in spite of her repugnance—whom she left, and was soon afterwards divorced from. See Fétis's *Biographic Universelle des Musiciens*, tom. v. pp. 415-16.

whole family—all of whom, old and young, are singers,* *tant bons que mauvais*—to establish an Italian Opera in America, where, it is said, she is married; so that she will probably never return to this country, if to Europe.†

Amongst the most useful orchestral players of this period was Signor Puzzi, whose horn-playing was justly celebrated as the most perfect that had ever been previously heard in this country. Useful, however, as were that gentleman's orchestral services, they were dispensed with for a time, in order that he might secure foreign *artistes* of intelligence and repute—for which he had shown himself peculiarly well adapted—by the exercise of whose talents it was hoped the failing fortunes of the King's Theatre might be retarded, if not wholly overcome.

Having returned from Paris, in 1827, after the engagement of Zucchelli and Galli, he was immediately commissioned to undertake a journey of greater importance, and to search the Continent for such disengaged performers of merit as he could

* " The company with which he (Garcia) crossed the Atlantic consisted of himself and the younger Crivelli, *tenors;* his son, Manuel Garcia (an eminent teacher still well and deservedly known in London), and Angrisani, *bassi cantanti;* Rosich, *buffo caricato;* with Mdme. Barbiere, Mdme. Garcia, and her daughter Marietta, *soprani. Il Barbiere,* the opera which they chose as their introduction to an American audience, was almost entirely performed by the family party. Garcia playing Almaviva, his daughter Rosina, his son Figaro, and his wife Berta. In the course of the season they successively brought forward *Otello, Romeo, Il Turco in Italia, Don Giovanni, Tancredi, La Cenerentola,* and two operas of Garcia's composition, *L'Amante Astuto,* and *La Figlia dell' Aria,* the latter written expressly for his daughter and Angrisani." From New York Garcia and his company went to Mexico, and succeeded in forming and maintaining so respectable an operatic company, that he often said " he would exhibit his Mexican performers before a Parisian audience, and they would not be unworthy the honour." See *Harmonicon* for 1833, p. 22.

† The Earl of Mount Edgcumbe's *Musical Reminiscences,* pp. 149-50.

meet with. This step was in some measure taken on the recommendation of Rossini,* who characterised Signor Puzzi as possessed of great intelligence in theatrical affairs, active, and zealous. Signor Puzzi was by no means eminently successful in his undertaking, so far as the interests of the great lyrical theatre in the Haymarket were concerned ; but "from Turin he wrote to" Mr. Ebers, "to say that he had the fortune to engage Mdlle. Toso, "belle comme une ange, jeune de dix-neuf ans, élève du Conservatoire de Milan." The animation of his expressions perhaps indicated the embryo flame which subsequently gave to Mdlle. Toso the name of Puzzi.†

On the lady's arrival in England she was received with a warmth proportioned to the accounts which had preceded her, and was everywhere invited and admired, although she had never sung on any stage before her first attempt at the King's Theatre. The eminent critic, to whom I have already‡ referred with so much advantage, thus spoke of Mdlle. Toso's talent on her appearance before the London public :—"In person she is very tall and well shaped, with delicate yet strong and expressive features, and is altogether a fine stage figure ; but for want of acquaintance with the boards, as well as from her

---

* Rossini had come to London in 1823, with his wife Madame Colbran-Rossini, who was a *prima donna* of considerable eminence. Here he remained five months, giving concerts and lessons, and receiving enormous sums from both these sources as well as from an engagement as musical director at the King's Theatre, for which establishment he did literally nothing, although entailing expenses which never could be repaid. Vide Fétis, *Biographie Universelle des Musiciens*, tom. vii. p. 323 ; the *Quarterly Musical Magazine and Review*, vol. vii. p. 179. As I never came in contact with either Rossini or his wife, or heard the one or saw the other, I merely name these circumstances as incidental to the above period.

† Ebers' *Seven Years of the King's Theatre*, pp. 314-18.

‡ See pp. 26, 41, 98.

superior stature, rather awkward in her gait and demeanour, and unexpressive in her gestures. Her voice is a soprano, very powerful, and of brilliant quality, and equal in its formation, except that the higher notes of her compass—which is not very extensive—seemed forced and somewhat harsh. With such endowments, the first impression she made was, 'that she ought to be a great singer ; yet from the delivery of her voice, which was often by sudden and forceful bursts, this notion soon gave way to the assurance that she was not a great singer ; for the constant exertion of the same power, and the want of transition —the lights and shadows of the art—betrayed either too little experience, or the absence of that intellectual dignity which alone leads to true greatness in art. Throughout the season this impression increased ; and although the lady possessed many of the elements which lead to exalted rank,' time was not given her to determine whether she had mind enough to train and polish these aptitudes, to overcome some technical errors, and to exalt her whole performance with that important but minute finish, which leads to superior station in her very arduous profession," inasmuch as almost immediately after her appearance she married, and in a few months retired from the stage.* Another authority offers the same opinion; for he says, " at a party given almost immediately after Mdlle. Toso's arrival, her talents were exhibited to great advantage, but she failed to make any impression upon the public, and very soon afterwards becoming Madame Puzzi, retired into comparatively private life,"† not, however, to disconnect herself wholly from operatic affairs, in which from that time to the present she has

* *The Quarterly Musical Magazine and Review*, vol. x. pp. 52-3.
† Vide Ebers' *Seven Years of the King's Theatre*, pp. 314-15, 318.

been so intimately connected—and especially during the period of Mr. Lumley's management—that the information which it is to be hoped she will at some time or other communicate to the public could not be otherwise than curious, amusing, and instructive. Madame Puzzi has been most successful as a teacher of singing, and has turned out some of the most proficient sopranos, both in public and in private life, during an energetic and active career—none more so than in the instance of her own two daughters, young ladies of as great proficiency as intelligence—and continues to give musical *réunions* during every season, the quality of her engagements being of the very best, and the selections for performance invariably artistic and worthy of consideration.

. Another *prima donna*, of whom great expectations were formed, also came before the public in the year 1827 :—Miss Fanny Ayton, who was at first engaged at the King's Theatre upon the enormous salary of 500*l.* ; but having failed there, she betook herself to Drury Lane Theatre, where I heard her in an English version of Rossini's *Il Turco in Italia;* Braham appearing as the hero, and Harley, who had but very small singing powers, attempting the principal buffo character. The circumstance of this lady being an Englishwoman was a considerable disadvantage to her; for although she had studied under Manielli at Florence, and had been well received in Italy, the public were from the very first disinclined to accept her as belonging even to the second rank, chiefly on account of the thinness of her voice, which was neither to be overcome, nor rendered agreeable, in spite of a certain amount of sweetness and considerable flexibility. She *débuted* in *La Gazza Ladra;* but it was at once felt that Signor Puzzi—one of

whose importations she had been—had overrated her powers
for filling the Opera-house, and had not 'discerned that her
method fell below the level of mediocrity. She speedily
retired from the musical profession, and was so soon forgotten
that it might almost have been doubted whether she had ever
existed.

Amongst the numerous singers to whom my attention about
this time was directed, not one made a more profound impression upon my mind than Zuchelli, whom I have already mentioned as having *débuted* at the King's Theatre in 1822.*
This celebrated *basso profondo*, from having, like Mori,† been
born of Italian parents in London, in the year 1792, met, upon
his arrival here as an accomplished *artiste*, with that kind of
reception which at once compels a man to feel that " a prophet
is not without honour save in his own country, or in his father's
house." Not only was he accused of having changed his name,
which the public insisted was " Joe Kelly," but he was said to
be a relative of the celebrated Michael Kelly—whom Sheridan
branded—from his having been a wine-merchant as well as a
musician—as " an importer of music and composer of wines "—
but his pretensions to celebrity were to a very considerable extent ridiculed. The excellence of his method, combined with
a round and full quality of voice, the volume of which was
immense, quickly placed him, however, in the first rank of his
profession, and established him as a legitimate successor of
Ambrogetti. Although possessed of a tall and handsome person,
and well qualified both to play the part and sing the music of
Mozart's *chef-d'œuvre, Il Don Giovanni*, Zuchelli failed to
make the title *rôle* one of his best impersonations, the recollec-

* See p. 97.   † See p. 100.

tions of that eminent predecessor, no less than of Garcia, being too indelible to give him a chance of escaping the disadvantage of an unfavourable comparison. I must myself confess to have been much disappointed with him in that opera, in which he seemed not to have grasped the fact, that however great and terrible a libertine Don Juan might have been, it was to do the character, no less than Mozart, injustice to represent him as anything else than a gentleman, whose manners were so bewitching, that he might indeed truly say of his successes with the fair sex, "*Veni, vidi, vici.*"

The part in which Zuchelli afforded me the most gratification was that of the Podesta in *La Gazza Ladra*, into which he threw much of the spitefulness which Ronconi afterwards manifested with so much characteristic reality, combined with somewhat of the unctuousness which a greater *artiste* than either of them, Lablache, displayed. In the celebrated trio—one of the most successful of Rossini's inspirations—"O Nume benefico," the manner in which his rich tones rolled through the theatre is indescribable. This, indeed, was a choice specimen of sustained singing in which he greatly excelled. It not only showed training of special excellence, but mind also, without which all the study and practice in the world are utterly useless. He made his *entrée* in London in the version of Rossini's *Mosè in Egitto*, which was then entitled, in order to satisfy English taste—prejudice, some people might call it—*Pietro l'Eremita*, as in after years it was changed to *Zora* with the self-same object. From that moment Zuchelli "made his public," in spite of the disadvantages with which he had to contend; and so long as he remained in England, he fulfilled his duties as a *primo basso profondo* to the satisfaction both of managers and *habitués.*

The year 1827, which, it has been seen, was peculiarly rich in the presentation of new singers in London, also witnessed the first appearance of a baritone, Galli, who, considering what his accomplishments were, ought to have been more noteworthy than he ever seemed able to become. I heard him early in April at the King's Theatre, in *La Gazza Ladra,* which was " mounted " almost exclusively for him, since it was determined, in order that no failure might be risked, that he should appear as Fernando, the disconsolate father of Ninetta, of that opera. Galli, who was a Roman by birth, having been born in the " Eternal City " in the year 1783, was no longer in his prime when he arrived in England ; but his long experience, and the reputation he had gained in most of the principal opera-houses of Italy, no less than in Paris, obtained for him a hearty reception. The need of such a voice was then greatly felt ; and without him this always popular opera could scarcely have been given. Although Zuchelli played the Podesta, neither the Ninetta (Miss Fanny Ayton) nor the Pippo (Mdlle. Toso) had force enough to carry it through satisfactorily. Besides—when *La Gazza Ladra* was got up for Mdme. Fodor's benefit at the Paris Académie, the year after it had been heard in London— Galli had excited such an extraordinary sensation in it as to have at once established both his present and future position.* In spite of the wear and tear he had encountered, both in his own country and in Paris, the volume of this *artiste's* once magnificent voice was very little impaired ; and when his tone was not formed so high as to make it nasal, it was round, rich, and

* Vide Ebers' *Seven Years at the King's Theatre,* pp. 338-40.

smooth. His execution, although less flexible than that of Zuchelli, was very facile, considering the weight of his voice. He was also a well-instructed musician. He was certainly less successful in buffo characters than in serious parts, there being a dryness about his manner which possessed but little of a mirth or laughter-provoking quality ; but the perfect accuracy with which, both in the comic and serious drama, he executed the music set down for him—except as appertained to uncertainty of intonation, which is but too often to be met with in Italian baritones and basses—made him always acceptable. His orchestral singing was chaste and excellent, whilst his stage presence was good, his figure being tall and commanding, and his features capable of strong expression.

' After having sung again in Paris in 1828, Galli returned to Italy, and appeared in 1830 at Rome and Milan. Then he went to Mexico, and remained there five years, after which he appeared at Barcelona. Again, but without success, he tried his failing powers at Milan, and finally accepted a place in the chorus of the Madrid and Lisbon Opera-houses, his extravagance having reduced him to the most abject poverty. On his return to Paris in 1842, in order that he might not starve, the Government made him professor of singing at the Conservatoire ; and until 1848 the *artistes* gave him an annual concert as a means of subsistence. With the Revolution of that year he was deprived even of this resource ; nevertheless he existed, in a most miserable condition, until June 3, 1853, when he died at the age of seventy, one amongst many instances in the world at large, no less than of music, of the inevitable consequences of reckless prodigality.

Amongst other notabilities of this year I had the gratification of hearing Curioni, of whom my earlier " Recollections " were by no means vivid. He had been " a standing dish " at the King's Theatre ever since 1822, and although never a very brilliant *primo tenore*, his talent was considered to be so valuable that his salary, which commenced at first at £600, was raised in 1827 to £1,450. His voice, which was well formed, was rich and sweet, but limited in compass, and he resorted— perhaps somewhat too freely—to the use of two or three notes of falsetto, with considerable effect. His method was purely Italian, but he by no means overloaded what he had to sing with too much *fioriture*. The opinion expressed concerning his talent on his *début* was, that he was by many degrees below Garcia, but superior to any other tenor who had appeared at the Opera since the time of Crivelli.* Curioni's general performances were said to indicate so much of mind, that credit was given him for more talent than he may truly be said to have possessed.

As Pasta had been re-engaged for the opera season of 1827, and it was necessary to produce some novelty, inasmuch as the public had become somewhat weary of seeing and hearing nothing else but the *Tancredi*, the *Romeo*, and the *Medea*, it was determined to revive the *Semiramide*. But where was an Arsace to be found, competent to support the great *prima donna*, and to give effect to her grand representation of the haughty, imperious, and wicked Babylonian queen ? Signor Puzzi had heard Brambilla, a very young, and not altogether perfectly-formed contralto singer, " at Milan, whilst she was a

---

* The contemporary at the Opera of Ambrogetti, Angrisani, and other celebrated artists in 1817, who was appointed the first singing master of the Royal Academy of Music on its foundation in 1822.

pupil of the Conservatorio, and on his representation she was at once sent for and engaged at a salary of £350, although she had never appeared on any stage. Her voice, however, was so great a recommendation in her behalf, being a genuine contralto of rich and beautiful quality, that in a measure it counteracted the weakness of her acting powers ; but, besides this, her personal beauty was so great, that this, in combination with her voice, was all but sufficient to insure the admiration of the public. For one so young, her scale passages were so neatly executed that she elicited the heartiest applause; so much so, indeed, that her older rival showed some symptoms of jealousy, totally unworthy of her, when her own and the new-comer's relative positions were considered. Even now, after that three such contraltos as Pauline Viardot, Alboni, and Trebelli-Bettini have been heard in the *rôle* of Arsace, the sweetness of Brambilla's voice, the artlessness of her manner, and the elegance of her face and figure, are by no means forgotten. Even had her voice been deficient, her popularity by means of the two latter qualities would have been sufficient to have made her a general favourite. 'She has the finest eye,' said a gay cardinal, 'the sweetest voice, and the best disposition ; and if she were discovered to possess any other merits, the safety of the Catholic Church would require her excommunication.'"[*]

Few years in musical progress were so eventful as those over which my "Recollections" have now extended. Were I to refer to the many other events of those years, as inclination prompts, the purpose of my undertaking would seem to be needlessly delayed, and might lay me open to the accusation of seeking unnecessarily to do so. I must, therefore, content my-

---

[*] Ebers' *Seven Years*, &c. pp. 340-1.

self with a mere reference to those English *artistes*, both vocal and instrumental, who vied with their foreign competitors in improving the public taste and contributing to popular amusement by the exercise of their undoubted talent; however unjust it may be to their memory to do so. Mr. Bishop—afterwards knighted on account of his acknowledged merit—a man to whom the appellation of "the English Mozart" has most appropriately been applied, was then in the zenith of his fame, working night and day with a hearty goodwill, and throwing off, as if by a process of inspiration, composition after composition for the theatre and the concert-room, the beauty of which—however it may indeed have been equalled, but rarely excelled—has secured for them a remembrance that cannot fade so long as music is cultivated as an art, or resorted to for recreation. Not only was Braham attracting crowded audiences to Drury Lane, of which he was one of the chief props and mainstays, but Sapio, his rival, was constantly before the public, being employed for the illustration of sacred no less than of secular compositions. Bellamy, although by no means a Bartleman, had not passed away, and although a "barking" singer, yet rendered the reminiscences of his renowned predecessor imperishable by reason of the adaptation of a method that was well suited, by way of illustration, to the demands both of the church and the theatre. Miss Paton* had risen to a position scarcely expected of her, because of her having been wise enough to listen to Weber's advice and instruction; whilst the minor departments of musical combination found most competent executants in the two Miss Cawses, Mrs. Geezin, and Miss

---

* Afterwards Lady William Lennox, and then Mrs. Wood, having married Mr. Wood, the Covent Garden tenor.

Carew. John Hobbs, the most elegant of orchestral vocalists, and one of the most efficient members of the three choirs of the Abbey, Chapel Royal, and St. Paul's, was in the full possession of those gifts which he so much adorned by his style and accuracy Attwood, the pupil of Mozart, was at the organ of St. Paul's, and contributing to the riches of its varied *répertoire* services and anthems, the exquisite quality of which had not been equalled since the times of the illustrious Henry Purcell. The demands, which the excellence of more perfect. pianoforte playing was making, were being considered and acted upon by those princes of manufacture, the Broadwoods, whose liberality—then, as now, as profuse as their construction is unrivalled—was winning for themselves, both within and without the musical profession, a respect and an admiration as widely diffused amongst their private friends as their professional acquaintances. But concerning these and many others, " story," rich in illustration and sincere in purpose, " though I could tell," I must refrain from speaking, not because " the will consents," but because there is not " ample room and verge enough " to do so.

CHAPTER VI.

1828-30.

MR. EBERS' seven years' management at the King's Theatre having been unpropitious, and all the negotiations for the renewal of his lease having failed, the management passed into the hands of MM. Laporte and Laurent—their offer of a rent of £8,000 for the season having been preferred to the proposals of Mr. Ayrton and Signor de Begnis. The former of these new *impresarios*, to whom the actual conduct of the undertaking was entrusted, had been well and respectably known as one of the managers of a French theatre in London, and also as a Parisian actor of deserved celebrity. M. Laurent had been for the two previous years engaged in theatrical speculations, by establishing a company of English actors in Paris, and subsequently by taking the Italian Opera off the hands of the French Government.* These gentlemen made a great blunder at the outset of their career, in selecting one of the greatest musical charlatans the world had ever met with as their musical director — M. Bochsa, a harp-player of considerable merit, but without the most moderate pretensions even as a writer and composer for his own peculiar instrument. Previously to Mr. Ebers quitting the post he had for so many years occu-

* See Ebers' *Seven Years of the King's Theatre*, pp. 349-50.

picd, with considerable advantage to a host of hitherto unknown *artistes* and the public, but with little else than continued pecuniary loss to himself, he had opened negotiations with Mdlle. Sontag, with the view of making her, as she afterwards became under MM. Laporte and Laurent, the *prima donna assoluta* of the year 1829. The unsuccessful termination of those negotiations—notwithstanding no less a sum than £2,000 and a benefit for the season were offered—had, in all probability, much to do with the refusal of a new lease to that *entrepreneur*; a decision by no means generous, inasmuch as the arrears of rent were comparatively small, in spite of his having carried on the concern at a ruinous loss, on account of the magnitude of the amount for which he had made himself annually liable. What that misfortune must have been may be inferred from his own statement, that although "the season of 1827 had been attended with the least loss of all that had passed under his management," he found himself deficient to the tune of "£2,974; the receipts having been £48,389, and the expenditure £51,363."*

Mdlle. Sontag was then the "coming woman" of her time, according to the opinion of those who had previously heard her in Paris, and were capable of judging of her acquirements. She had one great disadvantage to combat. She was German—not Italian. Hitherto the King's Theatre had been exclusively maintained by *artistes* nurtured in the sunny clime beyond the Alps, with the exception of Caradori, Garcia, and his gifted daughter, Malibran. The method of the two latter, however, was so thoroughly formed after the Italian school, that their Spanish origin was scarcely noticed. Now, however, Germany was to put in its full claim for celebrity; and it was no mean

---

* See Ebers' *Seven Years of the King's Theatre*, pp. 321, 349.

commendation of the new *débutante's* quality, that London immediately endorsed what Paris had already pronounced to be perfect.

This gifted lady, at an age unusually early, had attained a degree of reputation which the exertions of a life have often failed to secure, although the aspirant has been gifted with unquestionable talent. The beauty of Mdlle. Sontag also made a deep impression, and opened the way to a favourable reception of her singing, and might have insured success had her vocal abilities been far beneath the high standard by which they were sustained. Mdlle. Sontag was a native of Coblentz, having been born in that grand old mediæval Rhenish city May 13th, 1805. Her parents were connected with the theatrical profession ; so that she was at a very early period initiated into the mysteries of the stage, and even at six years of age appeared at the court theatre of Darmstadt, in an opera entitled *Donau Weibchen* (La petite Femme du Danube), with remarkable success.* On the death of her father, when she was scarcely nine years old, her mother placed her at the Conservatoire of Prague, whence she went to Vienna, where Mdme. Fodor was then singing as *prima donna,* and upon whose style she formed her own. During the four years she remained in the Austrian capital, she sang alternately at the Italian and National Opera-houses, but without producing any remarkable sensation. Not until 1824, when she appeared at Leipzig in Weber's *Euryanthe,* did " she make her mark ; " immediately after which she was engaged at Berlin, and from that moment success was insured. She continued in her native land till 1826, when she went to Paris, and made her first appearance at "Les Italiens," June 15th, as

* See Fétis, *Biographie Universelle des Musiciens,* tom. viii. pp. 63, 64.

Rosina in *Il Barbiere*, the personation of this character having been followed in that and the subsequent seasons by her undertaking, with equally eminent advantage, the parts of Desdemona in *Otello*, Donna Anna in *Il Don Giovanni*, Semiramide, and several others.

In accepting MM. Laporte and Laurent's terms for an engagement at the King's Theatre, Mdlle. Sontag stipulated to make her *entrée* in the same character (Rosina) by which she had taken the Parisians by storm. This event took place April 16th, 1828. She is said to have been but indifferently supported; but no one seemed to have had an eye, or an ear for anybody but herself. Of her personal appearance, as well as of her qualifications as an *artiste*, the following remarks, written by a severe critic at the time—inasmuch as they are perfectly in accordance with my own opinion, as formed on hearing her in the following year, when her reputation was thoroughly established—may not be unacceptable : " Mdlle. Sontag is of a middling stature and inclining to *embonpoint*. Her hair and complexion are fair, her eyes blue, with that kind of Roxaline nose—the *nez retroussé*—which often gives an appearance of great vivacity, though not in her case. Her mouth is well made, but she distorts it sometimes in singing; and it is lined by a set of teeth, the beauty of which she does not conceal. Her countenance indicates good temper, and is extremely pleasing, but has no pretension to what is properly called beauty, either as to feature or effect, and is not indicative of more than an ordinary degree of intellect. She is altogether well made, though there are defects in her person. Her hand and arm are beautiful, and her foot is not unworthy of the encomiums lavished on it. Her carriage is not objectionable ; but, to judge accurately of this, she must be seen in a character of more dignity" (than Rosina).

"Her voice is a true soprano of the full compass, extending from A below the clef to E in alt; though she does not display its utmost limits in this opera. Without being deficient in strength, it is not powerful, and its quality is anything rather than disagreeable, though not remarkable for its purity. Its greatest merit consists in its wonderful flexibility. Her *volate* (flights, or runs) are as graceful as they are perfect; she executes *arpeggio* passages with the neatness of a good finger on the pianoforte, and her *staccato* notes are not less finished; they are like drops of sound, each a whole in itself, and completely detached; but when playing thus wonderfully on her vocal organ, she abates its power, all such passages being given *à mezza voce.* Hence much of their effect is lost. Her style is essentially bravura. Execution is with her as everything, expression as nothing. The extraordinary pliancy of her voice has probably led to this; and that coolness of temperament which her acting seems to denote has most likely exercised a joint influence in determining the character of her singing. Hence she falls into the fatal error of striving to astonish rather than to delight, and concentrates all her force for the purpose of doing what instruments can always equal, often surpass; while, as an almost necessary consequence, she neglects what only the human voice can accomplish, and that which is, therefore, the triumph of the vocal art. The embellishments, of which she is so prodigal, often show taste and invention. She introduced two of these in 'Una voce poca fa,' that were not less pleasing than original. But her ornaments want variety, and are applied to everything alike. Her intonation is faultless; in public or in private, we have not heard her sing one note out of tune.   She is, beyond the possibility of a doubt, a good musician ; in all her *rifiorimenti* she never infringes on the time, loses sight of the accompaniments, or forgets the harmony.   Mdlle. Sontag stamped herself as a superior singer in her first aria, ' Una voce ' (on the occasion of her *début*), the second movement of which, ' Io sono docile,' could not but call forth a unanimous encore.   Nevertheless it was easy to discover that she had not here reached the expectations formed.   Her great effort, and most decisive success, was in Rode's air,* ' Ah, dolce canto.'   In this she luxuriated in all the *roulades, arpeggios,* and divisions that a florid singer most delights in, and her triumph was as great as her performance was unique."†

Mdlle. Sontag's particular merits were so exceptional, and her career upon her first appearance in this country so brief, that I am inclined to extend my "Recollections" concerning her, since, " take her for all in all," she certainly was at that period the most flexible vocalist it was ever my good fortune to listen to. I do not think that I can for this purpose do better than refer to that eminent critic whose valuable remarks have been hitherto of so much service to myself, whilst referring to other *artistes,* although they are somewhat similar to those already quoted.‡ He says : " Mdlle. Sontag differed from her great predecessors, Billington and Catalani, in the extreme lightness and rarity, so to speak, of her evolutions through the mazes of sound.   What they effected, the one by volume, the other by force, Mdlle.

* Mdlle. Sontag introduced this air as " the singing lesson " of the second act of *Il Barbiere.*

† *Harmonicon* for 1828, p. 120.

‡ See pp. 26, 41, and 88.

Sontag performed with a simplicity and ease that were perfectly captivating. Not only were all passages alike to her, but she appropriated some that were hitherto believed to belong to instruments—to the pianoforte and the violin, for instance—arpeggios and chromatic scales, passages ascending and descending, she sang in the same manner that the ablest performers on these instruments executed. There was the firmness and the neatness that appertained to the pianoforte, whilst she would go through a scale *staccato* with the precision of the bow. Her great art, however, lay in rendering whatever she did pleasing. The ear was never disturbed by a harsh sound; the notes trickled and sparkled like the diamond drops of the brightest fountain. Everything was rendered clear and liquid by solution, and the auditor listened to the melody as he did to the singing of birds, without attempting to appreciate, or, indeed, without caring for the nature of the intervals.* The velocity of her passages was sometimes uncontrollable; for we have observed that in a division, say of four groups of quadruplets, she would execute the first in exact time, the second and third would increase in rapidity so much, that in the fourth she was compelled to decrease the speed perceptibly, in order to give the band the means of recovering the time she had gained. But reflection was arrested by surprise, while the ear was satiated with the physical delight; for, we repeat, both the captivation of her singing and the superiority lay in rendering all those passages which fix the attention agreeable, and in making those pleasing which, when we have heard them from other singers, have

---

* Extravagant as this praise may seem, it is by no means exaggerated, but accurately describes the delightful peculiarities of Mdlle. Sontag's vocal capabilities.

inspired only wonder, mixed perhaps with sensations never pleasurable, and in some instances anything but pleasing. At the same time all this was effected with an ease that gave the semblance of nature. She appeared to sing, like a bird, from impulse, and to feel whilst she inspired delight. There was no distortion,—not even the heaving of the bosom was visible ; so that the auditor, although uncertain where a range of imagination and a facility of execution so extended would next carry him, was never exposed to the least apprehension of a failure. Thus the firmest sympathy was established, and confidence was never betrayed."

It will be gathered from these most striking facts attending Mdlle. Sontag's performance, both on the stage, in the orchestra, and in the chamber, that none of the more powerful faculties of the intellect were called into action. Nature, which generally prescribes a limit to attainment, seemed to have denied the qualities necessary to the display of the grander characteristics of style and manner, when this charming *artiste* exercised those lighter fascinations with which she was endowed. Mdlle. Sontag might unquestionably excel in tenderness and pathos, but all the more majestic and energetic characters were forbidden to her by her youth, the lightness of her figure, and her voice, not less than by the kind of study she had pursued. Nor could the judicious direction of her musical education be objected to. The highest praise perhaps that could be bestowed was in the admission that the guidance of Nature had been followed, and that her powers had been displayed in a manner most likely to lead to the greatest share of success. This praise was certainly due to Mdlle. Sontag. She had cultivated the imagination and the fancy to a degree they had never reached before. No singer had ever combined so variously, or executed in the light, brilliant, inventive, fresh, and, above all, in the pleasing manner she attained. In these particulars she stood alone.*

The second great success that Mdlle. Sontag made after her *début* in *Il Barbiere* was in *Il Don Giovanni*, on the 1st of May, 1828, at the King's Theatre. The cast on that occasion, when she was far better sustained than at her *début*, embraced the talent of Zuchelli (the Don), Torri (Don Ottavio), De Angeli (Il Commendatore), Pellegrini (Leporello), Porto (Masseto), Castelli (Elvira), and Caradori (Zerlina). It is almost needless to say, that the great object of curiosity was the new *prima donna*. It was generally thought that she would not be able to sustain the character chosen by her, either as a singer or an actress— the last especially—that she would overwhelm the airs by ornaments, and freeze the scene by coldness. But she could be charged with neither; for it would have been impossible to execute Mozart's music in a more correct, chaste, and perfect manner. Her method was of the German School, which best suits that master's intention; and the action, though it required to be animated by much more passion than the performer did, or perhaps could, throw into it, was not entirely devoid of warmth, and showed more feeling than was anticipated. The first duet, that fine burst of grief, "Fuggi! crudele, fuggi!" promised, at its opening, to excite the sympathy of the whole audience, but the feebleness of the Ottavio checked the exertion of his mistress, and diffused a chill over the whole scene. The recitative, describing the assault made by Don Giovanni, wanted spirit most certainly; but what lady could relate such wrongs with proper emotion to a lover who listened to them like a

* See *The Quarterly Musical Magazine and Review*, vol. ix. pp. 481-483.

stoic ?   The succeeding aria, however, "Or sai chi l' onore," was exceedingly well sung ; so was that exquisitely beautiful composition in the second act, "Non mi dir, bel' idol mio."   In each of these, the last particularly, was plenty of opportunity for both the flexibility and compass of Mdlle. Sontag's voice to display itself, and she indeed profited by the advantage offered.*

Mdlle. Sontag's continuance in the profession which she greatly adorned, and in the fulfilment of the duties of which she rapidly improved in vocal excellence, as she won the admiration of the public, was but of very short duration.   Having married the Count de Rossi at the beginning of the year 1830, she resolved to retire altogether into private life, and played for the last time in *Tancredi*, May 19th, 1830, at " Les Italiens," Paris.

In 1848, on account of a reverse of fortune, she returned to the stage, of which I shall have hereafter to speak.   The sudden disappearance of so bright and perfect a " star " caused general regret, although the circumstances of her retirement were, to all appearance, so unexceptionably prosperous, that congratulations poured in upon her from all sides.   The growing popularity of Madame Malibran, however, served considerably to fill the void which this sudden and unexpected event had occasioned.

On coming to England in 1828, Mdlle. Sontag had engaged the services of M. Pixis, as a pianoforte accompanyist—a gentleman who for a time created a sensation, more, however, from the reports that were circulated respecting his talent than from any very prominent demonstration of positive merit.   M. Pixis was a dashing player, and managed to overcome mechanical difficulties with some degree of skill ; but he was a musician of a very

* See *Harmonicon*, 1828, p. 144.

ordinary stamp, and shone by means of the reflected light he obtained from his association with Mdlle. Sontag. On her departure from London at the close of the season of 1829, M. Pixis likewise took his leave, and was no more remembered. He was chiefly spoken of as "a most rapid player, with an extremely neat brilliant finger and powerful hand," whilst "the velocity with which he executed his passages, and the accuracy also, were pleasing enough." But the pleasure, if such it could be called, which he created, arising more from astonishment than gratification, was but short-lived, and curiosity being very soon gratified by this sort of thing, ennui supervened, and it was asked, almost universally, "*Que me veux-tu, sonate ?*" *

Amongst the most remarkable *débuts* of the year 1829, that of Madame Pisaroni† must be mentioned, as being very nearly as

---

* See *Harmonicon*, 1828, p. 166.

† " Benedetta-Rosamunda Pisaroni, was born in 1793, and died August 6th, 1872, at Plaisance, her native city, in her seventy-ninth year. This artiste, although born in France, was educated in Italy, and made her *début* at Bergamo, in 1811, as a high soprano, but lost her upper notes during a severe illness at Parma, in 1813—small-pox—which greatly disfigured her. She then took to the contralto register. Meyerbeer, who in 1818 was travelling in Italy, heard her, and composed *Romilda e Costanza* expressly for her at Padua. At the San Carlo, in Naples, she sang in Rossini's *Ricciardo e Zoraide ;* and Mercadante wrote *Lodoiska* for her in 1819. It was in October of that year that she created a furore by her Malcolm, in Rossini's *Donna del Lago.* Meyerbeer again wrote for her *L'Esule di Granada* for Milan, in 1822, Lablache being included in the cast. In 1823 she sang in Rome and Lucca. At the last-mentioned city Pacini composed *Temistocle* for her and Sgnra. Tacchinardi—afterwards Mdme. Persiani.—Her next engagements were at Bologna and Milan. It was at the Scala that she electrified her audiences, in 1825, by her Arsace, in *Semiramide.* After being at Genoa, Leghorn, Florence, and Rome, Mdme. Pisaroni went to Paris in 1827, making her *début* as Arsace. The very first notes she sang, ' Eccome alfin in Babilonia,' roused the house in the same manner as Mdme. Alboni did in 1847, at the opening night of the Royal Italian Opera, also as Arsace. In Paris Pisaroni sang with Pasta, Malibran, and Sontag. In 1829 Pisaroni came to London, and at the King's Theatre

important as that of Mdlle. Sontag in the preceding season. Without exception this lady was the most ugly woman that was ever seen on the opera-stage; her appearance indeed was almost revolting. Besides the plainness of her face, she also limped, her figure was distorted, and her stature was short and squat. So well aware was she of her want of personal attraction, that when she was applied to by the management of "Les Italiens" to sing at Paris, she sent her picture, accompanied by an explanation that she was even uglier than that made her to appear. The moment, however, that she opened her lips, the feeling, that was little short of disgust at these imperfections, at once vanished. When she came to England, her voice had certainly passed its prime; but she could not sing six notes before it was perceptible that she was all sensibility, a model of devotion to her art, and alive to every breathing of passionate expression. Her voice naturally was a mezzo-soprano; but extreme cultivation had so improved its lower tones and extended its upper compass, that she imparted all the richness of a pure contralto to her deeper notes, and no inconsiderable portion of lightness, ease, and flexi-

under the late Laporte's direction, made her *début* here as Malcolm in the *Donna del Lago*, Sgnr. Donzelli—who is still living at Bologna—being the Roderick Dhu. Despite her physical defects, she brought down the house ; her voice was not what it had been in Italy and in France, but the genius of the *artiste* was supreme. Her Isabella, in Rossini's *Italiana in Algeri*, was marked by much finish, and her acting was so excellent, that the enthusiasm of her listeners knew no bounds. She subsequently played Arsace, first to the Semiramide of Sontag, and next to that of Malibran. Pisaroni returned to Paris and Milan in 1830, but quitted the lyric stage in 1836, Turin being the last theatre where she appeared. She was a great *artiste* in every sense of the word—histrionically as well as vocally : there was a grandeur and breadth of style, which always commanded the attention and enlisted the sympathies of her hearers. She had the tact to identify herself completely with the character she was sustaining, and it is difficult to state whether she shone most as a tragedian or a comedian."—See *Athenæum* for 1872, p. 284.

bility to its upper register. Notwithstanding that Madame Pisaroni's voice, as I have remarked, was past its best, her tone was pure, rich—particularly in the lower parts of the scale—sweet, and uniform. Her volume was also large, although not possessing the power of Catalani, or even of Pasta. With the purity and uniformity of her voice she associated a noble simplicity of declamation, a most accurate articulation, and the power of assimilation from the loudest *messa di voce* to the softest *pianissimo;* whilst she utterly rejected everything approaching to meretricious ornament, and contented herself with relying simply upon legitimate vocalization. But, after all, the union of intensely concentrated feeling with the most scientific understanding, and a most skilful employment of the resources of art, were her proper distinctions. No one could listen to Mdme. Pisaroni's singing without perceiving that she apprehended the entire scope of musical phrasing, the best application of her powers to its interpretation, and a sensibility which engaged her whole soul in the task. She was, to all intents and purposes, a great singer—the greatest contralto that had ever sung at the King's Theatre, and prepared the way for Alboni—whom she, more than any one else, resembled —for Nantier-Didiée, and, although last by no means least, Trebelli-Bettini.

At the opening of the operatic season this year (1829) a new tenor, named Bordogni, who had for several previous years held the first position at " Les Italiens," Paris, made his appearance in this country. The opera selected for the occasion was *La Gazza Ladra;* but although he was unquestionably an elegant singer and a master of his art, he failed to make any impression, chiefly from want of power. The area of the King's Theatre was too large for his diminished force ; yet, taking him for all in all, I very much doubt whether I ever heard a more finished or accomplished *artiste.*

During the season of this year, Mdme. Malibran was once more presented to the public, for the first time since her departure in 1825 with her father and the rest of her family to America.* She made her *rentrée* as Desdemona in Rossini's *Otello,* and at once "took the town by storm." Report had spoken very favourably of her reception during the previous year in Paris ; but no one anticipated that her voice would have attained the fulness or power which it now manifested. She was immediately accepted as the legitimate successor of Pasta, although pronounced off-hand to be inferior to her great predecessor in pathos and discrimination, both in acting and singing, and in the former particularly. Yet she was a more natural representative of the forlorn and helpless Venetian bride, except when—as she was always somewhat prone to do—she gave way to exaggeration, in order to intensify the situation of the scene, in which more than ordinary prominence seemed to her to be required.† In spite, however, of this fault, and the severe animadversions that were passed upon her because of it, Malibran at once established herself as a popular favourite, and never lost the influence upon

---

* See p. 145.

† As an instance of this propensity, I may mention that two or three years afterwards, when she played Leonora in Beethoven's *Fidelio* at Covent Garden—after Madame Schöder-Devrient had, so far as a London audience was concerned, "created" that part—she produced such an immense sensation by the manner in which she presented the pistol at the head of Pizarro in the prison scene, that she was again and again recalled. The next night, when the same scene had to be represented, she produced *two* pistols, and thus imparted such a sense of the ridiculous to the action as wholly to destroy its effectiveness.

the public she then immediately gained. Again and again did she repeat to me, "On that night, when the curtain went down, I was convinced, cold as you English creatures are, I shall always feel I can warm you."

On the occasion of this remarkable operatic event, the most accomplished *tenore robusto* of his times, Donzelli, was the Otello to Malibran's Desdemona. This singer was, indeed, justly pronounced as the very first of his class, if not the first absolutely in Europe, after Garcia. His voice had a clearness, a brilliancy, and a power—a *metallo* or natural vibratory power—that belonged to very few, either before or since his time. His tone was formed high in the head, his compass combining the falsetto to a very large extent; whilst he possessed such complete command over his vast volume of voice, that he could send it forth in all its body, or in its softest attenuation, at pleasure. He managed the junction of the chest and head registers with the utmost skill, so that it was quite impossible to discover upon what note the actual transition took place, although the fluty quality of the upper notes immediately made its use apparent. His conception was both vigorous and apprehensive, his manner being proportionately energetic or tender, as the expression or the occasion required. His style was in a great degree founded upon that of Crivelli and Garcia; more, perhaps, upon that of the latter than of the former, on account of its grace and fluency. His middle register was richly full, which, together with the concentration he occasionally used, and his facility and neatness of execution, were admirable. Yet, notwithstanding his possession of these remarkable qualities, Donzelli was by no means a faultless singer. One peculiarity was constantly apparent, which, after a while, not a little detracted from his excellence,

simply because it took from him the equality of his execution.
The ascending notes of his scales were generally given out from
his chest voice until he rose very high, and passed into the
falsetto, the almost inevitable consequence of which was, that
they were sometimes too strong by their comparative volume.
His descending divisions and *fioriture*, on the contrary, when
they commenced upon the higher notes of his voice, were taken
in falsetto, which he carried very low down before using his
mixed or natural voice. From such extreme contrasts the ear
was not seldom cheated into a belief of this having been done
expressly to convey the notion of an echo or distant sound, the
equality was disturbed, and the general effect of the performance
diminished. Donzelli was essentially a florid singer ; and therefore, although his invention might seem, or might actually be,
more extensively exercised, much of the nicety of touch and
finesse were lost in volubility, which produced the semblance, if
not the reality, of mannerism. After all, however, Donzelli
possessed all the requisites of greatness, both in nature and
art, in a super-eminent degree, and could but be regarded as
having come nearer to Braham in the perfection of his youth
than any other tenor that had been heard.* Donzelli sang for
several seasons in London, and was to the last popular, both as
a man and as an *artiste.* I knew him intimately; and although
he had by no means been well educated, he possessed and manifested the feelings of a gentleman. He was devoted to his art,
and what he was unable to effect by means of natural intelligence he succeeded in mastering by patient study and earnest
perseverance. He did not retire from his profession till the
close of the year 1841, when he sang for the last time in public

* See *The Quarterly Musical Magazine and Review,* vol. x. pp. 271-3.

at Bologna, and then retired upon the independence he had acquired by means of the exercise of his profession. That he is still living I have only recently ascertained.* Without question, his fame will never be forgotten so long as any musician, cognisant of the events of his times, lives to chronicle the excellences of so remarkable a man.

Amongst the lesser musical " satellites " which at this period revolved around the greater " stars," there were two singers, whose usefulness was of the highest order, and whose engagement was universally attended with advantage—Signors Pellegrini and Porto. The former came to London in 1826, and obtained an engagement at the King's Theatre during Mr. Ebers' management in that year ;† but being supplanted by Zuchelli in the following year, returned to Italy with the determination never to visit England again. Certain " considerations," however, induced him to change his mind, and he accepted another engagement in the same place during the seasons of 1828 and 1829, in the latter of which I heard him, on the 28th of May, at the King's Theatre, when he played, in *Il Don Giovanni,* Leporello, to the Don of Zuchelli, the Don Ottavio of Donzelli, the Donna Anna of Sontag, the Donna Elvira of Mdlle. Monticelli—a mere second-rate—and the Zerlina of Caradori—a most imperfect performance upon the whole, on account of the miserable condition of the band. The well-trained and established players had revolted against M. Bochsa's direction, and were superseded by a set of incompetents, who, whatever their individual talent might have been, were prevented from displaying it through the miserable ignorance of the harpist—or " harpy "—

---

* See p. 168, note.
† See Ebers' *Seven Years of the King's Theatre,* p. 282.

musical director, who not only could not read a score, but was totally ignorant of the smallest characteristics of his important office. The veteran Lindley had given place to a M. Rousselot, whose accompaniment of the well-known " Batti, batti," by the force of contrast, made every *habitué* feel how great was the loss the orchestra had sustained by the retirement of the most perfect violoncellist the world had then ever heard. Pellegrini's voice, being dull in tone, helped to render the performance of Mozart's *chef-d'œuvre* anything but a musical treat; yet he showed talent as a buffo singer, and certainly merited the reputation of being something better than a mere " utility man." Indeed, it is only to do this *artiste* the justice he certainly merited, to say that he was a capable performer and a steady vocalist. His talent was also versatile, and although his forte was chiefly in the comic line, he was by no means devoid of expression in serious parts.* His singing was altogether of a better school than that of de Begnis, and much more masterly, whether general sustentation, execution, or the power and science of ornament were concerned. His intonation, although

---

* One of the best performances, notwithstanding the inequality of the band, that was given during the season of 1829 at the King's Theatre was that of Rossini's *Il Barbiere,* in which de Begnis appeared as Bartolo, Pellegrini as Figaro, and Porto as Don Basilio, all of whom were equally admirable, making the necessary allowance for what each had to do, and the absence of those who had originally created those parts respectively. De Begnis, who had been one of the very best Figaros that was ever seen, was excellent as the jealous old Spanish doctor. Curioni, as Il Conte Almaviva, was at least, if nothing more, very respectable, although by no means equal to Garcia, in this, perhaps, his best dramatic performance. Caradori's Rosina was beautifully sustained. At that time I certainly gave her the preference over all the Italian and English actresses I had seen in that character, for rarely had there been such genuine native delicacy and naïveté mixed up with so much archness. The personation was alike elegant, natural, and effective. I had not then, however, seen Malibran, Persiani, Alboni, Viardot, or Patti in *Il Barbiere.*

at times faulty, was generally reliable, and his method formed
after the purest Italian school. Yet he scarcely ever rose above
mediocrity; for, notwithstanding he was a good singer and a
clever actor, he was, as it were, borne down by his companions,
who in several instances, with nothing like his talent, yet more
thoroughly succeeded in securing popular approbation. That
he really was a master of deserved celebrity may be inferred
from the fact, that upon his return to Paris, after his last
London season, he was appointed professor of singing at the
Conservatoire, which he retained until 1852, when he became
insane, and speedily afterwards died.* Porto was by no means
equal to Pellegrini. He might rather be termed the Polonini
or Tagliafico of his day, for he was perhaps more generally
employed than any other *artiste*, being the most useful performer on the boards of the King's Theatre. He could, in
fact, turn his hand to anything, and sing any part that was
required of him at an hour's notice. He was one of those men,
however, who never could be great, and yet such as are a
fortune to a management, when they are good-humoured and
anxious to be obliging rather than sticklers for dignity and
position. Porto's voice was loud in tone, but hard in quality,
with little facility of articulation. No sooner had he left
London than his absence was severely felt; for the means of
supplying his place were by no means easy, as the management
discovered both to its cost and disadvantage.

And now I approach an event which has had more to do with
the progress of music in England than had ever happened before
or since—the arrival in this country of the two greatest men in
their profession of modern times—Felix Mendelssohn Bartholdy

* See Fétis' *Biographie Universelle des Musiciens*, tom. vi. pp. 477, 478.

and Michael Costa, both of whom it has been my high privilege to have known intimately. The former of these justly celebrated musicians came first to our shores in the spring of 1829, and on May 25th, at the Seventh Philharmonic Concert of that year, produced his Symphony in C minor, of which the following just appreciation was immediately afterwards written :—"This admirable Symphony is in C minor, and in four movements— an allegro, a slow andante, a scherzo and trio, and a finale. Fertility of invention and novelty of effect are what first strike the hearers of this composition ; but at the same time, the melodiousness of its subjects, the vigour with which these are supported, the gracefulness of the slow movement, the playfulness of some parts and the energy of others, are all felt ; though from a first hearing, and without some previous knowledge of the score, it were in vain to attempt an analysis of the work, which can now only be described in general terms. The author conducted in person ; it was received with acclamation. The audience wished the adagio to be repeated, but M. Mendelssohn did not construe the continued applause as an *encore.* The scherzo and trio, however, were instantly called for a second time, and the band seemed most happy to comply with the command. It would be an act of injustice to the orchestra not to state that the execution of this entirely new work was as perfect as the most sanguine hopes of the composer could have taught him to expect. He was surprised at such accuracy of performance—which, indeed, was still more remarkable on the morning of rehearsal than at the concert itself—and expressed his satisfaction in terms that were highly gratifying to the most excellent band."*

* *Harmonicon* for 1828, pp. 173, 174.

As I was not present at the Philharmonic Concert when this event came off, I can only refer incidentally to the time, place, and circumstance of Mendelssohn's *début;* and as I did not become acquainted with him on the occasion of his first visit to London, I must defer what I have to say of him for the present. Not so, however, is it with reference to Costa, whom I am indeed proud to call the oldest of my musical friends now living. The Birmingham Festival of 1829 was held on the 6th, 7th, 8th, and 9th October; and at that great musical meeting he who is now,—upon the assertion of no less an authority than Meyerbeer himself,—the greatest *chef-d'orchestre* of the world, made his bow to an English audience, and met with a reception which, could those who accorded it have understood what he even then was, at the comparatively early age of nineteen years, or foreseen what he was to be, would have made them blush with shame. Costa came indeed to England under most inauspicious circumstances. Having received the rudiments of his musical education from his maternal grandfather, Giacomo Tritto—who seemed to have had the idea of forming a new school, or, rather, appeared to be desirous of uniting the soft melody of his own country to German harmony, in order to render it more fit for the expression of the great passions of the tragic opera—he was afterwards placed under the tuition of Nicolo Zingarelli, the fellow-student of Cimarosa, at the Naples Conservatoire. So great was the progress that he rapidly made in his art, that he was placed at the pianoforte in the theatre of San Carlo in 1828 as the accompanist, and produced an opera entitled *Il Carcere d' Ildegondo* at the Teatro Nuovo; and "*Malvina,* melodrama, in due atte, rappresentato sulle scena de R^{al}. Teatro de S. Carlo, le 7 Febb. 1829;" as also *Seldlachek*, for Tosi, Rubini, and Bendetti, at the same theatre.

It was the fashion at that time with the committee of management of the Birmingham Festival, as it has been ever since, to give " commissions " to composers of eminence to produce a new work for the occasion. Such a commission had been accepted by Zingarelli, who at the last moment, being unwell, and frightened at the long journey that was before him —he was then in his seventy-seventh year—sent over his favourite pupil with the score of a " Cantata sacra " upon the words of the 12th chapter of Isaiah, with the strict injunction that he was both to produce and conduct it in his stead. On Costa's arrival in Birmingham and presenting himself before the committee, those wiseacres concluded that such a mere stripling could but be wholly unequal to the task which he was ready to perform, and for which he was so much the better prepared, because he had scored every one of the four *motivos* of which the Cantata consisted. They one and all positively refused to allow him to fulfil his mission, and demanded whether he could sing ; for if he were able to do so, they would give him an engagement. Upon his reply, that conducting, not singing, was his province, and that he had never appeared in the latter capacity in public, they gave him to understand that, unless he did so, not one shilling of his expenses would they pay him ! There was nothing for him to do but to submit to those hard, miserly, and unjust terms. The consequence of this was, that he was put down to take part in various concerted pieces with which he was unacquainted, and to sing several solos both at the morning and evening performances, the latter of which were given in the theatre, most of the operatic selections being presented in character.

Costa's *début* in this direction—as unfair as it was unexpected—was with Miss Fanny Ayton in a scena from Rossini's *Donna dèl Lago*, "O mattutini albori." What with fright, as well as from the novelty of his position, he failed; and although, by dint of that innate firmness of character which had yet fully to develop itself, he made a far better impression than might have been anticipated, he did not escape from the cruelty of unjust criticism, by means of which the writer, without the slightest knowledge of the facts, assumed that " Signor Costa was, as it were, forced upon the committee by the request of Zingarelli, but that the singer was little, if at all better, than the composition." There were, however, other persons present at that Festival, who formed a far different judgment of the qualifications of the young musician, and predicted that the world would hear and know much more of him hereafter. Chiefly amongst these were Malibran,* Mrs. Anderson—the leading female pianist of her time—and the venerable Clementi. The latter, on looking over the song from Bellini's *Il Pirata,* "Nel furor delle tempeste," which Costa had scored

---

* At the morning performance (Oct. 6) Costa heard Braham for the first time in his life, and in his *chef-d'œuvre,* Handel's accompanied recitative from *Jephtha,* " Deeper and deeper still," in which no singer, either before or since, ever approached him. He sat, as I well remember, just behind Malibran, on the front of the orchestra, and, with open mouth, indicative of most earnest attention, lost not a note of that incomparable performance. When Braham concluded with that burst of agony, on the words, " I can no more," with which all who ever heard him were completely carried away, Costa, not understanding a word of the text, asked Malibran in a whisper, and in Italian, " What does the man say ? " To which that versatile creature replied in the same language on the instant, " Poor devil, it's all up with him ! " Not till long afterwards did he understand the information he had asked for.

with the utmost rapidity, that he might be accompanied by the orchestra while singing it at the third evening concert, quaintly remarked to him, " You are a composer, not a singer!"

The Birmingham Festival having come to an end, the various professors and performers went their several ways; but Costa took up his residence in the town, as a visitor in the house of a friendly amateur, who had become deeply interested in his welfare, quite as much on account of the talent that he perceived this mere youth possessed, as of the disgust he felt at the unhandsome manner in which he had been treated. Here Laporte, who was making his engagements for the opera season of 1830, heard of him, and at once engaged him as musical director of the King's Theatre, in the place of Bochsa, with whose ignorance and insolence it was impossible any longer to bear. When Laporte, at the first meeting of the company, presented the youthful musician to them as their future *chef*, they one and all burst into a roar of laughter, which made the house ring; and on the following morning he received a card with seven miniature razors affixed to it—which I have seen, and which Costa would not on any account whatever part with—accompanied by a written recommendation to him to shave. This practical joke he had the sense to take in good part; but both the singers and the band speedily discovered that, beardless as he was, they had found a master. Under previous mismanagement the orchestra had chiefly consisted of the pupils of the principal violinists, who made money by such engagements in addition to their own salaries. This state of things Costa determined at once to abolish; and the opposition he encountered would have broken down a less firm and resolute spirit. But he was resolved to have his own way, or retire altogether; and Laporte, pleased with the courage he displayed, and also having heard still more of what was in him, from Rubini and others who had known him at Naples, backed him up, and maintained his position with the utmost zeal. As a proof of his competency as a composer, a commission was given to him to write and produce a ballet entitled *Kenilworth*, the success of which was unequivocal.

Of this season Madame Malibran and Mdlle. Blasis were the *prime donne.* The latter is now wholly forgotten; but from what I remember of her, the impression remains that she had a powerful and well-toned voice, of fluty quality, and of considerable compass; that she was a fair musician and a well-trained singer, yet with no peculiar distinction or energy of talent to raise her to that eminence towards which she aspired. It was said of her, with the utmost truth, that " the intensity of character and feeling which formed a Pasta or a Malibran were not amongst the gifts nature had bestowed upon her."* Mdlle. Blasis's person inclined to *embonpoint;* her face was round and handsome, and her features bespoke a lively good-humour. In the Ninetta of Rossini's *La Gazza Ladra*—her chief *rôle*—her acting was superior; but she was eclipsed by the energy, imagination, and feeling of Malibran; although it was held by some that, by avoiding extravagance, she exceeded her rival in the purity of her personation. Mdlle. Blasis remained but a short time in this country; for although she certainly obtained a *succès d'estime,* she never " made a public " to give her cordial and undivided support.

On the 17th of April another *prima donna* and a new opera

* *The Quarterly Magazine and Review*, vol. ix. p. 277.

were both produced together. The name of the former was Meric-Lalande, and of the latter *Il Pirata,* "the work," as it was said, "of a young composer named Bellini!" Mdme. Meric-Lalande was a Frenchwoman, who left her country at a comparatively early age, and had been singing, previously to her engagement by M. Laporte, in various parts of Italy, where she had acquired a high reputation. This professional character reached London long before she herself arrived, and was heralded with the utmost pertinacity, insomuch that a rival to Pasta, Sontag, and Malibran was expected by such as either had not heard her, or were unaware of the source and objects of the commendation lavished upon her. All this would have been prejudicial to any singer, and unfortunately proved so to one who certainly could not be compared to any one of those "brilliant stars" without most disadvantageously suffering in the opinion of every tolerable judge. In personal appearance this lady was below the middle stature, and rather stout. Her face, without being handsome, was full of expression, and she became one of the most useful acquisitions the management had secured, although as a brilliant addition to the *corps opératique* it cannot but be said that she was comparatively a failure.

The year 1830 must ever be remembered as having witnessed the *début* of the greatest *basso profondo* the musical world has ever known—Lablache—who, on Thursday, the 13th of May, "was heard for the first time in England, in Cimarosa's clever opera, *Il Matrimonio Segreto,* the part of Geronimo having, as a matter of course, been assigned to him. The fame of his voice had previously reached England, and his character as an actor had been quite as loudly proclaimed." So high a reputation is not frequently maintained, but in this instance not one half enough had been told of the genius of this truly great and eminent man. Lablache made an immense hit in this opera, and in not the slightest respect fell short of the anticipations that had been raised respecting him. His triumph was complete. Indeed, he could not possibly have selected a better part to show off the pre-eminent qualities he possessed, both as an actor and a singer. His voice was of considerable compass, and its weight exceeded everything that was ever heard from a human chest. When put forth to its full power and extent, it not only overwhelmed every other upon the stage and re-sounded above the loudest orchestration, but entered into the most successful competition with the most sonorous instruments. This stentorian strength and gigantic power he, however, used with the utmost discretion, only now and then displaying it, and then most justifiably. Its quality was superb. So round, clear, and sympathetic was every note, that if he had only sung his scales—which he could do most perfectly—it would have produced the utmost gratification. It also blended well with other voices. Nothing could exceed the accuracy of his intonation, a quality that can never be too highly valued, whilst his steadiness indicated the superiority of his musical training. His style was of the purest—a model, in fact, of excellence, good taste, and feeling. As a comic actor, he was equal—indeed I might truthfully say superior—to what Ambrogetti was before he degenerated into coarseness, and superior to every one besides that had ever appeared on the boards of the King's Theatre. The character he had to represent was always uppermost in his mind ; to every minutiæ he paid the utmost attention. Thus, for example, his Geronimo—the character in which he *débuted*—was the dull, deaf, coarse, and ambitious *parvenu* from the very first moment to the last. He never seemed to be aware of the existence of such a person as Lablache, or of the presence of a large audience. He was the rich vulgar merchant, seeking an alliance with a foreign nobleman, and sacrificing his daughter in order to gratify his stupid selfish pride.

Lablache's next character was Assur, in Rossini's *Semiramide*, in which he scarcely made the same impression that his Geronimo produced. From that time forward, however, he went on " from strength to strength," acquiring greater and greater fame, the support and mainstay of every management that had the good fortune to secure his services and to rely upon his aid.

Amongst the many *débutantes* of this time, Mdme. Stockhausen* obtained a position as a concert singer by her intelligence and good taste. She was chiefly remarkable, however, as a singer of Swiss national airs, the peculiar quaintness of which, as they were quite new to English audiences when she introduced them, secured for her an extensive popularity. She was also a careful interpreter of sacred music, and sang, on one occasion that I well remember, at the —— Festival of 1830, Handel's song, " Ye men of Gaza, hither bring," from the oratorio of *Samson*, better than I ever heard it rendered either previously or afterwards.

* The mother of Herr Stockhausen, the German basso.

CHAPTER VII.

1830-32.

AMONGST the first fruits of the Royal Academy of Music in London, which had been established chiefly through the instrumentality of Lord Burghersh, afterwards the Earl of Westmorland, in 1822, there were three pupils, who about this period began to make a reputation for themselves as instrumentalists —Charles Lucas (violoncello), Seymour, and Henry Blagrove (violins)—whilst two, soon afterwards, distinguished themselves as vocalists, Miss Childe (soprano), and Mr. E. Seguin (bass). All of these were not only accomplished players and singers, but they bade fair to raise the reputation of the English *artiste*, and to show that this country is as well able to rear "well-built" musicians as even Italy or Germany. Foreign competition in the case of the two singers, who afterwards married, prevented their ever reaching the highest ranks of celebrity in their own country, although they obtained a much more marked success in America, whither, very early in their career, they emigrated; but the three instrumentalists maintained their ground, Charles Lucas becoming the successor of Lindley, when that veteran retired from the Opera, the London Philharmonic Society, provincial Festivals, and concerts; whilst Henry Blagrove, after having studied under Spohr in Germany, became

the legitimate follower of François Cramer as an oratorio and
concert leader, and of Mori as a soloist, and held his position
with unremitting perseverance and abiding honour to his name,
as well as to the school in which he was originally trained, until
ill health, a few years since, compelled his retirement from the
more active duties of his profession. Seymour, of whom the
promise was equally distinct, contented himself with settling
at Manchester, where he still remains, taking part in all such
performances as demand the exposition of superior talent,
in which very many provincial *artistes* unknown in the metropolis excel. The first occasion of my having become acquainted
with these three gentlemen was at the —— Festival of 1827,
when Charles Lucas held the post of second violoncellist, and
Seymour and Henry Blagrove together occupied the next desk
to that of François Cramer,* the leader of the morning and
evening concerts, out of whose book a little boy of only twelve
years of age played—a pupil of the organist of one of the principal churches in ——, who was afterwards well known in London, as Harry Westrop, a most efficient member of the Opera
and Philharmonic bands. Henry Blagrove on that occasion
played one of Meyseder's concertos, and obtained general approbation, more from the undoubted promise of future excellence,
which was thoroughly fulfilled, than from any remarkable finish
of style or warmth of execution. The interest in one so young
—he was scarcely seventeen years old—was increased by the
peculiarity of his dress, the most remarkable features of which
were a stiffly-starched frill that encircled his throat, and a blue
cloth jacket with R.A.M. gilt buttons. His name was inserted
in the bills as "*Master* Blagrove," but neither Charles Lucas

* See p. 71.

nor Seymour took the same prominent position. Charles Lucas was the only one of these three English musicians who obtained any fame by composition; but he essayed the highest flights, and so early as the trial night of the Philharmonic Society, January 8, 1830, produced a Symphony, that was pronounced to be "remarkably clever for so young a writer."* Charles Lucas afterwards became a partner in the firm of Addison and Co., and died four or five years ago, universally esteemed and respected, both by the members of his own profession and all others who had any acquaintance with him; but by none more so than by the then present and past pupils of the Royal Academy of Music, of which Institution he became a leading professor, and also principal.

Another English singer, whom it is impossible to forget, inasmuch as he was the legitimate successor of Bartleman, had about this time risen into permanent fame, and was creating a reputation, which never waned whilst he remained actively engaged in the duties of his professional career—Henry Phillips. Preferring an operatic and a theatrical career to the drudgery of a cathedral, under which he would never have risen beyond a mere occasional concert-room singer, this accomplished musician dashed at once *in medias res*, and, obtaining the favourable opinion of Sir George Smart so early as the year 1825, went on step by step, manifesting equal talent and excellence whether engaged upon the stage or in the orchestra. Henry Phillips' training as a boy had been neither that of the cathedral nor of the stage. Showing some aptitude for part singing, and being also possessed of a very promising bass voice, he came under the notice of Mr. Broadhurst, a tenor singer of very excellent

* See *Harmonicon* for 1830, p. 83.

taste, but of no important position, who engaged and instructed him in that class of vocal music which was then, and still is, in vogue at the great dinners of the various London City companies, such, for instance, as the Goldsmiths', the Mercers', the Drapers', the Merchant Taylors', and many others too numerous to name. Mr. Broadhurst had the arrangement of the after-dinner music of most of these entertainments, and was constantly on the look-out for novelty amongst promising male voices, since he had to depend solely upon these, the innovation of introducing ladies not having then been even so much as thought of—an innovation which, for many reasons, it would have been better never to have made. At the commencement of his career, "his voice" is said to have "presented a curious anomaly in description, inasmuch as it could neither be called bass nor baritone, heavy nor light, although it partook of all those several properties in its tone and compass." Its volume was considerable, but by no means vast, which he very soon discovered it would be alike to his interest and his advantage to improve by patient and assiduous study, cultivating finish and sweetness rather than grandeur or power, so far as tone might be concerned in the production of such effects. Henry Phillips' voice was certainly genuinely English, clear, natural, and capable of making an impression, whether it had been trained or not; but it was rendered all the more effective by the application of art, which imparted an influence without which he could never have risen above mediocrity, like a host of other aspirants, who, just before and about this time, "came like shadows," and like "shadows, so departed." From the very first moment of his making any impression, one point alone secured him an unqualified reception. The correctness of his intonation, which was so much the more remarked and approved because the Italian basses of that time—as they very often are still—were most slovenly and careless in this most essential particular. Another feature in Henry Phillips' singing, which secured for him unqualified commendation, was his use of appropriate declamation and dramatic fire. In this respect, without having at all copied him, he more resembled Braham than any other contemporary. Whether he had ever heard Bartleman I have had no means of ascertaining. I should rather think he never had that advantage, since he by no means inherited the powers of that most remarkable singer, and sang everything which he (Bartleman) had made his own rather after an original method, than according to imitation. Plain and simple, but perfectly natural, in his conceptions of his author, displaying a manly sensibility and energy in expression, yet without the least inflation or pomposity, his easy but feeling interpretation made its way to the good sense of his hearers, whilst there seemed to be "an ingenuous modesty" about all he did that won for him everywhere the reception which that quality alone obtains. He had likewise no slight versatility, but turned

> "From grave to gay, from lively to severe,"

with an equal air of nature and of truth. His execution was free and flowing—not, indeed, particularly remarkable for facility; nor was it till a considerable period after his *début* that his tone, at that time agreeable and solid, became as finished as it was, by many degrees, afterwards by means of study and practice during his mid-career.* It was feared that Henry Phillips might suffer disadvantage from the admixture of the

---

* See *The Quarterly Musical Magazine and Review*, vol. vii. pp. 465-6.

theatrical and orchestral manner when he first began to sing in each of these departments. But he was possessed of sufficient good sense to enable him to discriminate between the two, and to preserve a balance so even that it was impossible to ascertain in which he might be supposed to excel, so competent was he in each. For a long series of years this acknowledged favourite of the public held on his way as the first of English bass singers, no competitor having arisen to make him in the slightest degree anxious concerning the maintenance of his position. He was, however, unwise enough to leave his native country, and try his fortune in America, where he only partially succeeded. Although on his return he found the place he had left to all appearance unfilled, and as open for himself—and none other— as ever it had been before his departure, he had the mortification to discover that not only had absence not "made the (public) heart grow fonder," but that it had caused him to be all but forgotten. He appeared in his accustomed places again and again ; but the sensation he had once upon a time created had died out, and could never be resuscitated. He persisted, however, in working on, till at length failing powers indicated even to himself the absolute necessity of retirement ; since which time little has been heard of him, beyond his own publication of a series of musical anecdotes and *facetiæ*, which obtained no especial manifestation of popular favour. Henry Phillips, indeed, bought the sad experience which numerous other vocalists and actors have had since to do, and will, doubtless, continue to do—that if their talent is no longer available at home, no matter whether there be or be not any one competent to supply their places, they never will or can recover that position which no other cause would have forfeited, so long as they manifested neither decline of powers, nor failure of musical competency. Henry Phillips is still alive and resident in London. Four or five years ago he was actively engaged in bringing forward two daughters, the offspring of a second marriage; both of whom came before the public.* Even now, however, although this has happened, it cannot be truly said that Henry Phillips has yet found a successor. The only one in his actual line—and he is a baritone—who can be mentioned in comparison with him, is Santley; but between the two, equally excellent as the one still is and the other was, there is no more similarity than existed between Bartleman and Phillips.

During the year 1830, after an absence of forty years—he was then a boy of twelve years of age—the grandest male pianist I ever heard—Jean-Nepomuk Hummel—arrived in London, and, not having been able to come to terms with the directors of the Philharmonic Concerts to play there, gave two *matinées*—the first on the 29th of April and the second on the 11th of May. Of those events the following notice for the most part accords so much with my own impressions, "except as excepted"—I was present at the second concert, and afterwards heard M. Hummel frequently in the provinces—that I have no hesitation in reproducing it :—

"In his first concert M. Hummel performed a MS. concerto in A flat, a composition of which, both as regards science and taste, but one opinion was expressed, or, we should think, could have been entertained by all the judges in the room, who were very numerous. He likewise played a "new characteristic fantasia," founded on an Indian air, with orchestral accompani-

* One daughter has retired from the profession, being married ; the other remains on the stage.

ments, in which his fancy had more room for expansion than in the concerto, the style being truer and admitting higher flights of the imagination.* He concluded with an extemporaneous performance, in which he embodied the greater part of the finale to *Don Giovanni*—that of the first act undoubtedly—and two popular airs. The whole of this, except the latter part, which was a little *ad captandum*, showed no less than the preceding pieces Hummel's command over the instrument and the riches of his resources. At his second concert M. Hummel repeated his concerto, and afterwards played, with M. Moscheles, a duet for two pianofortes by Mozart, the execution of which was as perfect as was to be expected from two such masters. After this M. Hummel gave his new military septet (in C) for piano-forte, violin, violoncello, contra-basso, flute, clarionet, and trum-pet, which is full of masterly writing; and, what is of more importance, the effects are frequently original and throughout pleasing.† This concert, as the last, terminated with an extem-poraneous performance. He had previously invited the com-pany to furnish him with a theme. This request was repeated

* This opinion has certainly not been confirmed ; for while the concerto re-mains as popular as ever, and is still a favourite with various accomplished pianists, "the fantasia on an Indian subject" is never so much as heard of.

† Of this septuor I have but a very indistinct recollection ; his other septuor (in D minor), for pianoforte, flute, oboë, horn, viola, violoncello, and contra-basso, which I afterwards heard at a provincial concert, at the same time that he played his grand concerto in A, Op. 113, having made a much greater impression upon my mind. That impression has furthermore been since increased immensely by my having frequently heard it played at Mr. Ella's Musical Union Directors' *matinées*. Of the concerto I retain the copy which I myself lent to M. Hummel to play from at —— ; and of the septuor I have the recollection of his having said to personal friends of my own, on their compli-menting him on the manner in which he had played it, and especially the last movement : "Ah ! dat's what makes me schwet in winter !"

by Sir George Smart, and produced two subjects, neither of which M. Hummel appeared much to relish ; but he at length introduced them with some brilliant and learned descant, and finished with the very air—'The Ploughboy'—which he performed here when a boy, though he now treated it in a very different manner. The conclusion of this was one of the most splendid displays of pianoforte playing we ever heard, and left an impression on his auditory which will not easily be effaced." *

"M. Hummel," says the same writer, to whom I owe the above notice, " as a performer is master of all styles, but excels rather more in the brilliant than in the pathetic, though he never carries the former to excess. His touch is the true one, and more resembles (J. B.) Cramer's than any we have ever heard. The strength, and still more the equality, of his fingers are among the distinguishing features of his playing: and the pendulum-like accuracy of his time is too remarkable not to be noticed by all who hear him, though he occasionally makes this yield to expression ; not, however, quite so often or in so great a degree as those who have a strong predilection for that manner, which denotes much sensibility, would wish. His execution is perfect, but we believe he does not consider great rapidity as an essential quality. We observed, and with infinite satisfaction,

* Undoubtedly M. Hummel's improvisation on this occasion was clever ; but he was so put out by the incompatibility of the two subjects with which he had been furnished, that he made nothing but execution of the most difficult passages out of them, and gradually slipped into the commonplace air above-named, as a means of making up for his own feeling of failure. It was, however, to my mind, but a weak affair altogether. M. Hummel, indeed, improvised far better in private than in public, as I can testify without any hesitation, since I had not unfrequently, whilst he was in England, the gratification of listening to his " flights of fancy " when he was surrounded by his intimate friends, as well as when he played before much larger audiences.

that his allegro movements were considerably slower than most of the pianists of the present day would have taken them. His good sense teaches him that great velocity renders it next to impossible to discern the delicacy of an air or the beauty of a modulation; that racing and leaping on the piano are generally resorted to by those who are conscious of possessing none of the higher powers, and feel obliged to supply the want of pure taste and deep feeling by mechanical dexterity."*

Notwithstanding that such was the general feeling amongst musicians respecting the quality of M. Hummel's pianoforte playing, the general public certainly did not manifest the same appreciation towards him. That this arose from their not having been sufficiently educated up to the point, from which true talent can only be adequately discerned, is more than probable. Mrs. Anderson—than whom there never was a more conscientious or legitimate pianist—had been for several previous years doing her very utmost to make classical compositions force their way into esteem; but with so little comparative success, that she was even compelled upon occasion to put Beethoven aside for Herz and Kalkbrenner, and to be content to bide her time until genius should triumph over mere trickery and mechanism. The fight she had to make even against such professors as J. B. Cramer, Callcott, Attwood, and others, to obtain a hearing even for Mozart, and especially for Beethoven, was a hard one; but she has lived to behold her perseverance crowned with complete success, and to congratulate the public as well as herself that she did not permit her heart to fail her, or to yield before opposition, which was as unworthy, considering the acknowledged talent of her celebrated contemporaries, as it now seems to have ·

* The *Harmonicon* for 1830, p. 204.

been incomprehensible. When M. Hummel came to London, Mrs. Anderson was still "in arms against a sea of (musical) troubles " in this direction ; but she at once took that truly great man by the hand, and not only did her utmost to make him heard, but, after he had retired from England, continually introduced his concertos at her own concerts, and at such others where she was constantly engaged. Thus, by degrees, Hummel's compositions began to be admired and esteemed ; and although he has not taken, and never can take, any rank, except by many a degree lower than Beethoven, yet it has already come to pass that something more than that he was " a master in his art " is allowed, inasmuch as he is thought worthy to find a place amongst the greatest writers of his times.

M. Hummel did not long survive his sojourn in England. After a brief visit to Poland, he settled down at Weimar, where he merely followed his profession for the sake of amusement—a retirement which his prudence, if not his parsimony, had rendered easy and comfortable. He died at that place, October 17, 1837, at the comparatively early age of fifty-nine years.[*]

Of all the violinists I have ever heard, from Kiesewetter[†] to Joachim—and their name is "legion"—there is not one that has left such an impression upon my mind as Paganini did. It was —and is still, I have reason to believe—the fashion to denounce this most extraordinary man as little better than a monster of iniquity ; as avaricious to an extent scarcely ever before heard of, especially amongst musicians ; as a charlatan in his art; as a heartless father ; and as a false and treacherous friend. My own experience concerning him, except upon the score of money, was

* Hummel's Second Mass was performed at the Worcester Musical Festival in September, 1872.   † See p. 113.

in direct opposition to all such slander. During his career he
visited my native town, and as I had the good fortune then to
be able to converse in French, the friends who had engaged him
for a round of concerts in that place and its vicinity placed me
in direct communication with him somewhat in the capacity of
a secretary ; so that I not only travelled in his company and
heard him at every concert at which he appeared, but I lived in
the same hotels and lodgings which had been secured for him.
This kind of semi-official position necessitated my seeing much
of him during his leisure hours, when he threw off the suspicious
restraint which was always apparent in his manner when he was
amongst strangers, whom he imagined were bent upon getting
as much as possible out of him for their own advantage. Then,
indeed, he would evince anything but a hard and ungenerous
nature, his manner being not only kind but courteous ; whilst
any attention that was afforded to his wants or to his comforts
was sure to elicit not only looks but words of gratitude. In
public he confined himself almost exclusively to the performance
of his own music, which was in very many respects somewhat
crude, undigested, and extravagant, the sole purpose for which
it was written having been nothing more or less than to show
off " the meretricious trickery "—as it was not very generously
termed—of his marvellous execution. But in private—for he had
his violin constantly in his hand—he would sit and dash off by
the hour together snatches from the compositions of the best
masters, and give readings of such originality to passages that
had been heard again and again, as apparently have never been
supposed to be possible by any other player. As an instance in
point, he one morning, whilst I was writing several notes for him,
commenced the first *motivo* of Beethoven's magnificent violin

concerto. To write was then impossible; and he, perceiving how entranced I seemed, asked whether I knew what it was. On my replying in the negative, he promised, if it could be managed, that I should hear the whole of that movement before we separated. He then went off at a tangent, and I resumed my writing, speedily forgetting all about the promise he had given. On the last night, however, of the last concert at which he had played, several persons came to take their leave of him; and one gentleman, whom I never saw before or since, and whose name I never could learn, on a signal from the "master," sat down at a pianoforte, and drawing a piece of crumpled music from the inner pocket of a long black dress-coat somewhat worn and threadbare, began to play. Instantly I was on the alert, for I remembered the notes, and his promise rushed back upon me. Never shall I forget the smile on that sad, pale, wan, and haggard face, upon every lineament of which intense pain was written in the deepest lines, when I caught his eye, or the playing, into which a spirit and a sympathy were thrown that carried one wholly away. As soon as he had concluded, and before I could rush up to him to express my thanks, he glided away, more like a ghost than a human being, into his bed-chamber, without bidding myself or any other of the few acquaintances who were there good-bye. I never saw him afterwards. Although I had given express directions that I should be called early enough to take my leave of him and see him off, he had risen at daybreak, long before the hour he had named to me, entered a post-chaise that was drawn up, ready packed, at a short distance from his quiet lodging, where his faithful valet was waiting, and was many miles away before I so much as dreamed that he had gone. I have always believed, and shall be so convinced to the end of my days, that the sole reason for this strange departure originated in the desire to prevent his giving me pain. Whether it were so or not, the thought cannot but be as pleasurable as were those fourteen days in the most impressionable period of a young man's life, when I was the constant companion of the "prince of violinists."

That the love of money was a passion with Paganini, to which he gave the fullest vent, there can be no doubt. He loved gold, and the more he got of it, the more he coveted. But that it made him as brutal and contemptible as his numerous detractors asserted, I, for one, must positively deny; since to myself personally he would have been even generous, had he been permitted to be so. Others may have found him a different man from what he appeared to myself; but so far as I am concerned, I must repudiate *in toto*, except upon the score of pelf, the accusation that he bore the slightest semblance to the character with which he was universally charged.

It is necessary, however, to say something of the qualities which caused Paganini to be accepted as an *artiste* of the highest stamp, even by those who professed an abhorrence of his mercenary dealings. He was a Genoese by birth, having first seen the light Feb. 18th, 1784.* As early as the sixth year of his age he evinced so remarkable a talent for the violin, that a teacher was found for him in the person of Jean Servetto, who is said to have been a player of little merit. That, however, could have been of no moment, since he remained under him but a very short time. Giacomo Costa, director of the orchestra and first violin in the principal churches in Genoa, was next intrusted with Paganini's musical education, and under

* See Fétis' *Biographie Universelle des Musiciens*, tom. vi. p. 406.

him he progressed rapidly. At this period, Alexander Rolla was justly esteemed the first violinist in Italy; and Paganini, though yet but a boy, expressed the most lively desire to be placed under the guidance and direction of so competent a teacher. To gratify this wish, he went to Milan. But already this genius, who was destined to effect a revolution in his art, was unable to submit to the established forms of the schools which had preceded him. Disputes constantly arose between master and pupil concerning innovations, which the latter could only as yet conceive, without being able to execute them in a satisfactory manner, and which were condemned by the severe taste òf the former. Paganini soon abandoned himself in solitude to the researches with which his mind was occupied, and he then formed the plan of the "studies" that are known by his name, wherein he proposed difficulties which even he himself could not surmount without immense labour. Whilst, however, immersed in such inquiries, he suddenly interrupted them— leaving the possibility of increasing the resources of the violin to be at a future time considered—to study with the utmost seriousness and patience the works of Corelli, Vivaldi, Tartini, Pagnani, and Viotti. His chief object in doing this was to ascertain the successive progress of his instrument. He afterwards, with the same patience and assiduity, familiarised himself with the works of the best French violin authorities.

At the age of twenty-one (A.D. 1805) he entered the service of Napoleon's sister Eliza, Princess of Lucca and Piombino, in the capacity of concordist and *chef d'orchestre*. In consequence of a wager, he one night led an opera, and played a solo upon a violin having only two strings—the third and fourth. This was the origin of those *tours de force* which he was afterwards in the habit of making upon that instrument, and which, in his youth, as afterwards, he carried so far as to lay himself open to the charge of charlatanism. When the Princess Eliza became Grand Duchess of Tuscany, Paganini followed her to Florence, where he became the object of general admiration ; which was carried indeed to such an extent, as to have been termed little else than fanaticism. His talent kept developing itself daily in new forms, but he had not yet discovered the means of regulating its exercise. In 1810 he had, however, so perfected his mechanism, that he gave for the first time, at a court concert, his variations on the fourth string, the extent of which he had carried to three octaves by means of harmonic sounds. This novelty had a prodigious success, especially when he made it public at a concert given by himself at Parma, August 10th, 1811. From that date Paganini's remarkable career may be said to have commenced. Year after year he went from place to place in Italy, and thence to Germany, creating a *furore* in most instances, but astonishment, at least, in all. It was not, however, until March 9, 1831,* that he appeared in Paris, where he only remained until May, when he betook himself to London, and gave his first concert on Friday, June 3rd, in the King's Theatre, an orchestra having been erected upon the stage for the occasion. At that concert he played a concerto in E flat, of his own composition, consisting of three movements—an allegro maestoso, an adagio appassionato, and a rondo brilliante. To this he added a sonata militaire (upon Mozart's " Non piu andrai "), which he played upon the fourth string.† Although

---

* See Fétis' *Biographie Universelle des Musiciens*, tom. vi. pp. 412-13.

† The person of Paganini was thus described in the *Times*, June 6, 1831 :
" A tall thin man, with features rather emaciated, pale, a sharp aquiline nose,

great excitement had been caused in the musical world by Paganini's arrival, the results of his *début* were not altogether such as had been expected ; the cause of this chiefly being that the prices of admission were increased beyond the amount usually fixed for concerts at which the most celebrated vocalists and instrumentalists were engaged. The stalls and orchestra were fairly full, and also the pit, although by no means crowded. Few boxes were either let or occupied, so that the receipts were given out to be no more than £700 ! Paganini's reception, however, was most enthusiastic, his performances being greeted with the loudest acclamations, quite as much by the professionals as by any of the audience. Indeed, several of the former seemed to be entirely carried away by the astonishment this remarkable man's performance occasioned. At rehearsal he had been wary, and did not afford the slightest intimation of his powers, being content with merely giving directions, and skimming through his own *obbligato* passages. When, therefore, the progress of the first movement of his concerto proceeded, every face lighted up with enthusiasm, and at his conclusion not a single member

a keen eye, the expression of which is much heightened when he plays. His hair, dark, is worn long behind, and combed off his temples and forehead. His manner grotesque. His appearance is not improved by a tuft of hair which he leaves on his lower lip, neither does it derive any aid from dress ; his suit of black being ill made and loosely worn. The full length portrait of him in all the shops is an accurate likeness." This description is in every respect correct, except as to Paganini's " manner" being " grotesque." So far from that having been the case, his carriage was easy and, especially as he stood up to play, dignified. The tuft of hair on the chin was an innovation upon the custom of the times, which was regarded as something outrageous. The more recent and general habit for civilians to wear both beard and moustache would have driven our fathers wild with exasperation, the only hair permitted by them to be grown on the face being the " mutton chop " whisker. It was, however, then the height of fashion for every one, gentle or simple, to undergo the constant torture of shaving.

of the band refrained from applauding him to the echo. Mori avowed that, if he could not sell, he would at least burn, his fiddle ; Lindley stammered out,* that "it was the devil ;" whilst Dragonetti growled, in tones almost as deep as he himself drew from his own double-bass, "*She's* mighty *esprit !* " †

At his second concert, which was given at the same place on Friday, June 10th, Paganini introduced another concerto of his own composition, which has since been better known by the title of *La Clochette,* from the rondo, *à la Sicilienne,* being accompanied throughout by the repeated sound of a silver-toned small bell, the effect of which was increased by its having been most correctly played by Lablache.‡ He also played a fantasia, the

---

* Lindley used to tell many anecdotes of the consequences of this infirmity. The following I have heard him relate. Going through Wardour-street one day, his attention was attracted to a very handsome gray parrot exposed for sale. He stopped and said to the shopman, "C-a-a-n h-e-e s-p-p-e-a-k ? " who answered, "Yes, a *precious* sight better than you can, or I'd wring his *blessed* neck !"

† Dragonetti was the son of a Venetian gondolier, and having left his country in his youth, had not only forgotten his native language, but had never given himself the trouble to learn any other. His conversation, therefore, consisted of a most marvellous *lingua franca,* the component parts being made up after the above fashion. All *he's* were *she's* with him, and if any one offended him, his usual exclamation was, "*She* dirty blackguard !" He once applied this expression to an archbishop of York (Dr. Vernon Harcourt), who, as a director of the Ancient Concerts, he supposed, had put some slight on him. It was after this fashion : "You, signor, voyez dat Archevêque York ! Tell *lui, She* dirty blackguard ! " A well-known portrait of Paganini, surrounded by several of the best-known performers of the opera band, gives some idea of the nature of the scene of his well-remembered first appearance.

‡ When Paganini played this rondo at Dublin, at its conclusion, while an encore was being demanded, an excited Paddy in the gallery shouted out at the top of his voice, "Arrah now, Signor Paganini, have a drop of whiskey, darling, and ring the bell again ! " This concerto was played at the last Philharmonic Concert but one of the 1871 season by Sivori, the nephew

subject being the well-known "Carnival of Venice," and a sonata on the fourth string, consisting of an introduction, and the finale to *Mosè in Egitto*, with variations. In the latter, he tuned his string one note higher, in order to obtain an advantage in the harmonies. The receipts of this concert were better than at the first, no less than £1200 having been netted.

The third concert was given on Monday, June 13th, when Paganini introduced another new concerto, the receipts being £900. The fourth took place on Thursday, June 16th, in which he performed a cantabile of his own on two strings, which was followed by a rondo scherzoso of Kreutzer, a larghetto gajo, a sonata militaire on one string, and an andante cantabile, with variations on the rondo in *La Cenerentola*. The fifth and last concert was on Tuesday, June 22d, when stalls, orchestra, and pit were crowded to excess, and the applause was even more enthusiastic than it had been on any previous occasion.

That there must have been something much more out of the ordinary course of violin-playing in Paganini's method to have occasioned so much wonder and excitement, can but at once be obvious to any unprejudiced mind. I will endeavour, therefore, as briefly as possible, to explain "the reason why." The first surprise which the performance of Paganini elicited was his simultaneous production of bowed and pizzicato notes. Whilst the bow was employed in bringing out the air on the first string, he added an accompaniment, in harmony of two and sometimes of three notes, on the others, with such fingers, and also the thumb, as were not engaged in bringing out the legato passage. Then his harmonies were the next source of astonishment.

and pupil of Paganini, and elicited the liveliest "recollections" amongst not a few of the oldest *habitués*, of the first time of their having heard it.

Besides the ordinary method of producing them, he obtained a
new series in an instant by one single, sudden, and dexterous
turn of a peg, thus giving a different tension to his string. And
this was not all; for by making an artificial " nut " on any part
of a string, which he did with the utmost ease, he obtained, so
to speak, a new generator, which enabled him to command harmonies in every scale, and almost unlimited in number. These
he played in double notes, in thirds, and also in sixths and
octaves. He also executed double shakes in harmonics. His
performance on the fourth string, though by no means so astonishing as it was generally supposed to be, was nevertheless a
remarkable effort, as was also his *staccato* playing, which was
more distinct and crisp than was ever heard from any other
player, either before or since. He struck his bow once on the
string, and it seemed to run by a tremulous motion over as
many notes as he chose to include in the *staccato* passage. The
bow seemed indeed to act with the elasticity of a spring fixed at
one end, and made to vibrate. All this mechanism was peculiar
to himself; but in playing double notes of every kind, rapid
arpeggios, chords, or whatever passages other performers had
triumphed over, he was equally ready and perfect. His intonation, too, whether in double stops, high shifts, or harmonics, was
unfailingly true. His ear was indeed most acute, and a false
note so grated upon his sensibility that it produced a sensation
equal to the most intense pain. That he was by no means an
untaught musician or devoid of genius, his compositions go to
prove. They exhibit great boldness in search after effects, and
many original traits; but these are more to be observed in the
modern use he made of his own and other instruments, than in
his melodies; which, although generally agreeable, were by no

means remarkable for novelty, or in his harmonies, which bear little appearance of study, and indicate no great exertion of the inventive faculty.*

During the whole period of Paganini's stay in the British dominions, he was a martyr to constant pain, which the various annoyances he was subjected to greatly intensified. The attacks that were made upon him by the press and by means of various pamphlets, some of which were of the most scurrilous character, soured his temper, and only made him the more exacting in his terms, and more resolute to get as much money for his own share as it was possible to secure. He drove the hardest bargains, but he deceived no one as to his terms. "Take me or leave me," was, in fact, his motto, and those who availed themselves of his services had not, after all, much to complain of; for although in almost every instance he obtained the lion's share of the proceeds, they generally managed to realise a profit, which proved that the bargain which had been made was not so bad a one as they were but too apt to represent it.

On his departure from England, Paganini returned to Italy, and retired wholly from public life. By the advice of his physicians he went to Marseilles at the beginning of the year 1839, where he lived but a short time, his death having taken place on May 27th, from phthisis laryngitis, in his fifty-sixth year.†

In reference to Paganini's powers of execution, now, after no less than forty years' consideration, I can indeed truly say that they were little less than marvellous, and such as could only have been believed upon the evidence of the senses. They

---

* See *Harmonicon* for 1831, p. 165.

† See Fétis' *Biographie Universelle des Musiciens*, tom. vi. p. 413.

implied a strong natural propensity for music, with an industry perseverance, devotedness, and also a skill in inventing means, certainly without any parallel in the history of his instrument.

I have now to record the decease of one of the most promising young musicians that England has ever produced—George Aspull, one of the dearest friends of my youth, whose memory I shall never cease to regard and revere. This extraordinary genius—for so I must designate him—was born at Nottingham in the year 1813, and at a very early age gave proof that music could but be his vocation. Even at the early age of eight years his execution had become so brilliant and highly-finished, that he was able to play many of Hummel's and Kalkbrenner's most difficult compositions without the slightest diminution of time, and just as those authors had intended. He was brought before the public very early as a prodigy, and was worked so incessantly both in private practice and public performances, that his health entirely gave way, not, however, before he had travelled half over England, and obtained several gold medals as an acknowledgment both of his immediate manifestations of talent and promise of future celebrity. Young as he was, he not only excelled in the mechanical use of his instrument, but he gave every indication of unusual talent as a composer. Many, however, of his best compositions were never written ; for although he had played them in public as well as in private society, he could not find time to write, and so they are for ever lost. One of these, like an epic poem, would have served to hand down his name to immortality, had it ever been put upon paper. The orchestral accompaniments alone were written for its production at his last concert at Cambridge, as a compliment for the success and kind attention he had received both from members of the university and inhabitants of the town. He played this composition at Cambridge without a single page of it before him, as he also did but a short time before his death in his native town, Nottingham. He died at Leamington, August 20, 1832, in his nineteenth year, leaving behind him the assurance that, had he been spared, he would have proved the greatest musical genius this country ever produced, there being no similar instance on record here of any one so young having evinced the unquestionable superiority of talent which he possessed, and yet manifested with the greatest modesty of manner and simplicity of demeanour.

The promises at the King's Theatre for the year 1831 were by no means fulfilled ; for the arrangements, except with regard to the band and chorus, turned out for the most part badly, the *habitués* not being satisfied with the principals engaged, although they consisted of many remarkable names, including those of Mesdames Pasta, Meric-Lalande, and Rubini, as sopranos, of Signors David and Rubini as tenors, and de Begnis, after an absence of three years; with whom were conjoined Curioni, Pantini, and Lablache. Of these *artistes* the most prominent were certainly David and Rubini. Madame Rubini was a failure, and made no impression whatever. Not so her husband, who, from the moment of his appearance, created a sensation that was never afterwards allayed, although several critical cynics persisted in representing that " he flourished extravagantly, and was much too liberal in the use of that falsetto," which was the chief beauty of his remarkable organ. I was not within reach of London during the entire opera season of this year; therefore, as I did not hear Rubini till sometime afterwards, I am constrained to defer the consideration of my own opinion of his qualities to a future opportunity of expressing the reasons for my conviction that he was the most superb tenor that ever came from Italy to London.

There are two events, however, in this year that so fully live in my recollection, that I cannot be induced to pass over them without some slight reference. I refer to the production of Spohr's oratorio, the *Last Judgment*—or rather, as it should have been translated, *The Last Things* (*Die letzten Dinge*)—at the Norwich Festival, Friday, September 24th (1830), and his opera *Zemire und Azor*, which was brought out at Covent Garden, Tuesday, April 5th (1831). As I had the advantage of "assisting" at these "creations"—as it is the fashion nowadays to term one's presence at a first performance of any new and important musical work—a few words respecting them may not be out of place.

Spohr's inducement to write an oratorio originated with Mr. Edward Taylor, a gentleman who somewhat late in life, owing to the failure of certain business speculations, betook himself to the musical profession for a livelihood, and thus turned his talent, no less than the practice of the art he had hitherto followed, as an amateur, with unceasing devotion, to his own and his family's advantage. Mr. Edward Taylor was a native of Norwich, and had been the pupil of Dr. Beckwith, the cathedral organist of that city and a musician of the highest talent. He was also a sound classical scholar, and was so well acquainted with German, French, and Italian, that he could both read and write them with the utmost ease.* Having made Spohr's acquaintance during a visit to Germany in 1828, Mr.

---

* Mr. E. Taylor afterwards became professor of music in Gresham College, and made that appointment highly useful for the original purpose of its

Taylor placed before him the advisability of his trying his powers upon oratorio-writing, which had never been attempted with the smallest success by any composers, either foreign or English, since the days of Handel. The *Last Judgment* was the result of this recommendation, and, most appropriately, it was secured for the third musical Festival in Mr. E. Taylor's native city, in the inauguration and carrying out of which he had been specially engaged. On the occasion of this oratorio being first performed, it was not given in its entirety, it having been doubted whether a provincial audience could bear the strain of novelty in that direction, especially as it was not presented with the impress of metropolitan recommendation. Sufficient "numbers" were, however, given to indicate that it was a work of undoubted genius, and even worthy of being placed side by side with any of Handel's compositions—the *Messiah*, *Samson*, and *Israel in Egypt* alone excepted. That this is by no means an unwarranted opinion is fully confirmed by the following remarks, which were published almost immediately after the conclusion of the Norwich Festival by the best musical authority of the day.* "The *Last Judgment*, an oratorio by Spohr, performed for the first time in this country, we consider as one of the greatest musical productions of the age. It would be presumption in us, having heard it but once, were we to attempt a minute detail of all the beauties of this elaborate work, in which is embodied every passion, sentiment, and feeling that the power of music is capable of expressing ; and,

foundation. He died March 12th, 1863. For a thoroughly just and appreciative account of this gentleman's career, see Fetis' *Biographie Universelle des Musiciens*, tom. viii. pp. 494-5.

* The *Harmonicon* for 1830, p. 466.

however elevated the name of Spohr may justly be as a composer of the highest class of instrumental music, this sublime oratorio will add immensely to his reputation, and henceforward his name will be inserted in the list of those authors whose studies, efforts, and genius have been most conspicuously successful in this, the noblest branch of art."*

Although the greater popularity of Mendelssohn's oratorios— the *St. Paul* and the *Elijah,* of which I shall hereafter have to speak—in a great degree superseded the *Last Judgment* and other oratorios Spohr was afterwards induced to write, that work is still occasionally heard, and always with the liveliest satisfaction, repeated hearings having only served to confirm first impressions, and to render the earliest " Recollections " as vivid as they are gratifying.

The success of Spohr's oratorio at the Norwich music meeting having been endorsed at the Liverpool Festival, October 6, 1830, and fully confirmed at the third Philharmonic Concert, March 21, 1831, caused great excitement amongst the *dilettante* and professors of the metropolis, when it was announced that his opera, *Zemire und Azor,* was about to be presented at Covent Garden Theatre. The expectations that had been formed about it were thoroughly realised when it was produced under the title of *Azor and Zemira, or the Magic Rose,* on Tuesday, April 5, 1831. Indeed, it was said that the event " might be almost considered as a musical era in the history of that theatre, and reflected great credit on all who had been con-

---

* Not very long after the above unqualified praise was accorded to the *Last Judgment,* the same " musical authority " published an extended criticism on the entire work, consisting of an elaborate and learned analysis of every " number." See *Harmonicon* for 1831, pp. 142-4.

ccrned in bringing it before an English audience."* The cast
of characters was by no means so strong or effective as it might
have been easily made, but " the performers evidently took a
deep interest in their work, and their success was in exact proportion to their means." The *mise en scène* was also provided
with the utmost care, and, as regarded expense, with unprecedented liberality.

The prevailing characteristics of the *Zemire und Azor* were
found to be somewhat too scientific for the public taste ; Spohr's
harmonic combinations having been thought to be too elaborate,
although the existence of melody in the richest profusion could
not be denied. Indeed, whilst the harmonies were accused of
being overstrained, the melodies were said to be both cloying
and wearisome to the ear. The departure from the old method
of writing opera, so called, for the English stage, to which Mr.
Planché felt it needful to cause Weber to adhere,† was in many
quarters deprecated, the *habitués* of the national theatres of
that time being much more disposed to denounce .

" Everything new and strange,"

than to accept it with either welcome or approval. Those, however, who were best qualified to pronounce upon the quality of
the work, were decidedly of opinion, that " Spohr had shown
his strength more in vocal than in instrumental music ;" for
although " he was laborious in both, in the latter he was too
often obscure ; a fault from which the very nature of what was
to be performed by the human voice—an instrument of very
limited power—guarded him to a certain extent. The music,"

---

* See *Harmonicon* for 1831, p. 129.
† See p. 135.

however, " of *Zemire und Azor* was found to be practicable to any singers who had the advantage of being tolerable musicians —such as were to be met with in Germany, Italy, and England —although some of its "numbers" imposed a task of no little difficulty upon the performers. Whenever *artistes*—as is the case with so many of the Italians*—sing wholly by ear, after their respective parts have been drummed into them by incessant practice at the pianoforte, German opera cannot but be unintelligible, and, therefore, is but too often regarded with the utmost aversion.†

The cast of characters of Spohr's opera embraced the talent of Miss Inverarity, the two Miss Cawses, Mr. Wilson, and Mr. Morley, the last of whom was a mere nonentity, being scarcely able to act, much less to sing. Happily this was not the case with the other four, although not one of them could be classed as first-rate English vocalists. Miss Inverarity, who appeared as Zemira, was comparatively a novice, having only *débuted* a few nights previously, in an English version of Rossini's *La Cenerentola*, in the place of Miss Paton. She had, however, excited considerable sensation in the musical world, and was accepted

* See *Harmonicon* for 1831, pp. 129-30.

† This was entirely the case with Pasta, Grisi, Persiani, Mario, and many other *artistes* of the Italian school of the highest reputation. When, for example, the effort was made to produce Meyerbeer's *Les Huguenots* during the first season of the Royal Italian Opera at Covent-garden, the Italian members of the company resisted its presentation with the utmost pertinacity, calling it *la musique Chinoise*, because of their deficiency in being able to read their respective *rôles*. Had not "a Royal command" insisted upon the performance of that opera, it is very doubtful whether it would not have been postponed for a very indefinite period, so intensely hostile was the cabal against its production. The command, however, settled the matter, and *Les Huguenots* was not only *the* success of the season, but pulled the direction out of innumerable difficulties which would otherwise have been insurmountable.

as a young lady of great promise, which in a larger measure she afterwards fulfilled. She was Scotch by birth and education, and not until three years before her *début* had ever attempted to cultivate the early talent she had exhibited. Her first master was a Mr. Thorne, from whose tuition she speedily passed to that of a well-known Edinburgh violinist, Mr. Alexander Murray, who brought her to London, and obtained farther instruction for her from Sir George Smart, by whom she was introduced to a London audience. At this time Miss Inverarity was but eighteen years of age ; yet she was tall, well-formed, although her figure was somewhat slim, with an open, intelligent, and handsome countenance, to which was added a thoroughly easy and natural deportment. Her voice was a pure English soprano of considerable compass, the extent being from A below the treble lines to C above them — a range of more than two octaves—of tolerably equal quality, whilst it was freely delivered from the chest, full-toned, and of rich quality. Her style, although anything but completely formed, was good ; but it was not till many months after her first appearance, that she could be said to sing her divisions as clearly and distinctly as was needful to render her perfect in her art. The favourable impression she at once made on her coming out was much increased by her singing in Spohr's opera, and went on progressing for several years, when she suddenly retired into private life, and lived but a short time afterwards. The two Miss Cawses were pupils of Sir George Smart, and were possessed of considerable natural endowments, aptitude, and industry, which obtained for them a rank in their profession, to which the term " useful " rather than " celebrated " was most applicable. Each, after doing good musical service in both the theatre and concert-room, married, and wholly left the profession. Of the two, Harriet, the younger, was the more successful, chiefly by her persistence in preserving a natural manner, by pure enunciation and expression, and by the plainest use of an excellent voice.* Wilson was a tenor singer, who raised expectations upon his first appearance that were by no means fulfilled. He laboured under the disadvantage of never having been regularly trained; and although the beauty of his voice—which was of the purest quality—obtained for him many admirers, it was only as a ballad singer that he made his way or gave entire satisfaction. The best operatic part in which he ever appeared with anything approaching success was that of the Prince in Spohr's *Zemire und Azor*, for which he was drilled with the utmost perseverance by Sir George Smart, who at one time thought he might make something of him, so as to render him competent for that higher range of characters, which Braham was now becoming unequal to undertake. Wilson, however, removed all prospect of this expectation being fulfilled by leaving the stage, from religious feelings and conscientious scruples, about the year 1834 or 1835, and contenting himself afterwards with giving " entertainments " in the provinces, consisting of " illustrations of the music of Scotland," of which country he was a native. In this line he greatly excelled; and, truth to tell, it is doubtful whether the celebrated Jacobin airs of old Gael, or the few English ballads he occasionally introduced, have ever been so well sung as by himself—better they could not have been. His career was, however, suddenly cut short, if I remember rightly, by cholera, during its second visitation in this country in 1848.

* See *The Quarterly Musical Magazine and Review*, vol. viii. pp. 139-40.

It was considered unfortunate, on the production of Spohr's *Zemire und Azor*, that Wood was not in a position to assume the principal male title *rôle;* but circumstances about that period had arisen—to which a more explicit reference is unnecessary—which prevented him for a time from occupying the position he was able to claim because of his talent both as a singer and an actor. Wood had made his first appearance in London in the year 1837, in the character of Hawthorn, in the old and favourite—so called—English opera, *Love in a Village,* with a success which he greatly improved upon in the part of Aurelio in another English opera entitled *Native Land*—a work now wholly forgotten. In the latter part he was substituted at a very short notice for Sapio, whom he speedily superseded. Wood's voice was a purely legitimate tenor, extensive in its compass, and full in volume. Its great charm consisted in its sympathetic character, the tone being so touching, that few persons could hear it without being strongly moved by the mere physical pleasure it produced; whilst its adaptation to passages of pathos and tenderness rendered it more peculiarly worth that cultivation to which unfortunately he was never inclined to pay proper attention. As a singer, he was very far from being ever finished, although the soul of music was thought and said to be in him. That he did not persevere with his musical studies was, therefore, a cause of general disappointment amongst musicians, since, throughout his whole career—and it was a pretty long one—he invariably sang like one who had been taught a lesson and did not dare to venture beyond his very limited instructions, although he seemed now and then to feel all he did, and showed that he could have done more, if he had not been restrained by the dread of failure. In the union of his chest and head voices Wood was rarely if ever at fault ; but this was no compensation for a roughness of style which he never overcame. Not even when he had the advantage of being married to Miss Paton did he ever evince a disposition to raise himself to anything like a level with that lady's purer style, and more ample breadth of classical vocalisation. It was always a source of mortification to his best qualified hearers to discover that one who could have done so much effected so little. The consequence of this defect has been, that whilst the names of other male singers of his time are constantly spoken of as deserving creditable remembrance, his own is scarcely ever mentioned, and then only in combination with circumstances that are far better forgotten than revived. Having with his wife realised a handsome competency by singing in Milan Venice, and Naples, and in London, Dublin, and every city and town of provincial celebrity where music is cultivated, and afterwards in New York, Boston, Philadelphia, and other towns of the United States, Wood retired to an estate in Yorkshire, where, I have been informed, he still resides, and generously fulfils the duties of an English country gentleman. Mrs. Wood —who will always be better known as Miss Paton—died in 1864.*

* See Fétis' *Biographie des Musiciens*, tom. viii. p. 493, who is as inaccurate respecting Mrs. Wood as he has been concerning a great many other musical celebrities ; for he says, without the slightest warrant for such an unfounded and slanderous assertion, "Elle avait contracté, à cette époque (1829), une liaison intime avec Lord Lennox, et passait même pour sa femme ; depuis lors elle a épousé M. Wood, acteur du théâtre de Covent-garden ! " Miss Paton was Lord William Lennox's wife, and was so separated from him, that she was afterwards able to obtain the same relation with Mr. Wood.

CHAPTER VIII.

1831-1832.

A MUSICAL event of great importance took place at the Grand Opéra, Paris, in the month of December, 1831—the production of Meyerbeer's *Robert le Diable*, which had been so many months previously under rehearsal, that many persons were sceptical as to its ever being brought out at all, whilst many more, who did not quite go to such lengths, prognosticated little else than failure. Rumours were not only rife in Paris, but they extended to every capital in Europe, to the effect that, numerous and exacting as were the rehearsals upon which that " most fussy of composers " invariably insisted, they were by no means so wearisome as the music itself would be found ; the crudity of its rhythm, no less than the difficulty of singing and playing it, being more than enough to cause, if not its utter rejection, at least an equivocal reception. Only a few—and a very few—of the *artistes*, engaged for the interpretation of this opera had any faith in its composition, and, irritated by Meyerbeer's personal superintendence of the rehearsals and constant changes in the score, loudly condemned all that was set down for them ; so that if anything very like a cabal could have ruined a composer, that laborious and exacting master seemed to be in a fair way of having to encounter as disastrous a catastrophe as could well be contemplated. Meyerbeer had in a great measure changed the style he had relied upon in his *Il Crociato,* and given greater expansion to those extraordinary flights of fancy which the older and severer critics of the time were by no means slow to denounce. His system of instrumentation was also more quaint and peculiar than had ever been previously heard, whilst he resorted to what were called meretricious tricks for the purpose of creating effects that were said to be totally unworthy of a genuine 'master.' It was not denied that there was melody in abundance to be traced through every line of the score; but it was said—and with no small degree of truth—that it was by no means continuous, the ear having caught a phrase with which the mind was charmed only to be annoyed by its almost immediately going off at a tangent into crude and vexatious passages, as disappointing to the expectation as they were almost beyond the power of accurate execution. Meyerbeer heard all this and more to his disadvantage ; but he had faith in himself, and, although he pruned and added, lengthened and polished, his phrases, till at the last little or nothing of their originality remained, he showed that he had a far more extended idea of adaptation to scenic effects than any composer had ever possessed before him. The story, or plot, of his work was much against him ; but Scribe, who was his librettist, worked earnestly with him, and, although anything like excitement could by no possibility be extracted from the subject, Meyerbeer so managed to clothe the skeleton as to give it both form and substance.

At last the hour of decision came, and the result was a success that not only had not by any means been expected even by the composer's warmest admirers, but was unprecedented in the annals of operatic production. One fault alone was expressed on all hands—that the work was so lengthy, from undue elaboration, that there was enough in it for two evenings', rather than for one continuous, performance. Meyerbeer had, therefore, to undergo the unpleasant task of cutting his work down, to bring it within something like a reasonable time of presentation ; but, after all his efforts, it still continued to take up so many hours, that, I understand, it has never yet been presented in any foreign opera house without considerable additional abbreviations. At Vienna, where I heard it in 1851, the entire second act was mercilessly excised, whilst little or nothing of the last act was retained. At Berlin, where I had an opportunity, in 1862, of being present at a very respectable representation—much better than that at Vienna to which I refer—every act, except the great ballet scene, was so mercilessly cut, that the possibility of perceiving a ghost of the plot was out of the question. In London, both at the Royal Italian Opera, under Sir M. Costa's direction—where the excisions were submitted to, and also had the sanction of, Meyerbeer himself, after much discussion and deliberation—and at Her Majesty's Theatre, at least a third of the entire score has been put aside, and even then it has been, and still doubtless will be, pronounced by the general public to be both tedious and wearisome. Nothing but the exquisite character of most of the concerted music, the beauty of which is everywhere irreproachable, carries it through.

But I am entering upon the expression of an opinion upon the character of Meyerbeer's *Robert le Diable*, when I ought to be telling the story of my first hearing it in Paris. At the time of my arrival there, the whole town was in a state of *furore*

about *Le Robert,* as everybody was calling it. Stormy as the
period was with reference to politics—when was it, or ever will
it be, otherwise in the French capital?—little else was talked
about. Tastes differed, as they always will, as to certain parts
of the work, some expressing their preference for the first and
others for the last act, and but few saying much in favour of
the third, in which, to my mind, the gems of the work are set.
But the whole town was on the *qui-vive* about the ballet, or
" uuns' transformation scene "—one of the most daring, and, as
I am free to say, one of the most disagreeable and unhallowed
scenes that can ever be represented on the stage—not only on
account of its novelty, but for the sake of the music, which is
amongst the most charming that Meyerbeer ever wrote, and of the
dancing of Taglioni, Montessu, and Noblet. I went to the Rue
Lepelletier with the full expectation of being disappointed ; I
came away perfectly enchanted. In spite of a sitting which
lasted from 7 P.M. till past midnight, I was not in the least
wearied. The more I heard, the more I longed to hear ; and
every night that the *Robert* was given during the fortnight
I remained—if I remember rightly, five times—the doors
opened to no more willing or enthusiastic listener than myself.
What had at the first seemed strange to the sense speedily
became

" As tunable as lark to shepherd's ear ; "

and that which originally was a source of mystification came out
as clearly as the light of day. And so it is yet, whenever I
have the advantage of hearing this work. Whilst the ear
dwells upon the primarily-discovered beauties, which have lost
none of their pristine charm, but are rather enhanced, new ones
start into being, the effects of which, whilst they increase one's

delight, more and more serve to indicate the talent of the man who was so thoroughly competent to create them

At the Grand Opéra, *Robert le Diable* was mounted regardless of expense ; but the profusion of scenic effect with which every situation was clothed would have had little or no influence, if the music, charming as it is, had not been given by some of the most incomparable *artistes* the French *Académie* has ever reared. The four leading parts of Alice, Isabella, Robert, and Bertram were " created " by Mdmes. Dorus-Gras and Cinti-Damoreau, MM. Nourrit and Levasseur. Of the Alice, I have a most indistinct recollection, as the lady made no impression whatever upon me. The first *prima donna* who did this was Mdlle. Falcon, who *débuted* in the character July 20, 1832,* and whom I heard in the autumn of that year. I shall therefore combine that lady with the other four *artistes* I have named, as being more worthy of consideration. Each and all of those *artistes*, singular to say, are now very nearly forgotten ; but they were so justly celebrated in their day, that it is impossible to deal with so remarkable an event as the production and " run " of Meyerbeer's first really great work without offering some particulars respecting them. Of the four, Mdlle. Falcon is by far the least known to those Englishmen whose recollections trace back as far as my own. The chief cause for this fact arose from the brevity of her career, and from its having been exclusively confined to Paris. When but fifteen years of age—she was born on January the 28th, 1812—Mdlle. Falcon became a pupil of the Conservatoire, and at once attracted the attention of the professors of that most deservedly celebrated Institution, who universally predicted for her a most triumphant career, and

* See Fétis' *Biographie Universelle des Musiciens*, tom. iii. p. 179.

no one more so than M. Nourrit, from whom she received lessons, and with whom she was afterwards associated in several of the most remarkable events of the Grand Opéra of her day.* At the end of 1837, however, her voice wholly gave way. In the hope of regaining it she went to Italy, where she remained till the beginning of 1840. Having been somewhat benefited by change of climate, she reappeared in Paris in the month of March 1840; but it was so evident that her organ was injured as to be beyond recovery, that she at once retired from the profession she had adorned by such talent as, it is truly said, has never since been manifested by any one who has succeeded her from that to the present time.† Mdme. Cinti-Damoreau had a much longer, although by no means a more successful, career than Mdlle. Falcon. She was a Parisian by birth (Feb. 6, 1801), and was also a pupil of the Conservatoire. At the age of eighteen she became a member of the company which Mdme. Catalani engaged for "Les Italiens," where she appeared as Cherubino in Mozart's *Nozze di Figaro.* The favourable impression she at once made was so far increased, that she not only "made her public" in Paris, but was engaged (A.D. 1822) by Mr. Ebers for the King's Theatre. Here, however, she was but coldly received, although that gentleman declares that "she possessed all the qualities to form a good singer, in a situation where a less powerful voice would have sufficed than the Opera House required. Her knowledge," he says, "was good, her taste simple and chaste, and her acting, if not strikingly excellent, was highly pleasing and unaffected." To this Mr. Ebers

* Meyerbeer's *Robert le Diable,* 1832; Auber's *Gustave III.,* 1832; Halévy's *La Juive,* 1834; Meyerbeer's *Huguenots,* 1836; &c.

† See Fétis' *Biographie Universelle des Musiciens,* tom. iii. p. 179.

adds, that " from this it may be gathered that she was unsuited to win great favour in Paris "—an opinion by no means confirmed—" where she had previously been engaged at the Italian Theatre." The cause of her engagement was assigned to "a noble patron of the King's Theatre having seen her, and recommended her to London, where her success was, perhaps, hardly equal to her merit, though a portion of public approbation was uniformly bestowed on her performances."* When this lady appeared in London at the same theatre, under Mr. Monck Mason's management, she again failed to obtain that good opinion to which her merit justly entitled her. She had, however, to labour under a disadvantage at her first coming by comparison with Camporese, Caradori-Allan, and Ronzi de Begnis ; and was no better situated when ten years afterwards she was associated with Mdmes. de Méric,† Grandolfi, and Tosi, and had also the competition of Mdme. Schröder-Devrient to contend against. The opinion at the later period expressed by competent judges concerning her talent was, that she possessed "a voice not strong, but very sweet, and a style derived from the best vocal school, her execution being exceedingly neat, and not being tempted into redundancy of ornament, although possessing great flexibility of voice. Nature," the same critic goes on to say, "had supplied her with many personal charms, some of which ten years had of course abated. Her manner was also perfectly easy and genteel, whilst her knowledge of the stage appeared to be the result of much observation and experience."‡ In the

* Ebers' *Seven Years of the King's Theatre*, p. 142.

† See p. 139.

‡ *Harmonicon* for 1832, p. 144, quoting from the *Morning Chronicle*, May 29, 1822.

year 1825, the management of " Les Italiens " and the Grand Opéra at Paris being the same, Mdme. Cinti-Damoreau's services were secured at the latter for the interpretation of the works of Rossini, who wrote the chief *rôles* of his *Siege of Corinth* and *Moïse* for her. Owing to difficulties arising between herself and the management of the opera, she went in 1827 to Brussels, where she married M. Damoreau, an actor of no great repute, who failed to win public favour or approval, and from whom she speedily separated. On her return to Paris, she renewed her engagement at the Grand Opéra, and appeared with great *éclat* in Auber's *La Muette de Portici*— better known in England under the title *Masaniello*—in Rossini's *Comte Ory*, and, as I have said, in Meyerbeer's *Robert le Diable.** Until 1835, Mdme. Cinti-Damoreau maintained her position as *prima donna assoluta* at this theatre, and then seceded to the Opéra Comique, where Auber wrote for her his charming operas, *Le Domino Noir*, *L'Ambassadrice*, *Zanetta,* and several others, in each of which no successor has ever surpassed her. In 1843, having retired from the more arduous duties of her profession, this accomplished *artiste* again sang in London, and afterwards at the Hague, at Ghent, at St. Petersburg, and at Brussels, and then went to America, whence returning, she received the highest compliment that could be paid to her talent, in being elected professor of singing in the Paris Conservatoire, a position which she held till January, 1856, since which date nothing has been heard of her, so that whether she is living or not I am unable to chronicle.†

Amongst the numerous *artistes* who have been celebrated for

---

* See p. 221.

† See Fétis' *Biographie Universelle des Musiciens*, tom. ii. pp. 419—20.

their musical talent and acquirements, few have ever more thoroughly merited the fame they enjoyed than that tenor, M. Adolphe Nourrit, whom Meyerbeer had the good fortune to rely upon for the creation not only of the title *rôle* of *Robert le Diable,* but of Raoul in *Les Huguenots*—of which I shall have to write in a future page. Nourrit, the legitimate successor of Garcia,* and also his pupil, was not intended for the stage. His father, who had also been an *artiste* of considerable reputation, placed him in a commission house of business in Paris, against the drudgery of which he resisted with all the natural vehemence of his character. The bent of his inclination was towards the operatic stage; and being born an *artiste,* an *artiste* he resolved to be. Although Garcia, on his application to him for instruction, at first strongly advised him to think twice before he threw up his calling, and brought upon himself the anger of his father, he was at last persuaded that Nourrit's talent was of so high an order that it would be cruel to him to hold him back, and injurious to the art, of which he himself had been so competent an exponent. It took some time to reconcile M. Nourrit *père* to consent to the solicitations of his son; but on hearing him sing, the spirit of the old man revived, not improbably on account of the talent he had himself once upon a time so successfully cultivated and displayed. Adolphe Nourrit's *début* took place at the Paris opera house, September 1, 1821, before he had completed his twentieth year, the part selected for the occasion being that of Pylades in Glück's glorious *Iphigénie en Tauride.* Having been successful beyond his utmost expectations, the public not only receiving him with favour on account of their remembrance of his father, but because of his

---

* See pp. 102, 103.

own positive merits, and after appearing in several other operas, with increasing popularity, he permanently established his position both by his acting and singing as Néocles, in Rossini's *Siege of Corinth*, in which both his father (for the last time) and he himself appeared together on the 9th of October 1826. Feeling that a great future was now before him, Nourrit, unlike a host of singers of the present time, did not jump to the conclusion that his fortune was made, and that he had nothing more to do than to take life easily, accept all the engagements offered him, and earn as much money as he could, and as speedily as possible. He was convinced that to become a really competent actor and singer he must study, and that severely, because he had many difficulties to contend against, not the least of which was that, although nature had given him a magnificent voice, she had not equally endowed him with flexibility in its management. That he was entirely successful, may not be admitted ; but at least, by the determination of his will, and by incessant perseverance, he achieved all that study could accomplish ; and if he did not thoroughly overcome every natural defect, his excellence in every other respect was so positive that no fault could justly be found with him. In the whole history of the Parisian, or of any other operatic, stage, did any man ever, before or since, for ten years of his life work so severely as did Nourrit ? When it is said that in those ten years he created the principal tenor parts in no less than *eight* operas, and such operas as demand powers of the utmost endurance—the *Moïse, Comte Ory, La Muette de Portici (Masaniello), Le Philtre, Guillaume Tell, Robert le Diable, La Juive,* and *Les Huguenots* —some idea may be formed of what Nourrit really was in his day ; for although many other most competent successors have been found for the interpretation of characters which he brought out—not the least of whom were Duprez and Roger upon the French stage, and Mario and Tamberlik in the Italian versions— there can be no hesitation in saying that he was not surpassed by any one of them, and equalled by only one or two. It was not merely, however, that this justly celebrated *artiste* was great in his own peculiar line. Unlike the generality of members of his profession, he was still farther endowed with an appreciation and a power of evolving dramatic effects, which have done nearly as much as the music of the scenes itself, to which they appertain, to produce situations of the most intensely interesting character. It was chiefly to his suggestions that Meyerbeer certainly owed the thrilling characteristics of the great duet of the fourth act of *Les Huguenots* between Valentine and Raoul, which never can be played, if even by comparatively mediocre performers, without producing the most lively interest. He saw points, as it were by intuition, which had escaped the discernment both of Meyerbeer and Scribe, and they were both wise enough not only to listen to his advice, but to adopt it.

After a most brilliant career, the close of Nourrit's life was most unhappily clouded. So soon as his powers began to fail, and it was indispensable that he should be relieved of the weight of those labours which nothing but Herculean health and strength could have so long withstood, he began to show symptoms of mental aberration. Nothing could induce him to believe that he was no longer what he had been; and this idea so grew upon him, that he treated every arrangement for the relaxation of his labours as an intentional insult to himself. Breaking off at last from his Parisian engagements, he travelled and sang in Belgium and Italy, and afterwards in several of the French provinces, in all of which places he was received with respect; for the touch of the great *artiste* was manifest in everything he undertook, although he could no longer hold an audience entranced as he had been always able to do throughout his mid-career. His malady now took a morbidly religious turn, to relieve which he was advised to travel, and he therefore went to Italy. Still he would not give up his hold of his profession; and having induced Donizetti rapidly to write an opera, founded upon the *Polyeucte* of Corneille—which has since been better known under the title of *Les Martyrs*—he sang not only in that work, but in one or two others at the San Carlo at Naples. The idea then took possession of his disordered brain, that the public treated his efforts to please them with derision, and this has been thought by many persons who knew him well to have driven him to commit suicide; for on the early morning of the 8th of March, 1839, he fell from the roof of the Hotel de Barbaja at Naples, and was taken up dead. The general impression will always be, that this unhappy man both meditated and committed suicide. Such, however, was not the opinion of one of the most intimate of his friends, Madame Garcia, the mother of Marie Malibran and Pauline Viardot, who told me, as she had also stated previously to M. Fétis—she having been at Naples at the time—that she firmly believed, and always should do so, that Nourrit's death was accidental. He had gone, she said, to a corridor at the top of the house without a light, and having opened, by mistake, one of the windows which was level with the floor, instead of the door of the chamber he was seeking, had stepped out into the air, and so was hurled down headlong to his destruction. It is only charitable to hope that Madame Garcia's opinion of the cause of so terrible a catastrophe was the true one; and she was in every respect by far too excellent and conscientious a person to have made an assertion which she did not implicitly believe to be correct.*

As connected with the primary representation of *Robert le Diable*, one other excellent interpreter remains to be described —Nicholas Prosper Levasseur, the most important *basso profondo* the Parisian operatic stage has ever produced. He was the son of a common labourer resident in Picardy, and was born March 9th, 1791. How or why he came to Paris there is no authentic information extant, that can be heard of or met with. He is first named as having been admitted as a pupil of the Conservatoire on the 29th December, 1807, and as placed under the tuition of M. Garat, one of the then professors of singing, February 5th, 1811, soon after which he began to attract attention for the quality of his voice and his method of using it. Yet it was not till October 14th, 1813, that he appeared at the opera. Here he achieved a decided success, and from that day till his retirement in 1845, maintained the first position against all comers in that department, which, if not open to the possibility of the most brilliant achievements, is at least one of the most important and indispensable that any singer can occupy. During so many years it would be tedious, if not impossible, to tell in how many different operas he appeared, no less than what parts he created. Let it suffice, therefore, to say, that he was conjoined in nearly all the celebrated works with which Mdme. Cinti-Damoreau, M. Nourrit, and many others were connected, and that he was equally solid, useful, and good in all. Most certainly no better—if so good an—interpretation of the

---

* See Fétis' *Biographie Universelle des Musiciens*, tom. vi. pp. 334—338.

Bertram in the *Robert,* and of the Marcel in *Les Huguenots*, has ever been witnessed. Each was a grand personation never to be forgotten, and not less so was that of Baldassare, in Donizetti's *La Favorita,* in which I heard him with Mdme. Stolz and Duprez in the year 1843, a description of which will have to be given when that—as yet somewhat distant—period is reached. For some time after his retirement from the stage, Levasseur * occupied the responsible post of professor at the Conservatoire, whence, however, no single individual worthy of succeeding him has since come. As of tenors, so of deep bass voices, the dearth still continues to be as remarkable as it is inexplicable. †

Coming back to London after so interesting an event as that · of " assisting " at several performances at the Grand Opéra of Paris of Meyerbeer's *Robert le Diable,* whilst that great work—no less than its composer, in a musical sense—was in its *première jeunesse,* the " Recollections " I have to record of the following year cannot but be comparatively " stale, flat, and unprofitable."

On the 1st of December, 1831, Miss Shirreff appeared at Covent Garden, as a competitor for public approbation with Miss Inverarity.* About this promising young lady " much injudicious, if not coarse, puffing, in all the newspapers that were good-natured or weak enough to admit articles of such a character, was published. This so disgusted the thinking portion of the public, that a feeling—most undeservedly, as it turned out to be—almost amounting to prejudice, was excited against her," and, had she not really been possessed of exceedingly good

---

* Levasseur died only recently.

† See Fétis' *Biographie Universelle des Musiciens,* tom. v. p. 290.

‡ See p. 213.

qualifications for the position at which she aimed, and for which she had been carefully trained, would inevitably have crushed her out of hand at once. The character of Mandane, in Arne's once highly popular English opera, *Artaxerxes*, was that selected for Miss Shirreff's first appearance—a part at that time thought to be by no means an unfair test of the ability of a singer. Being a mixture of the bravura, the tender, the energetic, and the gentle styles, no one performer, without having arrived at some degree of proficiency in each, could either expect or hope to be patiently listened to as the heroine of this production. Miss Shirreff compassed all these requirements, if not with the utmost ease, at least with a facility which indicated an amount of promise that was altogether acceptable to the most fastidious critics of the period. Her voice, a pure soprano, was full in tone, and powerful in the upper register, but somewhat weak and clouded in the lower. There was an occasional hardness likewise about the *mezzo-voce*, which seemed to be rather the result of its delivery, than as arising from its natural quality. Her intonation was perfectly true—a point which never fails to secure a favourable hearing. At this period Miss Shirreff's musical training was evidently incomplete, for she sang as she had been taught, without showing any positive genius. To imagination she lent no wings. "Her embellishments," it was said, " were not only those of her master, but what had been her master's property, in common with many others, twenty years previously."

Her " shake " was for the most part defective, whilst her execution stood in need of much more finish, being, at the best, but that of a learner, who had, however, made a considerable advance towards a very respectable degree of perfection. The favour which Miss Shirreff thus early in her career was calculated to win, went on increasing as she progressed in the knowledge and discharge of her profession. As she did not excite any astonishment amongst her hearers at her *début*, so, during her somewhat brief career, she never excited any strong emotion. Compared with either Miss Stephens or Mrs. Wood, she had neither the clearness of voice, nor the naïve manner which were the chief attributes of the former, nor could she lay claim to the perfect knowledge of her art, or the fine taste and richness of the fancy of the latter ; yet, being devoid of any striking defect, possessing many valuable qualities, having no inconsiderable share of beauty, an advantageous presence and deportment, which, if not commendable, was at least, not censurable, she was unquestionably, and to a considerable extent, successful ; and continued to please so long as she appeared in public. Could Miss Shirreff have been induced to study her art—as it ought always to be studied by those who wish to become eminent—she might easily have placed herself among the first-rate singers of her time.

The comparatively favourable impression which Miss Shirreff certainly made by her first appearance in Arne's *Artaxerxes* was soon afterwards increased by her undertaking the character of Polly in the *Beggar's Opera*, wherein the difficulties were more easily compassed, although comparisons between herself and her predecessors and contemporaries could scarcely fail to be drawn, since no singer, of any pretension whatever, had ever considered herself safe with the public until she had been tried and accepted for her execution of music now deemed—and very justly so—to be not only void of all true merit, but little else than contemptible. To embellish such weak inventions, as the so-called songs of this specimen of English opera, was entirely out of character. If they are ever to please at all, reliance must be placed on their natural simplicity for such an end. Then they may be, to some extent, even at the present time, tolerated; but to overload them with not very accurately executed *fioriture*, as Miss Shirreff was unwisely induced to do, entirely destroyed the little effect they were calculated to obtain, and acted neither as a charm, nor as a surprise. Miss Shirreff* soon fell into the rank of a useful rather than a brilliant singer; and, but for the "hit" she made as the Page, when an English version of Auber's *Gustave III.* was, a year or two afterwards, brought out at Covent Garden, with Miss Inverarity as the heroine, and Templeton and Phillips in the two male leading characters, it is doubtful whether she would have left any abiding impression upon the public mind. Her personation, however, of that pretty little part, and her manner of singing its sparkling music, obtained for her a reputation which might be envied by any female *artiste* possessed of more considerable power and talent than she was ever able to manifest.†

The year 1832 was famous for one of the greatest operatic *fiascos* that was ever made in this country—the management of Mr. Monck Mason. The great fault of this undertaking was that that gentleman, who was thoroughly ignorant of theatrical or operatic matters, undertook too much, and so overweighted himself with engagements, that it was utterly impossible for him to bear up under their superincumbent pressure. Not satisfied with having brought together a comparatively strong company for the performance of Italian opera, although, so far, especially, as *prima*

---

* Miss Shirreff retired from the stage after her marriage, and is now a teacher of singing.

† See the *Harmonicon* for 1832, pp. 23—4.

donnas were concerned, the engagements under Mr. Ebers', as well as Messrs. Laporte and Laurent's direction were of a much more satisfactory kind, Mr. Monck Mason added to his embarrassments by providing a German company to give the works of the masters of that country alternately with those of a more exclusive southern *répertoire;* but that company, in spite of the excellence of its quality, failed to secure the appreciation either of the *habitués* or of the general public. At the very commencement of his career, this most unfortunate *entrepreneur* was met by the following damaging remarks, which, coming from a quarter possessing considerable influence, could not have failed to be most injurious both to himself and his undertaking :—

"Many weeks," said the *Harmonicon*,* " if not months, before the opening of the King's Theatre, expectation has been raised to a high pitch. A new manager had embarked his reputation and fortune in the enterprise, and commenced by promising reforms and ameliorations, much wanted and long called for by the subscribers ; among which were a considerable change in the operatic *corps*, as well as that of the ballet ; new musical dramas, the old ones, however excellent, having been heard to satiety ; and a renovation of the interior of the house, together with numerous other minor matters, which it is not necessary, to enter into. Mr. Monck Mason, the gentleman who now undertakes to sway the sceptre of this theatre, calculating by the demands of the town and his liberal wishes, rather than by the means of supplying the one and gratifying the other, certainly 'protested too much ;' he was not aware of the difficulties he would have to encounter, and, however conversant he may have been in the affairs of foreign theatres, could have

* Mr. Ayrton, ex-manager of the King's Theatre, was the editor.

been very little acquainted with the multitudinous details involved in the management of our Italian opera, in which the
activity and the address of the director are as much, if not more,
called for off the stage than on, and the obstacles he has to
struggle against are such as are utterly unknown abroad, where
the respective governments afford establishments of this kind
not only great pecuniary aid, but arm the 'administration,' as it
is called, with their authority ; thus bearing much of the expense
and preserving that order in the various departments which is
so difficult to maintain in an Anglo-Italian theatre. The continued agitation, too, of a great political question, and the threat
of a pestilential disease (the cholera) in the metropolis, were
additional impediments to the well-being of a concern which
depends entirely upon fashion, and the support of the higher
classes of society. Under these rather discouraging circumstances, the King's Theatre opened on Saturday, Feb. 4th, with
a new opera, and, with one exception (Madam de Meric), new
performers. So far, the management redeemed the promise
made."* A more thorough "wet blanket" than this could
scarcely have been applied to any undertaking, and, without
doubt, it had a most injurious effect upon Mr. Monck Mason's
interests.

The most important of the new engagements for the season
of 1832 were M. Nourrit and Signor Tamburini. The former
made little or no impression ; the latter at once established a
reputation that continued for nearly a quarter of a century.
Tamburini was first brought under the notice of the English
cognoscenti by the mention that had been made of his appearance in 1829 at the Kaernthnerthor theatre at Vienna, as

* See the *Harmonicon* for 1832, p. 68.

Figaro in Rossini's *Barbiere*, his voice being spoken of as of great compass and flexibility, and his method unexceptionable. This report having been confirmed, Mr. Monck Mason naturally considered himself fortunate in securing his services, and he made his first appearance, May 26th, in Rossini's *La Cenerentola*, meeting with a reception that augured well for his own permanent success, no less than for the welfare of the management. But as "one swallow does not make a summer," so one intelligent and brilliant vocalist did not constitute a company that would give satisfaction to the *habitués*, who had become exacting on account of the excellent quality of the engagements that had been for so many years made by Mr. Ebers, and afterwards by MM Laporte and Laurent during a much shorter period of their management.

From the first moment of Tamburini's appearance in London to the end of his career, he was a general favourite. The same good fortune seems to have, for the most part, attended him throughout his entire professional career. He was born March 28th, 1800, at Faënza, and from his childhood was brought in contact with musicians of greater or less degree of talent and acquirement. His father, Pasquale Tamburini, was a professor of music at Faënza, and a clarionet, horn, and trumpet player. Leaving Faënza for Fossombrone, in the Marches of Ancona, to undertake the direction of the military musical affairs of the former place, he took his son with him, with the fixed purpose of making him a horn player, although he was then no more than nine years old. That instrument very nearly killed him, causing an illness from which he was scarcely expected to have recovered. His father was sufficiently wise not to persevere, after his son's convalescence, with his studies in that direction, but placed him under the care of Aldobrando Bossi, a chapel-master at Fossombrone, who gave him singing lessons for the next three years ; when, returning to Faënza, he at once became a member of the chorus at the opera of that town. Young as he was, he had the intuition to discern what are those qualities which best serve to make an *artiste*, both as a vocalist and as an actor ; and having had the advantage of hearing Mombelli, David, and Donzelli, as also Mdmes. Pisaroni * and Mombelli, he was at the utmost pains to form his own method upon that of one or other of these celebrities. His voice, having settled down as a baritone, induced him, at eighteen years of age, to leave his paternal roof, and betake himself to Bologna, where a director of spectacle at Cento having fallen in with him, at once engaged him, and, in spite of his youth and inexperience, discovered that he had found a treasure. Going at first from place to place of no note, he readily learned the rudiments of his profession ; but before he was sufficiently instructed to take "leading business," he ventured upon a *début* at the Teatro Nuovo at Naples, where being but coldly received, he tried his fortune at Florence, only to meet with similar misfortune. The chief cause of his failure at each of these places was his disposition to sing flat—a defect which he never thoroughly overcame, and which in the later period of his career, at the Royal Italian Opera, Covent Garden, was often so painful as to make his appearance anything but desirable. In spite of the cold reception that Florence had accorded him, he obtained an engagement at Leghorn for the Carnival of 1820, and completely had his revenge against the decision of the more important Italian city by reason of the warmth of his reception, and the favour that was at once shown him, and continued so

* See p. 167.

long as he remained in that position. During the time of his engagement at Leghorn, he pursued his studies with the utmost assiduity, in order to fit himself for an appearance at Turin, whence, after having been thoroughly successful in the spring of 1822, he went to the Scala at Milan in the autumn of the same year, and secured the same result. After Milan, in the following year, he visited Trieste, and, in passing through Venice, sang at the Fenice, and at a concert given by the court, which Rossini directed. From that hour Tamburini's fortune may be said to have been made; for from Trieste he went to Rome, where he remained two years, and then, returning to Venice, sung in Rossini's *Moïse*, and divided the applause with Mdme. de Meric-Lalande* and M. David. His steps, were not bent, however, towards Paris or London till some time later, inasmuch as he accepted engagements at Palermo, Naples, Milan Vienna, and Genoa, as if he had no intention or design of ever trying his fortune elsewhere. At length the way opened for him to go to Paris; where, in October 1832, he *débuted* at "Les Italiens," as Dandini in Rossini's *Cenerentola*, and at once established himself as belonging to the first rank of trans-Alpine *artistes*.† During his engagement at that opera-house, I heard him in his *rôle*, and was at once struck by the beauty of his voice, which, but for his propensity even then occasionally to sing false, was pure and round in quality, and not long afterwards was farther improved by considerable facility of execution, but much more so by the excellence of his phrasing.

Concerning Tamburini's later career, I shall have hereafter to speak at some length. I content myself, therefore, with observing that, in spite of his accomplishments, he was one of

* See p. 182.

† See Fétis' *Biographie Universelle des Musiciens*, tom. viii. p. 178.

those *artistes* who were never wholly satisfactory to a well-instructed ear. Accomplished, clever, and reliable as he was, there was always something apparently wanting to render his vocalisation and the personation of the characters he undertook thoroughly acceptable. Those who had never seen or heard Ambrogetti or Garcia in the title *rôle* of Don Giovanni, are in the habit of asserting that Tamburini was a thoroughly competent exponent of that most difficult character. With this opinion I entirely disagree. From his first appearance in the struggle scene with Donna Anna to the alarm of Leporello, to the concluding note of the second act, Tamburini was by no means the high-born and chivalric Spanish Don, but a mere French *petit-maître*, of the most finicking manners and attitudes. He rather—especially in his later days—"barked" than sung Mozart's music, and gave, both to the impersonation and the vocalisation, a tone which might indeed have been the best of his time, although bad was the best. Thus, also, in Rossini's *Barbiere* he was a Figaro without hilarity or animation, his fun being as heavy as lead, and his *finesse* of such a complexion that it would never have been possible to outwit so crafty a schemer as Beaumarchais's jealous and unprincipled Dr. Bartolo. His mannerism was likewise of the most distinct type ; upon which characteristic he was sore, if it were, as he thought, in any wise mimicked or ridiculed. Of an instance of this peculiarity I have a lively recollection. When Mdme. Viardot was one night singing with him at the Royal Italian Opera, Covent Garden, the once highly popular but somewhat vulgar duet, " O, guardate che figura," she so closely imitated, if not actually mimicked, him, that he could scarcely restrain his anger whilst he was upon the stage with her, and actually burst into a fury when the curtain fell. Mdme. Viardot was thunderstruck at such a manifestation of ill-feeling, and told me, the following day, that nothing should ever induce her again to sing that duet with a man, who had not the good taste or temper to understand that the imitation she had given of his manner was merely adopted in an artistic, and by no means in an offensive sense—a determination to which she resolutely adhered. Disinclined, however, as I am to award anything like the same amount of commendation to Tamburini which he almost universally enjoyed, and especially in this country, I should indeed gladly hail the appearance of any successor who is worthy of being brought into comparison with him, especially in those parts which he made peculiarly his own. Faure is the only man who may in this respect be now named; but neither his voice nor his method is Italian; and great and accomplished an *artiste* as he unquestionably is, this disadvantage—by no means a fault— cannot, as I think, be wholly set aside or overlooked.

There was one feature, however, in Mr. Monck Mason's management which, it was admitted on all hands, had received an amount of improvement as satisfactory as it was unexpected —the composition of the orchestra, which had been most grievously neglected under every other management. In the previous year, Signor M. Costa had made great changes for the better; but on this occasion he had received *carte blanche* to do as he pleased, and he was not slow to avail himself of such an opportunity. As a matter of operatic history, it may not be uninteresting to name its several members in their respective departments. Director of the music—Signor M. Costa. Leader of the orchestra—Signor Spagnoletti. Violins —Messrs. Mori, Dando, Watts, Murray, Nadaud, Pigott, Ella, Kearns, Wallis, Baker, Reeve, Bohrer, Tolbecque, Griesbach, Zerbini, Littolff, Anderson, Watkins, Thomas, &c. Viole—Moralt, Warre, Alsept,

Daniels, Chubb, Nicks, &c. Violoncelli—Lindley, Rousselot, Hatton, Bohrer, Crouch, Brooks, &c. Contrabassi—Dragonetti, Wilson, Howell, Anfossi, Flower, Taylor, &c. Flauti—Nicholson and Card. Oboe—Cooke and Barret. Clarini—Wilman and Powell. Fagotti—Bauman and Tully. Corni—Platt, Ray, Calcott, and Tully. Trombe—Harper and Irwin. Tromboni—Mariotti, Smithers senior and junior. Timpani—Chipp. The chorus was also placed under the direction of an approved master, subject to the supervision of the director in chief; but the improvement in this department was not equal to that which had been made in the band. One of the expected profitable speculations of the season—the introduction of Meyerbeer's *Robert le Diable*, with very nearly the same cast with which it had been presented in Paris—turned out a complete failure, one cause of such a disaster arising from its production having been much too long retarded, and from two most ineffective attempts being made at the two patent theatres to anticipate its more legitimate representation at the King's Theatre. The opera was brought out in a most liberal manner; the dresses were superb, and the *mise en scène* beautiful. I was present on the first night of its performance; but it was so unlike what I had listened to in Paris, that, had I then heard it for the first time, I should have utterly condemned it, as did by far the greater number of the audience. Although this opera is confessed on all hands to have been Meyerbeer's *chef-d'œuvre*, next to *Les Huguenots*, it has never made a thoroughly favourable impression in this country, and is said scarcely ever to have paid for the mounting it absolutely requires. There seems, therefore, to be very little doubt that much force was prevalent in the following remarks, which were written very soon after its first performance, under Mr. Monck Mason's management, in the leading musical organ of the times :—

"This opera," says the accomplished critic of the *Harmonicon*, "it should be considered, was written for the French stage. Without entering into the question of which is right, it must be admitted that the taste of the two countries—of France and England—or rather the notion of what is and what is not true dramatic music, differs in many respects materially. Meyerbeer composed *Robert* for the meridian of Paris. His melodies, then, are French, and he has succeeded in pleasing those to whom he addressed his music in a manner that has surpassed the expectations of the most sanguine of his friends ; and, with all our national prejudices against the music of our neighbours, which has been strong, and is still kept up by a few, it will be admitted by impartial judges that of late years, the French have made vast strides in composition, particularly in that for the stage. They have left the living Italians, Rossini excepted, far behind, and are nearer and nearer approaching the best school of Germany. If, then, Meyerbeer has been fortunate enough to produce an opera that has not only obtained the suffrages of all Paris, but actually made a *fureur* in that capital, there is *primâ facie* evidence of its superior merit ; and the reception it has met with here is a proof that the English give their sanction to the verdict pronounced in favour of the work by a great and very critical nation. That the opera is too long for us, is admitted by all ; and that its effect here would have been much greater had it been cautiously abridged, cannot be doubted ; but its production was so much retarded, that the composer had not an opportunity of attending a single rehearsal, or he would most likely have profited by the advice of his experienced friends, and reduced it to dimensions calculated for a town to which the language is foreign."*

As I had very little opportunity of attending the performances of German opera at the King's Theatre during this season, I shall defer giving an expression of my " recollections" of Mdme. Schröder-Devrient and M. Haitzinger—who were the best members of that company—till a later period, and content myself with saying that, on the 9th of May, when the *Der Freischütz* was given, and on the 18th of May, when Beethoven's *Fidelio* was substituted for the former work, everything that could militate against satisfactory performances seemed to have combined. The choruses were tolerably well sung, but the band, although led by Spagnoletti, was not sufficiently efficient to produce a perfect *ensemble*, by reason of the unavoidable absence of those members who were engaged at the Ancient, Philharmonic, and other concerts on nights not exclusively belonging to the Italian theatre. The taste also for German opera had not then been created ; the consequence of which was, that the pit was only half filled, and that chiefly by Germans, whilst the boxes and amphitheatre were quite as sparsely occupied. Singular, also, to say, the reduction of the prices for the German off-nights militated against the gathering of crowded houses. The subscribers would not patronise the performances because they were cheap, and the less fortunate public, who mostly frequented the theatres, were not yet sufficiently educated up to the enjoyment of classical music of the highest class. It required nearly a whole generation to pass away before the masses could be brought in crowds to listen to Mozart, and Beethoven, and Weber, with the quiet enjoyment they now night after night patiently mani-

* See the *Harmonicon* for 1832, p. 160.

fest.   Mr. Monck Mason was assuredly the means of sowing this
good seed ; but the harvest of enjoyment it was to produce was
not brought to maturity until the remembrance of his name had
wholly ceased to exist, except amongst a few, who refer to his
brief career as an operatic director as the dawning of the day,
whence such excellent results primarily emanated.

During the season of 1832, Mrs. Bishop, the second wife of
the celebrated composer of that name—and afterwards Sir
Henry Bishop—came prominently before the public.   She had
been previously heard, and spoken well of, as Miss Rivière ; but
it was not until her appearance at the second Ancient Concert,
of March 14th, that she could be said to have made a reputation,
as a singer qualified to occupy a foremost rank in her profession.
Miss Shirreff also appeared at the same concert, and certainly
bore away the palm from her rival ; for, whilst she was said to
have sung in tune, and to have possessed feeling—two material
points in the formation of a vocal performer—Mrs. Bishop was up-
braided in very strong terms for the faultiness of her intonation.*

At the first concert of the Philharmonic Society for this year,
February 27th, I had an opportunity of hearing a clever pianist,
Mr. Field, who played a concerto of his own composition, which
was favourably received, the performance being pronounced as
in every degree gratifying.   This gentleman was the favourite
pupil of Clementi, and had been absent from England nearly
thirty years, and, having established himself at St. Petersburg,
had never, till this year (1832), visited his native country.   The
opinion expressed, concerning his concerto and his playing, so
thoroughly accorded with my own, that I adopt it with the
utmost satisfaction.   "Mr. Field's concerto in E flat differs
materially from the more prevailing style.   It is clear, melo-

* See the *Harmonicon* for 1832, p. 90.

dious, and not so overloaded with what are called brilliant, but are, in fact, confused passages, as we are now so much accustomed to hear. The middle movement—'a pastorale'—is exceedingly delicious, and excited a unanimous encore. The finale is very lively, though the whole was perhaps rather too long, the first movement particularly, which admits of abridgment. Mr. Field has a rapid finger, and executes with the utmost degree of neatness. His taste is pure, and in expression he every now and then reminds us of the great master of this style (J. B.) Cramer."*

A composer of considerable pretension, but of very ordinary capacity, about this time pushed himself into notoriety; and having been warmly taken up by several musical enthusiasts, and pronounced by them to be a second Haydn or Mozart, managed to keep his name for a year or two before the public, but then wholly and hopelessly died out of everybody's remembrance—the Chevalier Neukomm. With the exception of one song, "The sea, the sea, the open sea," which he wrote for Henry Phillips, and which that singer rendered popular, not a single composition made the slightest impression upon the British public. An oratorio, or rather a Sacred Cantata, as it should have been called, which he had a commission to write for one of the Birmingham Festivals, and from which great things were expected, fell completely flat upon its performance in that place; and to the best of my recollection, was never again heard. Neukomm was already an old man when he first appeared in London, but he lived to be eighty years of age, and died on the 3rd of April 1858, at Paris, whither he had returned after a voyage to the East.†

* See the *Harmonicon* for 1832, p. 92.
† See Fétis' *Biographie Universelle des Musiciens*, tom. vi. pp. 303—5.

At the latter part of this year's season Miss Romer*—a lady of whom I shall afterwards have to speak—made her appearance at Covent Garden as Clara, in the *Duenna*, with Mr. Wilson, the Scotch tenor, as Don Carlos. Miss Romer was the original Zerlina in Auber's *Fra Diavolo*, Braham being the Brigand, and was as well received as she deserved to be, on account of the great promise that to a considerable extent was speedily fulfilled. Mdme. Vestris was also much before the public, maintaining the position she had several years previously secured as one of the most accomplished actresses and useful vocalists that had ever appeared in this country. It was indeed truly said of this remarkable woman, who was equally at home upon the Italian, German, and English stage, that "in every sense she belonged to all Europe." Her father—F. Bartolozzi, R.A.—was an Italian engraver; her mother a German, and a good pianoforte player; her (first) husband, a member of the illustrious dancing family of France; and herself an Englishwoman, who was able to speak several languages with the utmost facility. Her voice was a pure contralto of the richest quality, and had it been cultivated up to its full requirements, would have rendered her the most perfect singer of her times in this specialty. After having been of the utmost service, especially at a pinch, to various operatic managers, she finally quitted the lyric stage, and devoted herself exclusively to the English drama, and both as an actress and a manageress continued to deserve and enjoy the favour of the public so long as she lived. She married Mr. Charles James Mathews July 18th, 1838, and died August 8th, 1856.

* Miss Romer, afterwards Mrs. George Almond, is no more.

CHAPTER IX.

1832—33.

THE circumstances under which Mendelssohn first came to London in 1829 have been already mentioned.* Immediately after the close of the musical season of that year he went to Scotland, and thence proceeded to Italy by way of Munich, Salzburg, Linz, and Vienna. In that "land of song" he remained till the month of July in the following year, visiting Rome, where he remained five months, and was at Naples for two months; thence returning by Rome, Florence, Genoa, and Milan, through Switzerland, to Munich in October. His stay in the Bavarian capital was but of short duration; for he arrived in Paris during the month of December, and remained there till March, meeting with nothing but disappointment, on account of the coolness with which his compositions were received in that city of frivolous pretence and heartless gaiety. So vexed, indeed, was he at such unexpected and most undeserved treatment, that on leaving it he wrote to a friend, that he considered "Paris was the grave of every reputation."† A far different reception awaited him in London, where, imme-

* See p. 176.

† "Paris sei das Grab aller Reputationen." See Fétis' *Biographie Universelle es Musiciens*, tom. vi. p. 78.

diately upon his arrival, he was received with open arms, meeting with a welcome so heartily enthusiastic, that he never ceased to speak of it as amongst the happiest reminiscences of his life.

Whilst at Munich, on his return from Italy, he had produced his pianoforte concerto, No. 1 in G minor, Op. 25, playing it himself for the first time in public on the 17th of October. An extract from a letter to his father, dated the following day, is so characteristic of this eminent man, that it is well worth recording. At the several rehearsals both of this concerto and his C minor Symphony he had been greatly disheartened; for the former, he said, "had taken two hours to study," whilst the other—the new concerto—"did not go at all"—a very different state of things from what he had met with in London in 1829, when the Symphony was played by the Philharmonic band at first sight, as the concerto also was to be, at the date to which I am referring, by the same orchestra. However, "on Saturday night there was a great ball, which was very nice," and put him in spirits again, and encouraged him for the next rehearsal on Monday morning ; and at last, at the concert itself, the concerto was a perfect success. "When the time," he further wrote to his father, "for the concerto came, I was very warmly applauded over and over again. The orchestra accompanied me well, and the whole thing went like mad. It gave the people immense satisfaction, so that they tried, after the Munich fashion, to clap till they brought me back ; but I was shy, and would not go on again."

This Munich concerto was one of the new works Mendelssohn brought with him to London, and he played it for the first time at the Philharmonic Concert, May 28, 1832, where it met with such a reception, as to lead to its repetition at the concert of the 18th of June following. What its effect was upon the audience may be gathered from the following remarks :—"The great novelty and high treat of the evening was M. Mendelssohn's concerto, never before performed in public." This, of course, referred to England, because it must have been known to the writer that the work had already been produced, as above stated, at Munich eight months previously. "He (M. Mendelssohn) is a composer who spurns at imitation ; for he is original almost to overflowing, and to the very last note of a piece is inexhaustible in new effects. The first movement of this [concerto] is in G minor, and glides, without any break, into an adagio in E major, a composition of surpassing beauty, in which the violoncellos are more than vocal : they sing better than most of those to whom vocal powers are said to be given. The finale, in G major, is all gaiety; the composer seems to have been hardly able to keep his spirits within moderate bounds; they flow over, and half intoxicate his hearers, till the close arrives, which is all calmness—a pianissimo. Such an ending is without example, and exceedingly delightful it was admitted to be by universal consent.* It may be worth while recording that of this concert Mr. Weichsel was the leader, and Mr. Cipriani Potter the conductor.

I had not the opportunity of hearing either the overture to *The Isles of Fingal* (Fingalhæhle) or the concerto on the occasions of their first performance (May 14 and May 28, 1832) ; but the description given of the former as of the latter composition by the same musical authority already quoted seems to be worth reproduction, as indicating the estimation in which

---

* *Harmonicon* for 1832, p. 152.

Mendelssohn was held by English connoisseurs at this period of his incessantly, and, as it turned out to be, much too active, life. "The overture by Mendelssohn, written for these concerts, was now heard for the first time—a circumstance which ought to have been noticed in the programme, for the dry announcement contained in the letters 'MS.' says little ; indeed it might signify that, whatever the age of the composition, it had never been thought worth printing. The idea of this work was suggested to the author while he was in the most northern part of Scotland, on a wild desolate coast, where nothing is heard but the howling of the wind and the roaring of the waves, and nothing living seen except the sea-bird, whose reign is there undisturbed by human intruder. So far as music is capable of imitating, the composer has succeeded in his design ; the images impressed on his mind he certainly excited, in a general way, in ours. We may even be said to have heard the sounds of winds and waves, for music is capable of imitating these in a direct manner ; and by means of association, we fancied solitude and an all-pervading gloom. This composition is in B minor, a key well suited to the purpose, and begins at once with the subject, which more or less prevails throughout ; for unity of intention is no less remarkable in this than in the author's overture to *A Midsummer Night's Dream*, and indeed is a prominent feature in all he has produced. Whatever a vivid imagination could suggest, and great musical knowledge supply, has contributed to this, the latest work of M. Mendelssohn, one of the finest and most original geniuses of the age ; and it will be but an act of justice to him, and a great boon to the frequenters of these concerts, to repeat the present composition before the conclusion of the season. Works such as this are like angel's visits, and should be made the most of." *

The great treat I had missed by not being in London at the seventh Philharmonic Concert (28th of May, 1832) was thoroughly compensated for by my presence at the eighth and last concert of the season (June 18th), when the directors again put the G minor concerto into the programme, and added the "Midsummer Night's Dream" as well; Signor Spagnoletti being the leader, and Mr. J. B. Cramer the conductor. Gratified as I had been by Hummel's concerto in A, Op. 113,† and his manner of rendering it, which I had hitherto considered to be the *ne plus ultra* of pianoforte playing, I was not at all prepared for such an extraordinary manifestation of power, combined with marvellous brilliancy and delicacy of mechanism, and unsurpassed sensibility of expression, as Mendelssohn exhibited. As for the composition itself, it seemed to make its hearers, as it made myself, perfectly wild with delight. The beauties of the three several *motivos*, crowding one upon another, left every one in a perfect state of bewilderment, without the power of deciding which to admire the most —whether the playful fancy of the allegro, the flowing sweetness of the andante, or the rushing brilliancy of the finale. The instrumentation also, so florid and varied, yet never too much overlaid, especially in the last *motivo*, took every one by surprise. As was well said at the time, "it seemed as if the brilliant passages for the solo instrument were not sufficient, but were accompanied by the loveliest little subjects for the violas and clarionets, which positively entranced the ear, quite

---

* *Harmonicon* for 1832, p. 141-2.
† See p. 192, note.

as much on account of their novelty as their adaptability to make the leading part more conspicuously perfect." With Mendelssohn's performance of this great work, the first act of the concert ended; and with many others—a crowd, indeed, of enthusiastic admirers, both professionals and amateurs—I hastened to the apartment whither he had retired, in the hope of being presented to him, as I had been to many of his predecessors, by the kindest friend of my youth, Sir George Smart—a hope that was gratified, but not until the greater part of the second act had been finished, inasmuch as it was all but impossible to get near that amiable and unpretending man, upon whom all the enthusiastic praises he was well and worthily receiving excited no other feelings than those of humility and gratitude. All that he could utter, as one after another reiterated his expressions of delight in speaking to and congratulating him, was, "You are too good." When, however, my turn came—which I began to think was never to come at all— and I tried to speak, I could not find a word. I could only grasp his hand, and look what I felt. With a smile never to be forgotten, and patting me on the cheek, he said, " Little man, you too fond of music, I think. Do you follow it ? " Upon my answering " No," " So much the better for you here," pointing to his head. He then turned to speak with Mesdames Schröder-Devrient and Cinti-Damoreau, who, with Tamburini, were the vocalists of the evening; and I, bowing my thanks, took my leave, and retired to a quiet nook at the end of the concert-room, to wait for, and listen with the utmost attention to, the overture, equally as new to myself and others as the concerto had been ; the perfect enjoyment of which was not prevented by the abominable habit of a large portion of the audience hastening away; for though the directors had placed this orchestral prelude at the end of the programme, where it would have little chance nowadays of meeting with the attention it deserved, scarcely a person left the room.

It has been my good, or my bad, fortune—who shall decide?—to hear the G minor concerto played by a host of pianists, good, bad, and indifferent, foreign and English, male and female, professionals and amateurs, since that ever-memorable Monday night, June 18, 1832; but not a single one has ever approached within "a shadow of a shade" of the manipulation of its gifted writer. The exquisite precision of the first *motivo*, lighted up with impulsive bursts of passion, bringing out a meaning which no one has since seemed capable of realising, together with the delicacy of the manner in which the instrument was, in the andante, made to sing, as if it gave out a combination of exquisitely attuned voices,—it is not within the compass of words to describe; whilst the intensity—nay, may it not be said, the fury?—with which the *presto* and *molto allegro e vivace* were dashed off, can never find any other illustration sufficiently exact than that which Mendelssohn himself used, after its first performance at Munich, when writing of his triumph to his father,* "the whole thing went like mad!" Whilst in the delicate *nuances* his fingers seemed to be like feathers, in those of more forcible and impetuous character there was a grasp and an *élan* which almost took away one's breath. Not a single note was slurred, notwithstanding the stupendous difficulties of passage after passage, which he seemed to sweep from the keys with a dash and a bound, that gave not the slightest indication of mere scale practice. Great

* See p. 248.

as Mendelssohn was as a composer, I believe he was far greater both as a pianist and an organist. Under his hands each instrument " discoursed " after a manner as original as it was captivating. Scarcely had he touched the keyboard than something that can only be explained as similar to a pleasurable electric shock, passed through his hearers and held them spellbound— a sensation that was only dissolved as the last chord was struck, and when one's pent-up breath seemed as if only able to recover its usual action by means of a gulp or a sob.

An anecdote relative to this feeling I may here introduce as told to me by Sir Michael Costa. On one occasion of Mendelssohn being in Switzerland, he and Sir Michael met at the church of Friburg, in which building the organ is of such world-wide celebrity, that few persons—especially those who lay claim to any musical taste—leave the town without going to hear it. At the time referred to the custodian was somewhat of a bear, and most determinedly refused, either for love or money, to permit any stranger to place his fingers upon the keys, although he himself had not the slightest pretension to the designation of an organist; and so far from showing the capabilities of the instrument, induced very many to go away under the impression that they had been "sold," and that all "Murray" and other guide-books had stated was nothing better than "a delusion and a snare." Mendelssohn was resolved, by hook or by crook, to ascertain what the Friburg organ was made of. For this purpose he drew the custodian out, working upon his weak points of character—for the old man really loved the organ as if it had been his child—but as to getting his consent to touch it, that seemed to be beyond the probability of realisation. Every one, who ever had the good fortune to be acquainted with Mendelssohn, must have been attracted by his winning manners, his courteous bearing, and his manifestation of decided character. Whether he won upon the old man by any one of these peculiarities of his "native worth" in particular, or by their combination, can only be inferred. Suffice it to say, that after long parley he was permitted to try one range of keys. One hand he employed at first, quietly using the other in drawing the stops, as if to test the variety of their quality; and when he had thus got out as many as seemed applicable for his purpose, he made a dash, which completely staggered the old man, and began to play as he alone could play. The old man gasped for breath. He clutched the rail against which he was standing, and for an instant seemed as if he would drag this bold intruder from his seat. That impulse was, however, only momentary; for he soon stood, as it were, spellbound, until a break in the gushing harmony enabled him to make an effort to ascertain who the master-spirit was that made the organ speak as he had never heard it speak before. Sir Michael Costa, at first scarcely knowing whether it were better to smile at the old man's astonishment, or to let events take their course, or to enlighten him at once, decided upon the former course; but at this moment the old man seized him by the arm, and gasped out, " Who, in Heaven's name, is that man ?" But when he answered, slowly and deliberately, " Felix Mendelssohn Bartholdy," he staggered as if struck by a tremendous blow. " And I refused him to touch my organ !" he sorrowfully said. But as Mendelssohn began again to play, he gave an impatient sign that he should not be disturbed, and listened and listened as he never listened again, as if some mighty spirit had entranced him. The object gained, Mendelssohn spoke a few kind words to the old man, and so departed, leaving an impression upon his mind and heart that, without doubt, during the time that he was spared was never for an hour obliterated.

The dead failure of Mr. Monck Mason's operatic enterprise in 1832 having been so disastrous, both as to pecuniary results and musical performances, precluded the possibility of his again occupying the position of director for the coming campaign of 1833. A season without the doors of the King's Theatre being opened was not, however, to be heard of by those noblemen and gentlemen who, as *habitués*, constituted themselves the exclusive patrons of the lyric drama, but did very little else than trammel the unhappy manager, who had to endure their interference on the one hand, and the caprice of the *artistes* on the other. M. Laporte, undaunted by the losses he himself had made, came to the rescue; and on Saturday, Feb. 6th, opened "the great house in the Haymarket" with Rossini's *Cenerentola*, his *prima donna* being Madame Boccabadati, who had recently appeared in Paris, without, however, commanding that remarkable success which had been anticipated by reason of the popularity she had won, not only in most of the opera-houses of Italy, but also at Munich, where, it was said, "her sweet voice and excellent method had made a most favourable impression." This opinion had been indorsed by Berlioz, when writing in the *Revue Musicale* his once celebrated *"Lettres d'un Enthousiaste,"** by means of which he made himself felt more as a critic than he was ever able to do by his compositions as a musician.† How great was the *fiasco* she made in London may be judged of by the following very severe but somewhat vulgar specimen of criticism:

---

* Tom. xii. p. 75.
† See Fétis' *Biographie Universelle des Musiciens*, tom. i. p. 450.

"Madame Boccabadati possesses a soprano voice, of that kind which makes its way into the house, though it sometimes forces people to make their way out. This potent quality is a piercing thinness; and, as commonly happens with a vocal organ of such description, is accompanied by an apparently total absence of all feeling. As counter-balances, however, her intonation is good, and she sings with that firmness, that self-confidence, which leads one to suppose that she understands music—at least, the modern opera-music; for the chances are, that this lady never sang, never dreamt of, any other. In person she is much shorter than her name; but what is wanting in height is made up in breadth. As to age, a well-bred critic would guess her at half of that allotted by the Psalmist to man. The less polite manager of an office for insuring lives would add seven or ten years to this, and be much nearer the mark."* As to the quality of this lady's voice, it cannot be disputed that the above remarks were as true as they were severe; for she was one of the most unpleasant—and yet I cannot say unsatisfactory— singers it ever was my lot to hear. She was well supported by Donzelli and de Begnis; but in other respects "the opera was got up in a manner highly gratifying to those who wished to see that kind of amusement put down by force of public opinion." Madame Boccabadati afterwards appeared in Rossini's *Matilde de Shabran*—one of Rossini's least interesting operas—and undoubtedly improved on her *début;* but she never rose beyond the rank of a *prima donna* in second-rate theatres, whilst her engagement could only be esteemed useful rather than agreeable.

The female novelties of this season were doomed to be unfortunate, inasmuch as another competitor for fame—a Madame

* See *Harmonicon* for 1833, p. 66.

Schiasetti, who was introduced to the public for the first time in this country as Malcolm, in Rossini's *Donna del Lago*—failed to make the slightest impression. It was evident that this lady was what is commonly called " an old stager : " and the fact speedily oozed out, that she had, several years previously, sung at Paris, and there again, more recently, with doubtful success, appearing at Dresden in the interim, whence no report, either to her advantage or disadvantage, had been received. Her voice was originally a mezzo-soprano, which she had spoiled, as many others, both before and since her time, have done, by attempting to force it down to a contralto compass, which no effort could accomplish. Thus, whilst her higher notes were hard and unsympathetic, those of her lower compass were crude and harsh. Her intonation was also anything but perfect ; her personal appearance too —she had nothing to recommend her—being masculine and muscular, the latter qualities more prominently so than her vocal strength. The only occasion of my hearing this lady was when Mozart's *Nozze di Figaro* was played, soon after her *début*; the part of Susanna being given to her, whilst that of the Countess was taken by Madame Boccabadati. Cherubino was personated by Mdlle. Nina Sontag, a German *artiste* of no pretension, remarkable for little else than want of animation both as a singer and an actress, yet inoffensive, unless great coldness and slowness of manner could offend. Of Madame Boccabadati's Countess it was indeed truly said, that " the music was perfectly strange to her ; but, like a stranger, she did not give it welcome, although she got through it better than might have been expected ; that Susanna seldom had so inadequate a representative ; and that the Cherubino ought not to have excited any doubts in the mind of Almaviva,"—which character, by the bye, was played by Donzelli, for whom, as for Madame Schiasetti, the music had to be transposed, to the manifest disadvantage of those charming effects which Mozart's vivacious creation is calculated to manifest when well given, and interpreted in the respective keys in which it was originally " made."

The dreariness of the operatic season of 1833 is in some measure to be inferred by the following remarks, which, severe as they may seem to have been, were not one iota too much so :—
" After nearly a season had passed away, in which nothing but old, mostly feeble, operas, filled by second and third-rate performers, had been given to the subscribers—for the *public* had been too wise to pay their money for nothing—the theatre was all at once found to be so crowded with singers that they actually jostled each other in the lobby. When the house stood in need of attraction, when the best management, the utmost activity, would hardly have enabled the lessee to pay his expenses, he furnished neither opera nor singer, ballet nor dancer, that drew enough to meet the rent. When Easter was turned—when that season had arrived in which, if the doors are opened, the house is lighted, and a set of puppets are placed on the stage, multitudes will go to see them—at that season, a double troupe—Italian and German—was formed, and fragments of operas given, in order that the performers might have some employment, and not to lose their voices for want of use!"[*]
" A change," however, then " came o'er the spirit of " M. Laporte's " dream ; " for he managed, on the 27th of April, to give Rossini's *La Cenerentola* as it had scarcely ever been heard in London before, Madame Cinti-Damoreau being the Angelina, and charming her hearers with her musical and flexible, though

* See *Harmonicon* for 1833, p. 139.

not very strong, voice and refined taste, the result of a perfect knowledge of her art ; Donzelli, the Ramiro ; Tamburini, Dandino ; and Zuchelli, Don Magnifico, all of whom were thoroughly competent for the task they had undertaken to perform. Not to "let the grass grow under his feet," M. Laporte brought forward Madame Pasta, after an absence of two years, in Donizetti's *Anna Bolena,* the title *rôle* of which that great *artiste* had "created" on the 8th of July, 1831, for her benefit, and in which she had never been surpassed. The effect of this improvement raised the drooping hopes of the subscribers and the public, and gave the manager a better prospect of success than he was said to have deserved, on account of the previous too evident shortcomings of his primary engagements. Pasta was in better voice then than she had been for several years, and was influenced, as it seemed, by a determination to make her greatness acknowledged on every hand previously to her approaching retirement. She, therefore, a few nights afterwards followed up her *Anna Bolena* triumph by appearing in Rossini's *Tancredi,* in which opera also she had not only never been excelled, but never touched by any successor whatever, not even by Alboni. In this *rôle*—one of her grandest efforts—she was well supported by Mdme. Cinti-Damoreau, Zuchelli, and Rubini. As I then for the first time heard Rubini, I must pause for a while in my narration, to give some account of the most remarkable tenor the Italian school ever produced, whom no one but Mario has ever approached, but to whom that superb *artiste* was "no more like than he to Hercules."

Gian Battista Rubini was born at Romano, a small town in the province of Bergamo, April 7th, 1795, and was the youngest of three brothers, all tenors of considerable celebrity. His father, like Tamburini's,* was a professor of music, a horn-player in the theatre, and the conductor of religious musical services in various churches and chapels, having a complete corps of singers and players, with a collection of masses, vespers, motetts, and litanies, all at the service of any chapter or convent that chose to hire them. His three sons were enlisted in this corps, the eldest being taught to play the organ, and the two younger the violin. The young Gian began his career as a vocalist at the early age of eight years, and showed such talent and aptitude that his father, diffident of his own powers as a singing-master, placed him under the tuition of a priest, an organist of Adro, in Brescia, named Don Santo, who sent him back to his parents at the end of a year with the consoling assurance that nothing would ever make him a singer, and that, as this was the case, it would be as well to look out for some other more likely means of livelihood for him. The father, better understanding the boy's capacity, at once set to work to instruct him, and not long afterwards invited his discouraging master to hear him sing a *Qui tollis*, which he delivered in such a style as to enable both to have their revenge, and to force from the old organist the confession that he was utterly wrong in his conjecture. At twelve years of age Rubini made "his first appearance on any stage" at Romano, in a female character and for his own benefit, with considerable advantage both as to fame and pecuniary results. Soon afterwards he went to Bergamo, where he played the violin between the acts, and sang during the operatic season in the chorus. Whilst fulfilling that engagement, a *petite comédie* was put in rehearsal, in one scene of which a cavatina had to be sung, which not one of the troupe was competent to

* See p. 236.

undertake. Somebody, in a lucky moment, having suggested that young Rubini might be able to serve the purpose, the manager liberally offered him a five-franc piece if he would undertake the task. He did as he was requested, and created a *furore* at once, which was in all probability the first step to his future success in life. This cavatina was the composition of a Signor Lamberti, who was born at Savone, Oct. 22, 1769, and went to Paris in 1806, where he dedicated some of his compositions to the Princess Pauline, sister of the Emperor Napoleon Bonaparte, but made no position for himself, and was still living in 1817, most probably in poverty.* Rubini never laid that cavatina aside, but frequently sang it, both in private and public, to remind him, as he said, of his first success. Very little, however, seems to have immediately come of that success ; for until 1814 he seems to have held no better position than that of a mere stroller, whose earnings were necessarily precarious and miserable. At Milan in that year he fell in with an engagement-broker, a so-called Marquis Belcredi, who, perceiving that there was something to be made of him, offered him an engagement at Pavia for the autumn season, at the liberal salary of eleven crowns—about £1 18*s.*—a month, which " the poverty, not the will, of the indigent stroller compelled him to accept. Here he made so great a sensation, that he was heard of at Milan, which caused the scheming Marquis to engage him at once for the Carnival of 1815 at 1000 francs for the season. Having first of all sent him to Brescia, he next transferred him for the spring season to the San Moire Theatre at Venice, at a salary of 2000 francs. Rubini next entered into an engagement with Barbaja, the director of the Neapolitan theatres, for six

---

* See Fetis' *Biographie Universelle des Musiciens,* tom. v. p. 178.

months, at eighty-four ducats (about £18) per month, with a
proviso in his engagement, that at the end of the first three
months, the engagement should be renewable for a year, at the
increased salary of 100 ducats a month. He sang at the Teatro
del Fiorentini with Pellegrini,* and was rising in public favour,
when Barbaja, instead of renewing his engagement at a higher
salary, proposed to dismiss him entirely, and only consented to
retain him on condition of his terms being lowered to seventy
ducats. Rubini had many cogent reasons that made him
anxious to remain at Naples. He naturally desired to improve
the hold he already had upon public favour there. He found
himself also in the society of the celebrated tenor Nozzari,† his
own countryman, from whom he received most valuable hints
and lessons, watching his method and imitating his manner so
carefully, as to derive almost as much benefit from each as from
his instruction. He, therefore, accepted Barbaja's terms, saying,
however, at the same time, " You take a mean advantage of my
present condition ; but before long you will have to pay for it."
During the Carnival of 1819 he made an immense hit in Rossini's *La Gazza Ladra* at Rome, which he confirmed at Palermo,
where he sung with Donzelli and Lablache ; so that upon his
return to Naples he was able to make his own terms, as he had

* See p. 173.

† Andreas Nozzari, born in Bergamo, 1775 ; studied first under the Abbé
Petrobelli, the second chapel-master of the cathedral of that town ; and next
under David, senior, and D'Aprile. Having *débuted* at Pavia, he went to Rome
and Milan, and in 1803 to Paris, which he left for Naples, where he fixed his
residence, after having sung in the principal cities of Italy. He was said to
be an *artiste* of the highest qualifications, for whom Rossini wrote the chief
tenor parts in his *Elizabeth, Otello, Armida, Moïse, Ermione, La Donna del Lago*
and *Zelmira,* which he " created." In 1822 he retired from the stage, and died
of apoplexy, December 12th, 1832, in his fifty-sixth year. See Fétis' *Biographie
Universelle des Musiciens,* tom. vi. p. 340.

prognosticated would come to pass. In 1824 Barbaja, having been removed from the direction of the Neapolitan theatres, took his entire troupe with him to Vienna, including Rubini and his wife,* whom, as Mdlle. Chomel, he had heard on his return to Naples, and recommended that an engagement should be given her. Barbaja followed this advice, and was repaid by her popularity during two or three seasons at the San Carlo and Fondo theatres. After singing together for some time, they were married in 1819. Madame Rubini was a Parisian by birth, having been born in that city May 31, 1794. When sixteen years of age she was admitted as a pupil of the Conservatoire, and at first placed under the instruction of M. Gérard for vocalisation, but afterwards of M. Garat. Having remained eight years in that academy, she quitted France for Naples, and obtained there a brilliant success in Rossini's *Elizabeth* and Morlacchi's *Gianni di Parigi*, which her after-appearance in "the sweet swan of Pesaro's" *Maometto* completely confirmed. On the 26th April, 1831, she sang with her husband at the King's Theatre, in Bellini's opera *Il Pirata;* but, failing to make any impression,† she immediately retired from her profession, and was never again heard in public, either here or abroad. Madame Rubini's want of success in London was the more remarkable, inasmuch as she was described, by critics of the most competent knowledge and fairness, to have possessed "a voice of vast compass, which, although certainly not of a fine quality, was by no means displeasing, especially as she did not sing out of tune. Her person likewise was much in her favour, and her action not only correct, but even noble, when the character she represented required it." Because of her

* See p. 265.   † Ibid.

having been criticised in most decided terms, a competent writer stated that he had " paid more than ordinary attention to her performances, and could not discover those enormous faults which had been so undisguisedly condemned. We have, it is true," he adds, "heard her only seldom. Our opinion, therefore, is not unalterably formed ; but we will go so far as to assert, that many a performer inferior to Madame Rubini has received lavish praises, and been ranked amongst the first of the day."*

The operatic company which Barbaja took with him to Vienna was perhaps the most numerous and splendid that was ever united at one time in any city. There were no less than nine *prime donne,* most of whom had established a high reputation, whilst the remainder attained the very first rank in their profession—viz. Sontag, Fodor, Mombelli, Rubini, Eckerlin, Ungher, Giulia Grisi, Dardanelli, and Grimbaum. How these ladies, most of whom were celebrated for their capricious conduct, both towards the public and one another, got on together, no record seems to have been made ; but that they quarrelled, after the manner of *prime donne* of every age, not excepting our own, " to the top of their bent," and " led" their husbands—but more especially the *entrepreneur*—" a life," may easily be imagined. The tenors whom Barbaja had brought together were Donzelli, David, Rubini, and Cicimira, each of whom, except the latter, was of world-wide reputation ; while the basses, equally strong in number, but not in talent, were Lablache, Ambrogi, Botticelli, and Bassi. At the close of this remarkable season, which for brilliancy has never been equalled, Rubini returned to Naples, whence he speedily made his way to Paris—taking Milan in his

* See *Harmonicon* for 1831, p. 157.

journey—and sung at "Les Italiens." for the first time, Oct. 6, 1825, in the part of Ramiro in Rossini's *La Cenerentola.* Whilst at Milan, Bellini wrote the part of Gualtero in *Il Pirata* especially for him. He also sang in the same composer's *La Sonnambula,* and Donizetti's *Anna Bolena,* in 1827; and in 1831 and 1832, freed from Barbaja's clutches, made as great a *furore* in London, if not greater, than he had produced in all other theatres. From that time until 1843 he alternated between Paris and London, with the exception of the year 1838, when he passed the summer in Italy, chiefly at Bergamo. In 1843 he went with Liszt to Holland and Germany ; but after arriving at Berlin, made his way alone to St. Petersburg, where he not only added immensely to his fortune, but so far captivated the Czar Nicholas, that he raised him to the rank of colonel, and nominated him as musical director-in-chief in the Russian dominions. On his return to Italy he purchased an estate near Romano, where he continued to reside till March 2, 1854, when he died.*

Rubini's voice was of the richest quality, of a compass of eleven or twelve notes, from about E flat or F to B or C. To this was added a falsetto certainly reaching to E or F. His intonation was of the purest, and his delivery free from all impediment ; but he may be said to have introduced that system of *tremolo,* of which there has been so much reason to complain in hosts of modern singers, male and female—a fluctuation of tone, so to speak, which rather excites the idea of age or weakness than as indicative of the effects it resorts to for the purpose of producing passion. His shake was excellent, and he was never weary of introducing it, accompanied with an overwhelming

* See *Harmonicon* for 1833, pp. 23, 24 ; and Fétis' *Biographie Universelle de Musiciens,* tom. vii. pp. 242-4.

multitude of roulades, latterly adopted to conceal the ravages of wear and tear, which, after a time, was apt to produce weariness amongst his hearers. He had also the habit of suddenly forcing out his voice, as it were, in gusts, and so suddenly withdrawing it, as to be nearly inaudible. This was done upon no fixed principle, or in order to express any particular sentiment or epithet, but merely to produce a succession of contrasts, that were thought by not a few, who, from the experience of the past, preferred a more level method of vocalisation, to be violent and unmeaning. In his *fioriture* there was much undoubtedly that might be called vicious, whilst his roulades were for the most part destitute of variety. Whoever heard him once, it might be said, heard him always; for he poured out the whole store of his embellishments in a single air, employing them indiscriminately—according to the then Italian fashion, which is now altogether lost and gone—in "grave and gay, in lively and severe." He nevertheless often sang in a highly impassioned manner, and especially in the well-known airs, "Tu vedrai la sventurata," and "Vivi tu," exemplified an amount of intelligence and passion that has never been surpassed. He was also void of affectation, and by his unpretending manners conciliated many of those who were unwilling to accord to him the undoubted merits to which he was justly entitled.

After the production of Bellini's *Il Pirata*, which never made any permanent impression upon a London audience, the same composer's *Norma*, as I have already recorded,* was brought out for Pasta's benefit—the first attempt of the kind during the season, which had been remarkable for everything else but actual novelty. The cast for this occasion comprised the talent

* See p. 138.

of Madame de Meric* (Adalgisa); Donzelli (Pollione); V. Galli (Oroveso); with Pasta as the "Diva." The two subordinate parts of Clotilde and Flavio were filled by Madame Castelli and Signor G. Galli. The Gallis—brothers, if I remember rightly—were but two makeshifts, of whom the least said the better. *Norma* itself, popular as it has since become—it has been played perhaps more frequently in England than any other work in the *répertoires* of either of our opera-houses—was but coldly received. It was said—which was by no means untrue—to be a direct imitation of Meyer's *Medea*, the title *rôle* of which was, without exception, the greatest of all Pasta's personations; and, but for her being the life and soul of the whole work here—as she had been at Milan, where it was originally played—with Giulia Grisi, afterwards to be Pasta's only successor in the same character, as the Adalgisa—in the previous year—would have been a failure. The music, "considered as a whole," although said to be "not censurable in regard to the rules of composition, possessed the most fatal of all faults, that of being deplorably uninteresting; so that, except the *motivo* of the duet, 'Deh! con te li prendi"—which, but for the skill of Madame de Meric, would have been a complete *fiasco*, owing to Pasta's imperfect intonation†—the aria, 'Norma! che fu?' and the finale, there was not a 'number' that had the slightest pretence to originality, or was productive of the least effect." As for the overture and *introduzione*, they were pronounced as only calculated to "stun one with all kinds of noisy instruments, whilst half, or more, of the first act is accompanied by the same intolerable din." It was, in fact, the general opinion that "the music of the last scene, and the acting of Pasta, might keep this opera on

---

* The mother of Mde. de Meric Lablache, the contralto.   † See p. 139.

the stage while she remained to fill the part; but without her, or her equal, if such should ever be found, it had no chance of being listened to in London; and even with her, it was with half-reluctance permitted."[*]

The miserable practice of giving fragments of operas was brought much into vogue during the season of this year (1833), and gave, not unnaturally, great offence, inasmuch as it was not confined to the comparatively smaller works of Bellini and Donizetti, but was also applied to Rossini's *Semiramide*, which was positively, on one occasion, compressed into one act! *La Cenerentola*, however, given in its entirety for the *re-entrée* of Malibran, who had become but occasionally a bright star in the Italian operatic hemisphere. Singular, however, to say, neither this gifted woman, her associates, nor the opera itself, produced any very marked sensation; the chief cause undoubtedly being that it had become so hackneyed that the *habitués*, no less than the public, had grown completely weary of it. As, however, the clamour for novelty was not to be suppressed, except by bringing forward something good, bad, or indifferent, the management introduced Bellini's weak and incomplete opera *I Capuleti e Montecchi* (Romeo and Juliet), on the 20th of July, with Pasta as Romeo, Madame de Meric as Julietta, Donzelli as Tebaldo, and V. Galli as Capuleto. Pasta's acting, grand as it was, however, could not save it. In all my remembrance, I never witnessed anything that surpassed the furious manner in which she, as it were, hurled herself upon Tebaldo, when the news of Mercutio's death was imparted. Donzelli, apparently wholly unprepared for what was coming, positively cowered before the onslaught, and went down before it, as being utterly powerless

* See *Harmonicon* for 1833, p. 160.

to contend with such a foe, whilst the action of the scene was all but suspended, and would have been so entirely, had not the plaudits of a crowded house given the actors time to recover from their bewilderment. Nothing in the grandest of Edmund Kean's most brilliant efforts ever surpassed this incident. Yet neither that point, nor any other excellence which the greatest *tragédienne* the Italian stage ever knew manifested, could save the opera itself. It was played but twice, and then gave up the ghost, to be " buried in the tomb of all the Capulets."

On the 10th August the season of 1833 was brought to an end with a performance of Paer's finest work, *Agnese*, an opera now never given, founded upon Mrs. Opie's tale entitled *Father and Daughter.* The principal part, Uberto the father, was one of Tamburini's most finished personations, and the impression he made upon me on this, the first and last occasion of my ever hearing the work in its entirety, lives in my remembrance as if it had happened only yesterday. Dull, heavy, and painful as are the incidents, with which the music for the most part throughout accords, the pathos this clever *artiste* imparted to the scenes in which he was chiefly engaged was so true to nature, that the idea of acting was wholly displaced. But one general regret could be expressed, that the opportunity of witnessing such a performance had not been more frequently accorded ; whilst for the production of other less-meritorious means of amusement, Tamburini was permitted to remain during the greater part of his engagement comparatively idle. The season of 1833, indeed, was eminently distinguished by the performance of thoroughly worn-out operas, and the production of only two, imported fresh from Italy, which proved less endurable than those that preceded them. Nearly half the subscription nights passed with scarcely a tolerable performer upon the stage; and for the other moiety, from Easter to the close, twice as many performers were engaged as could properly be employed. No wonder that M. Laporte's losses were immense; especially as he had been so rash as to repeat Mr. Monck Mason's unfortunate speculation of the previous year, in giving German opera at Covent Garden contemporaneously with the performance of Italian opera in the Haymarket. Those losses were said to have considerably exceeded £30,000. This statement, however, was not only thought to be exaggerated, but by many, better informed than their neighbours, to be false; it being naturally surmised that M. Laporte would not have been disposed to risk another season had his receipts been so singularly disproportionate to his outlay.

A kind of mania for operatic performances seemed to have seized upon the managers of the patent theatres during this very remarkable year. Thus, on the 5th of March, Mozart's *Il Don Giovanni* was brought out at Drury Lane, with the following cast: Braham, Don Juan, as the English version was entitled; Templeton, Don Ottavio; Paul Bedford, Don Pedro (Il Commendatore); H. Phillips, Leporello; Seguin, Masetto; Madame de Meric, Donna Anna; Miss Betts, Donna Elvira; and Mrs. Wood, Zerlina. The orchestra, in order to do justice to such a work, was augmented by the principal instrumentalists of the King's Theatre and Philharmonic bands, Sir H. Bishop being the conductor, and Mr. T. Cooke the leader. Braham's Don was a clever personation, his singing being better than his acting. H. Phillips made but a heavy Leporello, comic humour and archness being wholly out of his line. Of Paul Bedford's version of the Commendatore, it was said truly that, as the statue, both equestrian and pedestrian, his voice, figure, and firmness told surprisingly well, but of the music he did not seem to have the smallest comprehension. Mrs. Wood's Zerlina was much admired, although she persisted in singing almost all the solo and duet music of the part much too slow. In the concerted portions, however, she atoned for this fault, and displayed her knowledge and power to more decided advantage. Madame de Meric made an excellent Donna Anna, and Miss Betts did more justice to the part of Donna Elvira than it commonly received at the King's Theatre.

There being literally nothing for Malibran to do at the King's Theatre, that gifted woman transferred her talent first to Drury Lane, and afterwards to Covent Garden, appearing at the former house in an English version of Bellini's *La Sonnambula*, with great success, May 1st, and June 4th in a nondescript piece called the *Student of Jena, or the Family Concert;* but the latter was so decided a failure, that the house was closed immediately afterwards. M. Laporte and Mr. Bunn having entered into an agreement for the performance of German opera, transferred their company to Covent Garden, which they opened with a performance of Mozart's *Zauberflöte.* As I was not tempted to witness this or any other representation of German opera during the season of 1833, I must content myself with saying that the principal singers were Mdmes. Schröder-Devrient, Stoll-Böhm, sopranos, and MM. Haitzinger tenor, Dobler and Uetz basses. The most remarkable occurrence, however, during this untoward management was the representation at Covent Garden, June 29—for the first time in England —of Weber's *Euryanthe,* which made no greater impression than had been brought about by the older and better-known work of Mozart. Full of beauty as the score of this opera is, and by no means less showing the hand of a master than the *Der Freischütz*, it never has been, and never will be, equally popular. The libretto is dull and insipid, and is not to be made interesting by the beauties which the music at every turn displays. Had the music been set to " a book " that possessed only a scintillation of cleverness, it would in all probability have been stamped by general consent as Weber's *chef-d'œuvre*. Its presentation at Covent Garden this year by no means added to its chance of ever obtaining permanent popularity.

Until 1833, although he had been in London during several previous seasons, I had not the advantage of hearing one of the most remarkable violin players of the present century—Charles Auguste de Beriot. I must confess to have been—unwisely, as it turned out—prejudiced against him and every other violinist after having heard their greater master, Paganini; and for this cause I had taken no trouble, nor gone out of my way to meet with what I had fully made up my mind would certainly turn out a thorough disappointment. I was again and again most justly ridiculed for my obstinacy, but this only served to render me more perverse ; and I, at this distance of time, confess, with no small degree of shame, that it was not in London, but at the Norwich Festival of the year 1833, that I first came in contact with this man of talent and capacity. As an executant, I found him, as I had anticipated, far below Paganini, but to all intents and purposes quite the equal of, if not superior to, Kiesewetter and Mori. Of genius, I cannot record an impression that I discovered any particular manifestation ; but as an executant he was assuredly finished and exact, and able to produce a tone which, if not altogether rich and round, was at least devoid of thinness or scratchiness. Elegance rather than *tours de force* was the characteristic of his playing. That he could have rendered either Beethoven's or Mendelssohn's violin concertos satisfactorily, I no more believe than that he could have written a single note of either the one or the other. He formed a distinct violin school, and for that he wrote exclusively, confining himself almost wholly to the performance of his own compositions, which consisted chiefly of prettiness, rather than high merit, as the groundwork for variations intended to display his mechanism to the utmost advantage. It would be folly to call his writings concertos, so long as the two great works already mentioned and those of Spohr remain. Their construction was as weak as their purpose was trifling, and when he had played them, the impression could but remain that " the game was scarcely worth the candle." Yet De Beriot has taken, and will continue to hold, rank in the forefront of the many celebrated violinists of the last fifty years. If only on account of his perseverance, his intense study, and his laborious career, he would deserve honourable mention ; yet he had talent supervening upon these qualities of a high order, and, therefore, has left an imperishable fame behind him.

De Beriot was by birth a Belgian, having been born at Louvain, February 20, 1802. At nine years of age he became an orphan, and, fortunately for his immediate wants as for the success of his future career, found not only a tutor for the violin, but a second father, in M. Tiby, a musical professor of some eminence. For ten years he practised incessantly to overcome the mechanical difficulties of his instrument, with the steady determination of improving upon the school of his master Jacotot, which was held by his countrymen in the highest estimation.

On reaching his 19th year, De Beriot left Louvain for Paris, his first and chief desire being to play to Viotti, who at that time was the musical director of the opera. So much satisfaction did he afford to this old and celebrated master, that he encouraged him to persevere with his studies, whilst he commended him for what he had accomplished, and strongly advised him to imitate no one, but to form a style of his own. Although the impression such sound advice made upon him sank deeply into his mind, it did not prevent him from entering the Conservatoire, that he might there have the advantage of obtaining lessons from De Baillot, professor of the violin in that institution. He remained but a month under this tuition, since his master felt that he was already capable of going out upon his opening career without farther aid or instruction. Having broken ground at Paris, and met with every encouragement, he left that capital for England, where he established a reputation that went on increasing so long as he was before the public. Having travelled in company with Malibran to Italy, he eventually married her, and derived the greatest advantage from the advice that gifted woman was able to impart. She, indeed, was the means of very considerably drawing him out of the comparatively cold manner which was always associated with his playing, by imparting somewhat of that spirit and animation to him which she, more than any *artiste* of her time, possessed. After her lamented and lamentable decease—of which I shall have hereafter to give the true version, as I heard it from her mother's lips—De Beriot settled at Brussels, and only once previously (in 1840) to his death, which took place in the year 1870, left it for Vienna, where he gave one or two concerts. In the latter days of his life he became wholly blind ; but to the very last his instrument was his constant companion and solace, although his playing, like his life, was but the wreck of what it had been before the greatest calamity he ever had to bear fell upon him. I knew but little of him, although I was frequently meeting him in society. His manner, like his playing, was cold and unsympathetic ; and as on every occasion of being with him it seemed as if one had to make his acquaintance afresh, he obtained but few friends, whilst he raised up a host of enemies, whom he found, to his cost, were not to be appeased by any explanations that either he, or those who knew him best, could offer concerning his strange conduct* immediately after the decease of the woman who loved him with the utmost intensity of affection, and to whom he was as warmly attached as his naturally cold temperament permitted him to be.

I cannot close the "Recollections" of the year 1833 without mentioning my having made, during the earlier part of it, the acquaintance of Clara Anastasia Novello, an *artiste*, who alone, of all the English female singers I ever heard or met with, was worthy of being compared with the Billingtons and Salmons of earlier years. Clara Novello was about sixteen years old when she was introduced to me. Having at nine years of age been first taught the rudiments of her art at York by Mr. Robinson —the organist of the Catholic chapel in that city—she was transferred by her parents to a religious musical institution at Paris, where, being well grounded, she returned to London, and was placed under the tuition of Moscheles and Costa. Her father, himself an eminent musician, feeling that the time was come

---

* In leaving Manchester, after giving directions for his wife's funeral before she died at the Moseley Hotel. De Beriot left for Paris to secure her property.

for her appearance in public, if she were ever to "make her mark," brought her out at first by means of concerts in the provinces ; and it was at Oxford, in the spring of 1833, that I first saw and heard her. The song by which she made an impression there, as elsewhere, was written expressly for her by her father, and entitled "The Infant's Prayer"—a composition of considerable merit, the chief points of which were rendered most impressive by her manner of delivering them, no less than by her juvenile appearance, although the peculiarity of her dress, but more especially the singular arrangement of her hair, caused no small amount of ridicule. She remained with her father and mother several days at Oxford, and was so charmed with the beauty and grandeur of that find old city, that in all after time, whenever I met with her, she never ceased to dilate upon the impression the colleges, halls, and other public buildings made upon a mind then peculiarly impressionable. After having made a highly successful *début* in London, Liverpool, and Ireland, Clara Novello departed for Germany, singing and increasing her reputation, as an *artiste* of the highest rank, at Leipsic, Dresden, Munich, and Vienna, studying all the while with the utmost perseverance, and with the determination to do well in everything she undertook. From Germany she went to Russia, and at St. Petersburg confirmed the favourable reports that had preceded her. Returning homewards she sang at Dusseldorf and Weimar, and had the good fortune to obtain the approbation and friendship of Mendelssohn. On her arrival in London she sang for a short time at her Majesty's Theatre, and then again left for Italy, where, at Padua, Bologna, Genoa, Modena, and Rome, she excited more enthusiasm than she had even roused in Germany. At the latter place she became engaged to the Count Gigliucci, an Italian gentleman of good fortune and excellent position, to whom, after the Birmingham Festival of 1843, she was married. She then retired from her profession, to the regret of all, who had foreseen in her the English *prima donna, par excellence,* who would restore that prestige which had been in abeyance since the decline of Mrs. Salmon, and the retirement of Miss Stephens and Mrs. Wood. From political circumstances, in which the Count Gigliucci became involved, and the deprivation of his fortune by the tyranny of the Austrian Government, it became necessary for Clara Novello once more to return to the practice of her art ; which she did not only with undiminished powers, but with a largely increased amount of excellence, taking her part in the performance of oratorios and sacred music, as well as appearing at concerts both in London and the provinces—but not again returning to the stage—and giving the utmost satisfaction to a host of admirers ; so that it came with truth to be said of her as it had been of Braham in his day,* " There is no such soprano as Clara Novello in Europe." But as her after-career belongs to years in advance of the period about which I am now writing, I defer consideration respecting her for future illustration.

* See p. 67.

CHAPTER X

1833—34.

BEFORE wholly concluding the " Recollections," that are most vivid respecting the musical events of 1833, I ought to have made mention—and this record indeed would be imperfect without my doing so—of an event which to myself was one of the greatest enjoyment, the witnessing the presentation of Beethoven's *Fidelio*, for the first time in London, according to the German score, on June 18th, at Covent Garden Theatre, with the following remarkable cast :—Leonora, Madame Schröder-Devrient; Marcelline, Madame Meissinger; Don Fernando de Selva, Herr Gunther; Don Pizarro, Herr Dobler; Florestan, Herr Haitzinger ; Rocquo, Herr Uetz ; and Jacquino, Herr Meissinger. The fame of Madame Schröder-Devrient had not only preceded her, but the effect of her performances in Mozart's *Zauberflöte* and Weber's *Euryanthe* had more thoroughly established her in popular favour than any testimony from abroad concerning her talent could possibly have effected. It was no enviable task on the part of this celebrated *cantatrice* to enter the lists against so formidable a rival as Malibran—and especially in the character of Leonora in Beethoven's only opera; but her reading was so widely different, and her method so much more suited to the music as

adapted to the German words—the only means of really
making any one thoroughly understand the composer's mind,
alike in Mozart's operas, as in this instance—that a discerning
public could scarcely fail to prefer the "new love" to the
"old."   It may well be conceived what were my impressions on
listening to the grandest specimen of modern opera, after *Il
Don Giovanni*, as represented in its entirety according to the
German intention of the colossal master of harmony.   Impassioned as Malibran's version was—especially in the prison
scene of the second act—and much as I desired to believe that
great *artiste* to be the best interpreter that could be ever met
with of the affectionate and courageous wife, who consents to dig
her husband's grave, if she can only thereby be the means of
saving him from the vengeance of his deadliest foe, I cannot
but confess that Madame Schröder-Devrient's version threw a
new light upon the entire character, the charm of which was its
thorough realism in every look and word, and especially in the
rendering of the most eloquent music that has ever been noted
down.   The sudden burst of resolute determination with which
she confronted the would-be assassin, and the piercing manner
—half shriek, half vocal tone—with which she flung, as it
were, the words "Sein weib!" at him, was truly electrical.
It made one's blood curdle—a sensation not removed until the
stage was relieved of the presence of her antagonist, whom she
followed, pistol in hand, to the very edge of the dungeon stairs,
when she sank into her husband's arms, and was at once the
true, confiding woman, who, now that he was safe, gave up all
courage, all resolution, all farther strain upon her heart-strings.
Her singing of the duet that follows was a thrilling manifestation of all these feelings—hysterical, in fact, as could but be

the case had the scene been real instead of acted. Ably—most ably—was Madame Schröder-Devrient, supported by Herr Haitzinger, who, though not possessed of a sympathetic tenor voice—what German ever was?—was a true artist of the noblest stamp. The other characters were admirably filled; but the impression they might have left behind them was completely obliterated by the heroine, alike of the opera as of the evening.

The year 1833 closed with a tolerably successful manifestation of the new effort towards progress, which had been gradually increasing under many discouraging circumstances ever since the engagement of Weber induced Mr. C. Kemble to go out of the old and beaten track of operatic management. The directors of the two patent theatres were at first by no means willing to note the signs of the times, or to go heartily with them. But the fact was at length forced upon their somewhat stubborn minds, that English opera, hitherto so-called, was dying, as it deserved to do, of inanition, and that, if music were to secure its truly legitimate position, something more than three-act adaptations of popular novels, interspersed with a few songs and duets, and perhaps a concerted finale or two, must be mounted liberally, and creditably sung and acted. The *Gustave* of Auber having had a tremendous success in Paris, it was, after much deliberation and consultation, deemed advisable to fit it for the Covent Garden stage, and Mr. Planché was forthwith instructed to prepare English words, in the event of a concession from the composer and the Grand Opera being obtained. As Christmas was approaching, it was deemed advisable that spectacle, for which Covent Garden had become famous, should be resorted to, in order to gratify those whom the music alone might not have sufficient influence to please, that, both the eye and the ear being satisfied at the same time, "pleasure and profit might be the result." So extravagant, indeed, was the extent to which this inclination ran, that "former successes" in the same direction were said to "have been thrown into the shade;" whilst productions which were thought splendid before, now twinkled in the mind's eye like rushlights when compared with the gas of *Gustavus III.*[*] The manner in which Mr. Planché Anglicised the plot was deservedly spoken of as an instance of good taste and skill, since he studiously rejected senseless innovations, and proved himself not merely a clever dramatist, for that was shown before, but well entitled to the F.S.A. which was added to his name. The musical arrangements were placed in the hands of the veteran "Tom Cooke," who led the orchestra and conducted the performance. The female singers who "created" this English version were Mdmes. Inverarity (the Countess Ankastrom) and Shirreff (the Page), whilst Mr. H. Phillips (Count Ankastrom), Mr. Wilson,[†] Mr. Templeton, and Mr. Seguin supported the other leading male characters. Of the ladies it may be said that the one achieved a greater success than the other, and so captivated the general public, that not only were crowds drawn to Covent Garden almost expressly to hear her version of the "Invitation to the Ball," but the very errand-boys in the streets whistled that pretty and sparkling air as they had whistled nothing else since the introduction of *Der Freischütz.* Mr. H. Phillips had never appeared to greater advantage in any previous opera, and exhibited a degree of "interest and manly feeling" which would have made "a somewhat dis-

---

[*] See *Athenæum* for 1833, p. 780.
[†] See pp. 212, 214.

agreeable part" stand its ground well even without the powerful aid of his musical talent. "Messrs. Wilson, Templeton, and
Seguin also left nothing to be desired, and contributed greatly
to the general success by the able manner in which, they both
sung and acted. The costumes were magnificent, and with
the exception of one or two concessions to stage effects, were
generally correct. The *mise en scène* was appropriate and
beautiful throughout, and the ball scene, with which the opera
terminated, surpassed not only in grandeur, but in chasteness
and elegance, all that had ever been beheld either on our own
or on the Parisian stage."*

Whilst this English version of Auber's *Gustave* was having a
prosperous run, the manager of Drury Lane, not to be outdone
by his patented rival "over the way," brought out a version of
the same composer's *Masaniello*, with Braham as the Neapolitan
fisherman; but the music was so cut about and mutilated, and the
general arrangements were so imperfect, that it received anything but the hearty welcome that had been anticipated for it.
How fearfully the score was excised may be inferred from this
simple fact, that on the occasion when I "assisted" at its performance, it was given as an after-piece, Lord Byron's *Sarda-
napalus*—with Macready as the Babylonian Sybarite, and Miss
Ellen Tree—afterwards Mrs. Charles Kean—as Myrrha, the
Greek slave—having been previously performed. Until, therefore, *Masaniello* was given some years afterwards at the Royal
Italian Opera, Covent Garden—to which I shall have by-and-by
to refer—Auber's *chef-d'œuvre* may be said never to have been
heard in this country.

The season of 1834 opened by no means propitiously at the

* See *Athenæum* for 1833, p. 780.

King's Theatre on Saturday, March 1st, and gave no promise whatever of the brilliant prospects that were in store for the *habitués* and the opera-going public. The opera on that occasion was Rossini's *La Gazza Ladra;* but the Ninetta (Mdme. Fearon, a very second-rate *artiste* indeed) totally failed to win approbation, and the Pippo—Mrs. Anderson, a younger sister of Mdme. Vestris—was accepted as a mere stop-gap.

Madame Fearon was an Englishwoman, and first came before the public about the year 1811 or 1812, as the articled pupil of a violin-player named Cobham. " Her voice at that time was brilliant in its tone, very extensive in its upward compass, and of great volume. Her master " was said to " have drawn his ideas of vocal art chiefly from the branch he exercised, and cultivated execution principally, and that execution by no means in the best manner. Her talents were somewhat abused in the exertion to which he submitted them ; for she was taken round the country, announced with the cognomen of 'the English Catalani,' and exhibited wherever a few guineas were to be earned. Such a course of training was not likely to confer any great celebrity, and Miss Glossop—that was her real name— quitted England for Italy, where she remained for a considerable time, enjoying good instruction and the advantage of singing in the first theatres, her husband having been joint proprietor with Signor Barbaja,* of those of Milan and Naples ; " so that, when she returned to England in 1827, she " did so with all this ripening practice and experience. Such a singer must, of course, have excited high anticipations." Nevertheless, she caused nothing else than disappointment to those best qualified to judge, inasmuch as " so completely had her Italian instruction

* See pp. 262, 263.

and taste been absorbed and neutralised by the practice of English," that she belonged neither to the one school, nor to the other. She, indeed, "presented the most curious and complete example" of this defect; "for after a residence of many years upon the Continent, surrounded by all that could change and denationalise the mind and the habits, after performing continually upon the Italian stage in Italy, and, of course, giving herself up entirely to Italian feeling and conforming herself to Italian manner, she came back to England, and at once took a supreme place upon the English boards, without any trace of foreign acquisition that disturbed even the prejudices of a native and mixed audience." *

But for the male characters—Curioni† (Giannetto), Giubelei (Podesta), and Zuchelli ‡ (Ferdinando)—the performance would have been positively unendurable. "Curioni was cordially greeted after his temporary absence; but time had told its tale on his powers, while it had dealt leniently with Zuchelli, who personated the deserter with great feeling and effect." Giubelei —whom I then heard for the first time—was considered wholly unequal to the part of the Podesta, having neither sufficient comic talent, nor histrionic capacity to compass its requirements.

The latter singer was a useful rather than a brilliant acquisition to the King's Theatre. He was one of those ready men, who could always be relied upon in an emergency, being thoroughly up to the necessary work he was called upon to

* See the *Quarterly Magazine and Review*, vol. ix. pp. 351, 359. Madame Fearon was the mother of Mr. Augustus Harris, the stage-manager of the Royal Italian Opera, Covent Garden, under Mr. F. Gye's lesseeship, for many years past. Her last engagement was at the Princess's Theatre, under Mr. Maddox's management.

† See p. 153.   ‡ See p. 149.

undertake; but he was apt to sing out of tune, and had the misfortune rarely to be placed in any position in which he could thoroughly do himself justice. He made his first appearance in London on the occasion of Mdme. Puzzi's—*née* Toso—*début*,* in the middle of March, 1827, in the version of Rossini's *Moïse* which was prepared so as to satisfy the scruples of the British public under the title of *Pietro l'Eremita.* On this occasion he played the "hermit," and was thus spoken of by a competent critic :—"Signor Giubelei's voice is agreeable, and his manner at once modest and good; but nature does not seem to have done enough to render him a great, though he may become a very useful singer. He is tall in person and easy in his manner, and his acting is of the same standard with his singing."† I did not hear him until the occasion already mentioned, and, although six years had elapsed since these remarks had been written, he had certainly made no progress to warrant a higher appreciation of his qualities. He was without question one of the ugliest men that ever lived, and in addition to this he squinted fearfully. In after time he was of great service in playing with Adelaide Kemble at Covent Garden in an English version of Bellini's *Norma,* and one or two other operas; but he did no more then and there than he had already accomplished at the Italian Opera House. After fulfilling this engagement, he retired to America, where he obtained much greater popularity than he would ever have won on this side of the Atlantic, either in England or abroad, and died there a few years afterwards.

Rubini and Tamburini having arrived, although somewhat

---

* See p. 146.

† See the *Quarterly Magazine and Review,* vol. ix. p. 53.

later than they had been looked for, M. Laporte was able to put
up the *Barbiere* on Saturday, April 6th, which, as it always is,
was sufficiently attractive to silence complaints that are ever
ready to be made about operatic mismanagement. The following
Tuesday, April 8th, 1834, was, however, to compensate for every
disappointment, and to remain for ever in the records of the
doings of the King's Theatre as a night " marked with white
chalk,"* for on that ever memorable occasion Giulia Grisi made
her *début* before a London audience.   It seems but yesterday
that I sauntered towards the Haymarket, as I was then so often
in the habit of doing, merely *pour passer le temps*, without
having the slightest expectation of hearing anything—or anybody—extraordinary ; for I did not even know what opera had
been *affichéd*, and if I had heard tell that a *débutante* was about
to try her vocation, it would have afforded me the smallest
amount of interest.   The reasons for this state of mind were
obvious, because I had heard little or nothing, so far as soprano
prime donne were concerned, during the previous season, and I
had, like many others, come almost to believe that there could be
no rival found to compete with the goddess of universal idolatry,
Marie Malibran, whose services M. Laporte had never seemed to
value—whether on account of his own or that excitable woman's
caprices, nobody seemed to be able to tell.   On entering the pit
on that memorable night, the first person of my acquaintance
whom I met was the late Mr. Edward Taylor, afterwards the
Gresham Professor of Music,† who, accosting me by my Christian
name—he had known me from my childhood—asked whether I

---

* " Cressâ ne careat pulchra dies nota."—Hor. Carm. I. xxxvi. 10.
         " Hunc, Macrine, diem numera meliore lapillo,
              Qui tibi labentes apponit candidus annos."—Perseus, ii. I. sqq.
† See p. 51, and p. 208.

had come purposely to hear the new singer. Great was his surprise, when I told him, that not only had I not done so, but that I was wholly ignorant both as to the opera itself, and who were to sing in it. The overture was played—and so well played that it received a hearty encore; notwithstanding, some signs of impatience were shown at the delay its repetition necessarily occasioned for the appearance of the new singer. Scarcely a note of the opening of the opera was heard, owing to the hum of conversation that was going on in every direction. The scene descriptive of the expectation of the young soldier's (Giannetto) return, and the teasing of the magpie by Pippo (Mrs. Anderson) only to get his fingers bitten, passed all but in dumb show until the moment arrived for the *entrée* of Ninetta, when the house was on the instant so hushed that the slightest whisper might have been heard. When Grisi came down the bridge upon the stage, there was on the instant such a burst of applause that made the house ring from end to end. Not one in a hundred who had come to hear her knew anything whatever about her musical qualities. They had listened to her sister, Giudetta Grisi, two seasons previously, only to be disappointed, and a similar repetition, for aught they could tell, might once more be in store for them ; but the personal beauty of that youthful Italian face, the slimness of her figure, and the modest confidence she manifested, seemed to act like an immediate charm, and to rouse even the most impassive into a state bordering upon little else than wild excitement. Scarcely, however, had she given the first bar of the "Di piacer," than her success was achieved. The peculiarity of her rich and full tone, the decision of her manner, and the undoubted signs of her proficiency, disarmed all criticism, and made her at once that favourite she never ceased to be so long as she remained in the full vigour of her powers. In confirmation of the accuracy of this impression, nothing can be more to the point than the following piece of just criticism, which was immediately afterwards written by one thoroughly qualified to express an accurate judgment :—

"And now, room for Mdlle. Giulia Grisi (*la jolie Grisi*, as the Parisians call her, to distinguish her from her sister). It is long since we have seen so triumphant an appearance upon these boards, or an audience so alive to every beauty of acting and singing as the audience of Tuesday evening assembled to pronounce upon the new *prima donna*. Mdlle. Grisi's appearance is sufficient to make a most favourable first impression. Her voice, and style, and (perhaps above all) her acting, to confirm it, all three leave little or nothing to be wished. She is gifted with a good figure, and a handsome and expressive face, in the first instance; in the second, she has a rich, clear, powerful, and extremely flexible voice ; her execution is at times exuberant, but it goes along with the passion of her part, and carries the hearer away with her. We were certain of her feeling in the first part of 'Di piacer ; ' we were not, however, aware of the fulness of it till the second act, when her leading of the quartet, 'Gia di pinto,' and the sudden outbreak of despair in the scene where she is led to execution, excited us to the highest possible degree."*

Grisi had the immense advantage of being most admirably

* See *Athenæum* for 1834, p. 274. The notice in the *Morning Post* of Grisi's *début* was written by Mr. C. L. Gruneisen, then a young and rising musical critic, whose just and appropriate remarks, that *prima donna* always insisted, helped materially to give her that position she so long and ably maintained.

assisted by Rubini (Giannetto), Tamburini (Fernando), and Zuchelli (the Podesta), each of whom seemed to vie with the others to render so auspicious an event one that never should be forgotten by those who had the privilege of witnessing it. The only drawback to the cast was the Pippo of Mrs. Anderson, who was utterly unfitted for the position she occupied; so much so, indeed, that, in consequence of her incompetence, the beautiful duet, "Ebben per mia memoria," one of Rossini's most touching compositions, had of necessity to be omitted.

Inasmuch as Giulia Grisi's appearance in Donizetti's *Anna Bolena* was one of the most important events of the opera season of 1834, a reference to the criticism of the *Times* on the following morning (Wednesday, April 16th) may not be without interest :—"If we could dismiss such a performance, as our limited space almost impels us to do, by a single sentence, we might be content with saying that she has confirmed by it the impression she made on her first appearance. To those who witnessed that, there cannot be higher praise, and it is honestly and strictly her due. Her singing and acting of the character are both so truly beautiful, that it is difficult to say which of them stands in the higher rank, or displays the greater genius. We feared at the commencement that this ungenial climate of ours had somewhat injured her fine voice ; and her first scenes, in fact, evinced a want of vigour ; but here was soon discernible the judicious reserve of a first-rate artist. As her subject rose in interest, she warmed with it; and her first interview with Percy ; her discovery with him by the King ; her detection of the King's motive in seeking to make her appear guilty ; the celebrated scene with Jane Seymour ; that with Percy, in which she reverts to their former attachment ;

and, above all, the scene previous to her being led off to execution,—were a succession of effects judicious in conception and masterly in execution. Her disdainful burst at the King's intimation that the judges would hear her defence, was remarkably fine; but the most beautiful point, we think, in her acting was in the last scene, where the horrible incident is introduced of the bridal procession of her rival close to the walls of her prison, as she is about to be conducted to the scaffold. She had sunk on her knees in a state of mournful abstraction in the front of the stage, and at the sound of the rejoicings is roused from it with the feeling that she is again free and happy with her former friends, till a review of the scene around her brings her back to the sense of her dreadful situation. All these transitions were depicted with a truth and force which could not be surpassed. Her singing was exquisite throughout, far too good for the music; but it might be said to give it a new charm, so much did the workmanship excel the material."

Having repeated the parts of Ninetta and Anna Bolena twice, if I remember rightly, in the interval, Grisi next undertook the *rôle* of Desdemona in Rossini's *Otello*, April 22nd, and completed the triumph she had most positively won in *La Gazza Ladra*,* although her conception and delineation of the old Venetian's daughter were, in some respects, wanting in that energy and *abandon* which were expected of her. It was not till some time afterwards that she refined upon her first personation of this character; but even when she had done her

---

* Grisi appeared on Tuesday, April 15th, in Donizetti's *Anna Bolena*, when Ivanhoff made his *début*; but as I had not the opportunity of being present on that occasion, I defer my " Recollections " of the latter to what I heard of him a few nights later. See p. 294.

best with it, it could never be compared for impulsiveness, passion, or tenderness, with Malibran's well-known version. The fact was, that the one was a genius of the most original and positive stamp—the other scarcely ever made a sensation except by reason of imitation. When Mdme. Viardot heard Pasta for the first time in her life, in her decay, she uttered a most forcible truth in saying, " Now I know where Grisi got all her greatness." It was from Pasta that the original Adalgisa obtained the impression how the *Norma* and *Anna Bolena* should be rendered ; as it was from Malibran that she gained an insight into the requirements necessary for a truthful delineation of the unhappy girl, " who loved not wisely but too well," and, as it likewise was many years afterwards, that she learned what was to be made of Valentina in Meyerbeer's *Les Huguenots*, by having witnessed Mdme. Viardot's perfect version of that interesting character. This, however, is not a matter to complain of, since in nothing that she imitated did she fail, except in the Fides in Meyerbeer's *Prophète*, which she had the good sense to lay aside so soon as she had ascertained that it was not within the compass of her means, either vocal or histrionic, to make anything of it. Grisi had the misfortune also to be no musician, as I have already said ; * but no *artiste* that ever lived was more conscientious than herself in mastering the details of any part she undertook to play; and when once she had got the notes and words by heart, and had impressed upon her mind the " necessities " of the scenes, she never forgot them. Her memory was as prodigious as her study was rapid ; and no *prima donna* that ever lived was so ready as she was on the instant to go upon the stage and act any one of the charac-

* See p. 120.

ters of her extensive *répertoire*, no matter how many months or years had elapsed since she had appeared therein. And this continued to the last; so that, save when prevented from fulfilling her duties by indisposition, she was never known, during the whole term of her long career, to have disappointed an audience because of her being imperfect in her " words " or music.

On the occasion of the *Otello* being given, the strength of the cast was fully equal to that which had marked the *début* of Grisi on the previous 8th of April. Rubini appeared as the fiery Moor, and sang the music with his usual exquisite taste; but in his acting he was by many degrees inferior to Donzelli, and not to be named in the same year with Garcia. Indeed, throughout most of the scenes Rubini may be said to have only " walked through the part," and gave scarcely the slightest effect to the first triumphant *intrata*, or to the recitative and duet of the last act, in each of which Garcia completely carried his hearers away with him, and to which Donzelli gave very considerable effect. Zuchelli played the part of Elmiro—the Brabantio of Shakespeare—and obtained some success in the denunciation of the curse, which was looked upon as unrivalled, until Lablache gave afterwards a version that made one's blood positively curdle. Tamburini's Iago was a finished performance, but manifested none of the villany of the character which Ronconi in after time imparted to it. His singing, however, was so equal, finished, and pure, that in every portion of the scene in which he had to be present, and especially in the trio, ' Te parle d' amore," nothing whatever remained to be desired.

To myself the appearance of Giulia Grisi in Rossini's *Otello*, was scarcely less remarkable than that in which she had made

her first curtsey before the *habitués* of the King's Theatre;
for it was then that I heard Ivanhoff—for the first time, in the
rôle of Roderigo—who had already taken a position scarcely
second to Rubini. In spite of the opinion, generally expressed,
that the new-comer had yet to acquire a fine pronunciation of
the Italian language, so difficult to all foreigners—he was by
birth a Russian serf—and that his exterior and physiognomy
were far from striking and prepossessing, it was admitted that
he was evidently a very good musician, and in all respects a
great acquisition to the King's Theatre. Ivanhoff's voice
although placed in the category of tenors, was, from its high
compass, more strictly an alto ; and when not too much exerted
was flexible and of good quality. In the upper part of his
scale he had greater force than Rubini possessed, and in the
union of the chest and head voices he was somewhat more
equal, whilst he also firmly sustained his notes ; but he most
certainly had to yield to the Italian in intensity of feeling and
facility of execution. He was, however, deficient in power,
which was easily enough discovered when he sang anywhere
else than at the King's Theatre ; so that whenever he put
forth any effort—which was, it must be confessed, but seldom—
the result was almost always injurious. He had, besides, not
the slightest idea of acting. It seemed to him to be enough to
walk upon the stage, to take up his cue whenever it came
round, and to sing what had been written for him ; but then he
sang so sweetly, and attracted approbation by the manner in
which, by means of a *diminuendo*, he reduced his tone to a
mere whisper, that it was scarcely possible to be vexed, or to
find fault, with him. He made little or nothing of the small
part of Roderigo in Rossini's *Otello*, much less than he had

done as Percy in Donizetti's *Anna Bolena;* but he was at once accepted as a singer belonging to the first rank; and this—without the slightest improvement of manner, method, or action—he retained to the last.*

The brilliant success of *La Gazza Ladra, Anna Bolena,* and *Otello,* combined with the general favour in which the two new *débutants* almost equally shared, did not induce M. Laporte to remain content with three such stock pieces to work upon; for on the following Thursday (April 25th) an admirable performance—as it was on all hands admitted to be—was given of Mozart's *Il Don Giovanni* for Zuchelli's benefit, who on that occasion condescended to sustain—and very admirably too—the character of Leporello to Tamburini's version of the title *rôle,* which, so long as the latter remained upon the stage, he continued to "hold against all comers." It was on this occasion that Giulia Grisi first sustained the difficult part of Donna Anna, and gave a version of it that has never since been surpassed—I might indeed add—and never by the "shadow of a shade" equalled. Whether she had ever seen any other *artiste* in this part, I cannot tell; but immensely as it was in advance of any other Donna Anna I had before—or ever since have—known, I am convinced that she must have done so, or at least have given herself up entirely to Signor Costa's tuition, advice, and direction. To have had such a conception of the requirements of the part as she manifested was not within the compass of her natural intelligence. Like everything else, it must have been "created" for her, since she never seemed to have the mental acquirements to strike out anything new for herself. However it might have been, no greater Donna Anna has ever

---

* Ivanhoff is still living, residing at Bologna.

been heard since Mozart wrote his *chef-d'œuvre.* The intensity
of passion she threw into the opening scene, wherein the out-
raged woman struggles with the libertine, was overwhelming,
and only surpassed by the following situation, wherein she discovered that the Don was her father's murderer. The screaming tone—yet perfectly in tune, as round and full as it could
possibly be—with which she uttered the expression, "Gran
Dio!" rings in my ears whilst I write of it, and never ceased
to electrify myself, as it did thousands of hearers, even up to
the time when, with decayed powers and failing strength, she
ought to have remained in that retirement she did not seek
one moment too soon, and from which she so unwisely again
and again emerged, and would again have done but a short
time before her death, if she could have met with any *entrepreneur* rash enough to have offered her an engagement. Of
Tamburini's version of the Don I have already expressed an
opinion,* which, formed on this, the first occasion of my seeing
him in it, I never changed. To those who had never heard
Ambrogetti or Garcia in the same opera, I can well imagine
that he will remain the best Don Giovanni of their day; but
as compared with the version of those two giants, Tamburini's
was weak indeed. His frantic struggling with the statue in
the last scene was spoken of very highly; but there was nothing
about it of the terror that Ambrogetti imparted to the incident,
and less of the heroic determination that Garcia manifested.
There was no mind, in fact, in the delineation, the struggle
being little else than a ridiculous wriggle to get free. The
start with which he evidenced the thrill the cold statue might
naturally be supposed to have driven through his frame was an

* See p. 239.

excellent "point," but all that followed was little else than mean and commonplace. The cast of this opera was of the strongest, for besides the *artistes* already named, Madame Caradori was the Zerlina, Madame E. Seguin the Donna Elvira; Rubini, Don Ottavio; and Giubelei, Masetto.

On Tuesday, May 27th, Rossini's *La Donna del Lago* was revived, for the purpose of introducing a new contralto, Madame degli Antoni, in the *rôle* of Malcolm; but neither the opera itself, although supported by Grisi, Rubini, Donzelli, and Curioni, nor the *débutante* afforded the anticipated satisfaction, the former having been given in anything but a complete state, and the latter scarcely obtaining a *succès d'estime*. And no wonder; for, although possessed of a mezzo-soprano voice of considerable compass, it was much too weak in the lower register to have been rightly called a contralto. Comparisons could not fail to be drawn between this lady and Pisaroni,* who had been the more recent exponent of the part, and these were greatly to the poor lady's disadvantage. It was feared that M. Laporte, being somewhat inflated with success, was about to resort to tricks similar to those with which the season had been inaugurated; and not even the brilliancy which had been apparent at every performance since the ever-to-be-remembered Easter Tuesday of Grisi's *début*, or the production of Rossini's *L'Assedio di Corinto* on Thursday, June 5th, with Grisi, Rubini, Ivanhoff, Giubelei, and Tamburini in the principal parts, served to remove this very general impression. During the progress of the scene of this opera, Grisi introduced a song, written expressly for her by Signor Costa, which, unlike most interpolations, was exceedingly well adapted

* See pp. 167, 168.

to the situation, and met with an enthusiastic reception. Of this opera—now never heard—it may be most appropriately and truly said, that its success did not arise from the mere brilliancy of a *scèna*, or the tunefulness of a melody, but from those concerted pieces and dramatic adaptations of sound to sense, which afford the greatest delight. There was, in fact, an *ensemble* in this opera, which made itself felt at once as an immense improvement on anything Rossini had previously produced. " In the first place, the introduction had a clearness, a force, and a freshness which none of Rossini's many *diluters* had ever reached."* As regarded the singers, Grisi was, except in the instance already mentioned, scarcely at her best; but Rubini appeared to greater advantage than he had yet been heard or seen, whilst Tamburini, as usual, was full of energy, and sang splendidly. Ivanhoff had little else to do than deliver an interpolated song in the second act, which was the only opportunity really of hearing him to anything like advantage, because his other music by no means suited his voice, and seemed as if it had been transposed. Much effort was made to give greater effect than usual to the chorus and *mise en scène;* but the time had not then arrived when perfection could be attained in this respect, and the public had to look—but look in vain—for principals, who could emulate the glories of those great *artistes*, who were, at the time of which I am writing, the sole prop and mainstay of the theatres wherein their invaluable services were engaged.

Soon after the introduction of Rossini's *L'Assedio di Corinto*, one single performance of the same writer's *Barbiere* was given, which was indeed an event to be remembered, since it embraced

* See *Athenæum* for 1834, p. 458.

a cast that since that time has not been surpassed. Indeed, it can scarcely be said how that cast by any possibility could have been improved, when it is stated that Grisi, Rubini, Tamburini, and Giubelei were included therein. No mean or incompetent critic told, indeed, more than the truth when he wrote of this performance, that " its perfection was such as to make him forget how often he had listened to ' Piano, pianissimo,' and how long he had been tired with ' Zitti, zitti.' It afforded a proof," he said, " if any were wanting—that the extreme of vivacity and the presence of refinement were quite compatible. Grisi and Tamburini "—although the latter was generally but a dull Figaro, as has been already intimated*—" seemed to act, from the inspiration of the moment, and to pour out their melodies and cadenzas, not because they were written, but as if they could not help it ; and the consequence was, as might have been expected, rapturous applause." " Worn out as the opera is,"—the same critic thus proceeds, expressing an opinion, with which very few indeed would now agree, since the *Barbiere* still " holds the stage," and is never unwelcome,—" Worn out as the opera is, it is worth coming any distance to see in its present cast ; and we shall accept of no other Figaro in place of Tamburini, who seems to revel in the part from the ' Largo al factotum,' with which it begins, to the ' Felicita,' with which every Italian *opera buffa* concludes, as a matter of course."†

The next novelty of the season was Grisi's attempt to play the part of Amina in Bellini's *Sonnambula*. I say "attempt," because, although to a certain extent successful, it was not to

---

* See p. 239.
† See *Athenæum* for 1834, p. 523.

be compared with Malibran's version, with which the public were then familiar, or with Pasta's, which had well-nigh been forgotten. Triumphant as the new *Diva's* career had been, from her first appearance to the eve of its close, she would have done well and wisely to have at least postponed her appearance in this character, if not to have declined ever to have appeared in it. But the spirit of rivalry was inherent in her nature, and against Malibran she at once pitted herself, as she also did against her sister, Pauline Garcia, afterwards Madame Viardot, as if on purpose to justify the decision of Severini, the manager of Les Italiens in Paris, in permitting the former of these great *artistes* to cancel her engagement in a moment of pique and discontent. Since Grisi then came to the rescue, as the only successful *artiste* of four, sent from Italy expressly to Paris to supply Malibran's place, it really seemed as if she were on set purpose bent upon keeping up a species of operatic "vendetta" that never was to cease. Without doubt her genuine success at the King's Theatre was a source of annoyance to Malibran, since it clearly enough demonstrated that her services, valuable as they were, could be dispensed with; and if they could be rendered anywhere at all, it must be on the English stage—which actually came to pass—where, although her *prestige* was infinitely less than had she been at "the great theatre in the Haymarket," the success was, to all intents and purposes, enormous. That Grisi, therefore, for the time being, crushed Malibran, there can be no doubt; but that the "Garcia" would have had her revenge is more than probable, since she was rapidly recovering her diminished position, when she was untowardly smitten by the hand of death at the Manchester Musical Festival of the year 1836.

The legitimate end of this truly brilliant season arrived on
Tuesday, August 12, with a performance of the *Barbiere ;* and
as it was without exception the most important of those performances I have already recorded, I could not refrain from giving
it all the attention it seems to have deserved, nor can I close
my " Recollections " without resuscitating some most appropriate remarks, which were immediately published concerning it.
" So far as regards the public, it (the season) has been a most
successful one, and that in spite of one novelty only having
been produced.   But the advantages of such a company as we
have had being stationary for the season, and its members thus
becoming perfectly familiar with the style of each other's singing, as well as the music they had to perform, and of a well-
disciplined chorus, have been appreciated as they deserved, and
have made us willing to overlook the tediousness of a many-
times-told tale. . . . And yet, with the remembrance of
La Gazza and *Il Barbiere* fresh in our minds, we cannot be
extreme in finding fault, and we must thank M. Laporte for a
new and very great pleasure, which his making us acquainted
with Grisi has afforded us.   Always efficient, always welcome
as she has been, it is our opinion that she is far from having
reached the fulness of her powers.   We should say that her
performance of the character of Ninetta was her best and only
faultless " serious " effort ; her Rosina left us nothing to wish.
In other parts she undertook there were brilliant points—as, for
instance, her splendid recitatives in *Don Giovanni*—but a want
of sustained energy.   In one or two cases she was more anxious
to show the perfect control she possessed over her voice than to
be Desdemona, Pamina, or Anna Bolena, and became in her
solos a mere singing-machine, instead of continuing the senti-

ment or passion of her part. But this fault time will correct.* Mind will rise superior to mechanism, and we look forward with confident anticipation to the day when she may challenge a Pasta or a Schröder on their own ground without the chance of a defeat. We are sure that every month that passes over her must mature her powers. As to voice, and skill in the management of it, she has nothing to desire or to learn. We must likewise notice with pleasure the introduction of Ivanhoff to an English audience, and his success. He, too, is to attain a far higher point of excellence than he has yet reached, if we are true prophets.† With such a perfect voice as he possesses, and such feeling as he has given evidence of, we have a right to look for much from this young *artiste.* With the rest of the *corps,* who are worthy of mention, the public is more familiar. Let the *entrepreneur* only add to their numbers Donzelli and an efficient contralto for the next season, and we shall be more than satisfied."‡

The " Recollections " of this year (1834) would be manifestly incomplete if some account were not recorded of the revival of so-called English opera in this country, with which the veteran Planché had much to do, since he fitted the libretto of Hérold's French opera, *Le Pré aux Clercs,* for representation at Covent Garden, under the title of *The Challenge,* on Tuesday, April 1st; the principal characters being sustained by Mesdames Inverarity, Shirreff, and H. Cawse; and Messrs. H. Phillips, Wilson, Seguin, and Harley. As a previous adaptation

---

* This was a defect, which in the course of a few seasons Grisi almost entirely overcame.

† This prognostication was by no means fulfilled.

‡ See *Athenæum* for 1834, p. 613.

of the work had been tried by the English Opera Company
at the Adelphi Theatre and failed, it was prognosticated that
similar misfortune awaited this second attempt. Mr. Planché
had, however, avoided one rock upon which his predecessor had
struck, by keeping the plot, which was one of an historical character, to its original soil, instead of transferring the scene and
the characters from France to England. Although this was a
decided improvement, there was one blunder in the adaptation
which English play-writers and English musicians were sure to
make, and for which they studiously and incessantly went out
of their way—the interpolation of scenes and music by different
writers, that had no more to do with either one or the other,
than a jig would be in place, if introduced before the " Halle-
lujah " chorus in Handel's *Messiah.* The English musicians of
that day could not shake off the propensity to introduce ballads,
which they seemed to think were the only means of securing a
favourable reception. They were tied and bound by the old-
fashioned system, which could not designate anything as of
an operatic character unless it had " length " after " length " of
wearisome spoken twaddle introduced by way of helping the
incidental music onward. Therefore, in *The Challenge,* a song
by some one called Blangini was given to H. Phillips in the
first act, another by T. Cooke in the second, and a duet with
Wilson by Auber in the third. The interest of the scene was
completely broken up by such interpolations, which only
served to weaken a plot by no means strong, and which would
never have lived through half a dozen evenings' performances
had not the music been most attractive. I saw this opera
twice, and was better pleased with Miss Shirreff than Miss
Inverarity ; for, whilst the former was always painstaking and

intelligent, the latter sang and spoke so low, that not one note or word in twenty that she uttered could be distinguished. Miss H. Cawse had not much to do, but what little fell to her share she did conscientiously, as was her wont. H. Phillips, although singing with his wonted taste and correctness, was without his usual animation, as if the part of the swaggering bully overweighted him ; but Wilson did himself more justice than he had ever done in anything he had previously undertaken, or afterwards attempted. Seguin was of infinite use, especially in the few concerted "numbers" that had been retained, but he never got beyond that "tip-top mediocrity" which prevented his making any position at home. When he went to America, I believe, he succeeded better ; but then the Transatlantic towns and cities were comparatively a new country, so far as music and many other matters were concerned, and what was considered bad or indifferent on this side of the three thousand miles of sea, passed for something that was oftentimes thought and said to be " better than good."*

The first real instance of the ridiculous notion about English opera being really and positively combatted was Mr. Barnett's production at the English Opera House, Aug. 25, of the *Mountain Sylph*, the libretto of which had been provided by a Mr. Thackeray upon *La Sylphide*—a ballet that had an immense run, and established the fame of Mdlle. Taglioni as the first *danseuse* of the world. It was noted as one of the most hopeful signs for the future of English opera, that the words of this libretto, both "for the songs, duets, choruses, &c.," were infinitely

---

* Mr. Wilson died in America, of cholera, whilst on a tour with his "Scotch Songs." He was originally a compositor, and was in the secret as to Sir W. Scott's novels.

superior to the run of those that had hitherto been in vogue. " There was no twaddle, no nonsense, no bad English," in these words, notwithstanding there was little or no rhyme in them that could be designated as positively good. " In short, there was really nothing to find fault with, a great deal to praise, and more than one thing to quote." As an instance, the following specimen was given as a fair example of this opinion :—

Air.—*Sylph.*

" Say, could I live, if he I love
An early grave must find ?
A lonely thing on earth to rove,
Like leaf before the wind.
O no ! if chilling death must come,
With him I love I'll die :
I fear not e'en the cold dark tomb
If on his breast I lie."

Of the manner of Mr. Barnett's setting this libretto, it is preferable to give the somewhat humorous description of a first-class critic of that day, because the opinions expressed are completely in accordance with my own, and intimate all that one could have wished to have then said, and that it is desirable now to recall :—

" We could begin at the beginning, go through to the end, praise everything more or less, and pause to give a reason for the faith that is in us ; but we must content ourselves with saying that Mr. Barnett has surpassed himself in the ballads, that he has rivalled the ballet in the concerted pieces and choruses, and that he has shown himself to be excelled by no living English composer in instrumentation. Full as all his compositions are of melody, he is certainly inferior to Mr. Bishop* in the

* See p. 155.

art of giving a descriptive character to his music ; but then so is, in our opinion, almost every composer, English or foreign, whose works are ever heard. There are several—more than several, many—of Mr. Bishop's compositions which are so curiously and minutely descriptive of the words they accompany, that we have often fancied that we could have written them underneath the notes without ever having heard them. We only mention Mr. Bishop here to show that, however we are delighted to hail such an arrival as this fine opera from what may, under the circumstances, be called a new quarter, we are not disposed to forget the merits of one who, for so many years, honourably held the place of champion in this department ; nay, who may keep it yet, perhaps, if he is inclined to fight for it ; but he must be active ; assuredly he never had so fair a chance as this which has fallen to Mr. Barnett. Let him then up, and look out for one. Let him put on his musical gloves, and in all friendliness pick a crotchet with Mr. Barnett, and try to strike him on the ear with a better opera. Mr. Barnett, who has showed that he is musically great enough to take his own part, will, no doubt, soon return the compliment. The exercise will be good for both the combatants, and the public will gain, whichever loses.

"If we are expected to call attention to any particular pieces, we must do so almost at haphazard ; however, we will mention the opening chorus. Mr. Phillips' scena, 'To me what's mortal happiness ?' the air, 'Thou art not he, whose looks of love ;' and the air, 'Farewell to the mountain,' sung in his very best style. So beautiful is this melody, and so melodiously was it warbled by Mr. Phillips, that its effect upon us was extraordinary. It was encored by a burst of applause which satisfactorily, proved the great strength of Mr. Beazley's walls; and at its conclusion the second time we felt an unaccountable inclination to lean over and pull Mr. Phillips into the box with us, though we should not have had the slightest idea what to do with him when we had got him. Mr. Thackeray is much obliged to Mr. Barnett for the admirable music in which he has enshrined his words. Mr. Barnett is much obliged to Mr. Thackeray for the opportunity he has given him of showing so much of the depth and extent of his musical resources. We are much obliged to them for the treat we have experienced, and mean to experience again; and we shall be much obliged to the public to go and judge for themselves if we are not right."* The cast of this opera included the combined talent of Mr. Aldridge (Bailie Macwhapple), Mr. Wilson (Donald), Mr. Keeley (Christie), Mr. H. Phillips (Hela), Miss E. Romer † (Eolia), Miss Novello (Etheria), and Miss Sommerville (Jessie), and had a consecutive run of unmingled popularity for a considerable period. Messrs. H. Phillips and Keeley's parts were afterwards supplied by Messrs. J. O. Atkins and Oxberry. Yet the only portion of the work which is now at all remembered is the trio, " This magic-wove scarf," and even that is rapidly fading out of memory.

Of the Philharmonic Concerts of this year there is but little to mention, beyond the fact that, if they did not add very much to their acknowledged superiority over every other instrumental performance of the time, they at least did not recede from that proud and well-earned position. At the third concert, on Monday, April 21st, Mendelssohn's MS. overture, intituled *Melusine, or the Knight and the Mermaid,* was played for the first time;

---

* *Athenæum* for 1834, pp. 644-5.

† See p. 246.

but although, like all the works of that gifted composer, it exhibited much skill and experience in the management of orchestral effects and in the treatment of its subject—which was said to be " sweet enough to be the song of any syren "—was, as a whole, less effective than most of his other compositions.* This opinion has never been reversed. This overture is indeed very seldom heard now-a-days ; but whenever it is played, it never for an instant rouses that enthusiasm which almost every other specimen of Mendelssohn's genius invariably produces. The seventh concert was only remarkable for the performance of an *air varié*, by De Beriot,† by Monsieur (or Master) Vieuxtemps, who was said to be only thirteen years of age, although he looked older, and whose playing was so extraordinary, and so little like that of the generality of prodigies, that some persons expressed a wish that Corelli's ghost could have been evoked to hear him, and others declared that "they did not think the excellent Arangelo would have ever slept quietly in his tomb again."‡

The chief musical event of the year 1834, after all, was the Handel Commemoration that was held in Westminster Abbey, on Tuesday, June 24th, Thursday the 26th, Saturday the 28th, and Tuesday, July 1st. The scheme of the first morning's performance embraced : Part I. Coronation Anthem, and the first part of Haydn's *Creation ;* Part II. the *Creation,* parts two and three ; Part III. Overture to and selection from *Samson,* with the Dead March in *Saul* introduced. Although the orchestral and choral effects of this performance were not by many a degree to be compared with what has since been effected by the Sacred

* See *Athenæum* for 1834, p. 297.
† See p. 273.
‡ See *Athenæum* for 1834, p. 435.

Harmonic Society in Exeter Hall, or at the Crystal Palace Handel Festivals, yet nothing at all like them had ever been heard by the audiences who filled the Abbey.

" *Il n'y a que le premier pas qui coûte,*" is a proverb which certainly had its immediate verification upon the commencement of the Coronation Anthem.   The gradual *crescendo* in the opening Symphony, which works one up into a much more elevated state of enthusiasm than any could be startled into by a sudden burst of sound, reverberated along the vaulted roof of the Abbey like the swelling of mighty waters, and the first unanimous exclamation of the chorus, " God save the King," although it did not burst upon the ear unexpectedly, seemed to give vent to a pent-up feeling which a few minutes more of protraction would almost have excited to pain.*   I had once heard—and taken part also in—this Anthem in one of our cathedrals some years previously to my being called upon to listen to it in Westminster Abbey, and then it produced the effect upon me of, as the saying is, " making my heart come into my mouth ; " but on this occasion I was completely overcome.   Nor was I by any means singular in this respect; for whilst I observed many a female face bedewed with tears, I also remarked the moisture standing upon the eyelids, ready to run over, of many and many a one of the sterner sex. I have again and again listened to the same chorus in Exeter Hall, and I think I remember its being given at the first Handel Festival at the Crystal Palace in 1859 ; but it made no such impression on either one or the other of those occasions. It wanted evidently the solemnity of the grand old fane, not only as regards its adaptation for the transmission of sound, but its association with all that is hallowed and time-honoured.

* See *Athenæum* for 1834, p. 490.

Perhaps in no place whatever in England are Handel's or Mendelssohn's oratorios given with less perfectness than in the cathedrals of Hereford, Gloucester, and Worcester at the triennial music meetings of the three Midland Festivals ; but nowhere else, in spite of all the deficiency of performance, do they produce anything like the same results. There is a grandeur and a dignity in the stately march of the choral " numbers " of such works, which we wait for in vain anywhere else, even when not the slightest fault can justly be found with the manner in which they are rendered. The Crystal Palace Handel Festivals have doubtless put an end to those Commemorations of the great masters, whose remains are interred within the Abbey's sacred precincts; and this is, indeed, the more to be regretted, since, with increased means and improved resources, effects could now be produced which would entirely supersede the remembrance of the event of which I am writing. A privilege indeed it was to have been permitted to be present in the Abbey on such an occasion as the Handel Commemoration of 1834, for, as it was the last occasion of that. grand gothic building being put to such a use, so was it the means of affording the richest display of the immensity of the colossal genius of that " master," whom every succeeding age pronounces to have been the grandest sacred " tone-poet " the world has yet, or is ever likely to, become acquainted with.

Into an elaborate narrative of the several performances of Handel's works at this Commemoration I shall not attempt to enter, as it will be enough simply to summarise the events of the four days, and to refer to such incidents as appeared to be most deserving of reminiscence. After such a thrilling performance of the Coronation Anthem, the *Creation* could but fall flat. Indeed, why it found its way into the " scheme " at all was inexplicable, since it had nothing whatever to do with the event itself, nor was it in any way whatever consonant with its end and purpose. It was said to have been on this occasion performed in its entirety for the first time in London, or, at all events, for the first time under such favourable circumstances ;* but this was by no means an excuse for its being thrust into the " scheme," as if to be a foil to what had preceded and was to follow it. The selection from *Samson*—although it would have been far more appropriate to have given that work, as a whole, in preference to the *Creation*—had a most imposing effect. Mr. Braham sang " Total Eclipse " as no one else could then or now sing it, so as to make his hearers *feel* the hopeless sorrow of blindness with every note and word he uttered. Mr. H. Phillips rendered the dashing and somewhat vulgar song of Hariphah, " Honour and arms," in his usual characteristic style, with perhaps a little too much exuberance of the *forzando* to be altogether satisfactory ; and Miss Stephens dealt with the recitative, " Ye sacred priests," and the following arias, " Farewell, ye limpid streams and brooks," and " Brighter scenes I seek above," as no other living soprano of that time, Malibran alone excepted, could have done. But, after all, as it always has been on these occasions, the choruses were the chief features of attraction no less than with reference to the worthiness of the occasion.

The second performance—of Thursday, June the 26th—was made up, with the same inconsistency, of various odds and ends, in which the Handelian Coronation Anthem, " The King shall rejoice," formed the only portion of Handel's music in the first and

---

* See *Athenæum* for 1834, p. 490.

second parts.   Beethoven's " Gloria," from his mass in C, with English words, Haydn's " Kyrie," "Qui tollis," and the concluding fugue of the " Credo," of his second mass ; Mozart's " Credo " and " Agnus Dei," from his first mass, the solos being respectively sung by Mdmes. C. Novello and H. Cawse,* and Messrs. Vaughan and E. Taylor,† Madame Stockhausen, Miss Masson, and Signors Rubini and Zuchelli.   Rubini also sang an air by Mozart from " Davide Penitente ; " Miss Stephens warbled Handel's " Angels ever bright and fair ; " Mr. H. Phillips introduced the dullest of dull songs—"The Snares of Death," by the late Sir John Stevenson ; and Miss Betts made her appearance in a song from *Joshua* apropos of nothing—" O, who could tell ? "—with violin and violoncello *obbligati*—the latter by Lindley—which were entirely lost on account of the vastness of the building. Grisi followed in a " Quoniam " by Haydn, which, although well sung, was wholly out of place ; and " Luther's Hymn," quite as much so, was declaimed by Braham, with trumpet *obbligato* by Harper.   The remainder of the morning was occupied by " the work for immortality," Handel's great and glorious *Israel in Egypt*, which was given very nearly as it was written, and compensated in a measure for the unmeaning display of that light and trivial Roman Catholic church music, which, rarely in the best taste, was most unsuitable for introduction on such an occasion.

At the Saturday's—June 28—performance there was an immense galaxy of vocal talent, so far as " the principals " were concerned, embracing the names of Grisi, Madame Caradori-Allan, Madame Stockhausen, Miss Stephens, Mrs. W. Knyvett,

* See pp. 212, 276.
† See pp. 208, 209.

Mrs. Bishop, Clara Novello, Miss Bruce, Miss Wagstaff, Miss Lloyd, and Miss Chambers; Signors Tamburini and Ivanhoff; Messrs. Braham, H. Phillips, Bennett, Vaughan, Bellamy, Sale, Terrail, Goulden, Seymour, and Stretton; and Masters Howe and Smith, two Abbey choristers. The scheme embraced Haydn's "God preserve the Emperor," with English words (!), a selection from Handel's *Judas Maccabœus*, and two acts of miscellaneous music, the only creditable portion of which was that which appertained to Handel himself, and a selection from Beethoven's *Engedi* or *Mount of Olives*, an anthem by Purcell, the march and Chorus "Glory to God," from *Joshua*, and the double chorus from *Solomon*, "From the censer."

Tuesday, July the 1st, was reserved for the *Messiah*, which was given by the express desire of Queen Adelaide. This was, in every sense of the word, a truly Handelian performance, and brought the event to a conclusion with more *éclat* than was merited, considering the inappropriate miscellaneous selections of the previous mornings. Much fault was found, and deservedly, with many of the engagements of principal singers, their number being much more extensive than the quality of their services. Upon the whole, the appearance of the foreign *artistes*, male and female, was much complained of, because they, with but one or two exceptions, failed to satisfy the audience, from causes which were held to be inevitable. Such English talent as was brought forward was likewise, for the most part, only of a second rate quality, to the general disappointment of the public. Great clamour had been raised against the hitherto exclusion of English singers, and the managers yielded to it; but, in looking forward to the future, such as were best qualified to express an opinion, universally insisted that those only should have then been engaged, whether they were British or foreign, who deserved such a distinction on account of their talent. The hope was also expressed "that, by such a time, many of our own artists would have earned a right to be included amongst the number, by patient and intelligent study of their art, which, after all, is something more, and of a nobler nature, than a means of amassing money or exciting the wonderment of the vulgar and sensual." Whether that hope was fulfilled or not I shall have to relate when I arrive at the period of the next Handel Commemoration, which took place at the Crystal Palace in 1859, on the occasion of the centenary of that "mighty master's" death.

CHAPTER XI.

1835.

But for the re-engagement of Grisi, Rubini, Ivanhoff, Tamburini, and Lablache—the latter in the place of Zuchelli—the opera season of 1835 must have been recorded as one of the most uneventful that ever had been known in the experience of the oldest *habitué*. The management relied almost wholly upon the old *répertoire*, which was worked to shreds, and presented no other novelty than the *Marino Faliero* of Donizetti, which was, not quite deservedly, a failure, and Bellini's *I Puritani*, which, having been expressly written for the exceptional voices of the grand *quatuor*, had achieved so great a success in Paris as naturally to obtain the same reception in London. Of these two novelties it was indeed with the utmost truth recorded, that " the worse was most decidedly the more popular, simply because of the strength of three catching melodies, and a libretto which more equally displayed the *artistes* than was the case with *Marino Faliero*. Nevertheless, from the beginning to the ending *I Puritani* was full of noise rather than sense, and bore no comparison with other music of the same composer, of a higher order and fresher fancy." But for the manner in which this opera was sung, it must have proved a *fiasco* from the very first, as it has invariably been whenever it has in later times been resuscitated. Except by four such interpreters as Grisi, Rubini, Tamburini, and Lablache, nothing can ever be made of it; and as it is not to be expected that there may be such a concentration of talent as this again met with, it will never be considered by those best competent to judge to have been a loss that it is now almost wholly laid upon the shelf.

During this season it seemed to be utterly useless to ask for any of Mozart's operas; and even had they been given, there was little chance of the entire *ensemble* being satisfactory. So far as leading parts were concerned, the *quatuor* were not sufficient to fill them; for, however good the Donna Anna, the Don Giovanni, the Don Ottavio, and the Leporello (Lablache) might have been, there was neither a competent Zerlina, a passable Donna Elvira, a good Commendatore, nor a respectable Masetto. A Madame Finckhlor, who *débuted* on Tuesday, April 28, as Semiramide, was thrust into the part of the village coquette, for which she indeed had very few qualifications; for " although her voice was of fair quality, compass, and power, and her action for the most part appropriate, her execution was unsteady and unequal; the style of her *cadenzas* and *tours de force*, upon which she obviously relied for producing an effect, being clearly enough indicative that she was even less at home in the solid melodies of her own countrymen than in the florid and figurative music of the modern Italian school." Of all the interpreters of Mozart's coquettish peasant girl it has ever been my fortune to hear, this lady was most assuredly the worst, since not only was her version of the music coarse and slovenly, but her voice was incessantly out of tune. This lady's sojourn in London was brief; but not one hour too soon, to the satisfaction of the public, did she quit the King's Theatre, where the "star system" was beginning to prevail, to the ruin of art and the destruction of anything like legitimate operatic performances. No wonder that at the close of the season, the following inquiry was pertinently made: "Why have we not had other of Rossini's works—his *Moïse,* his *Assedio di Corinto,* above all his *Guillaume Tell?* Some of his less hackneyed and lighter pieces, *Corradino,* or *Il Turco in Italia,* for instance, both admirably adapted to the strength of the company, would have been a welcome change from the tears and mad scenes of tragedy, with which the public has been somewhat satiated. Why, too, were we disappointed of Cimerosa's *Matrimonio Segreto?* It is impossible to be contented another season without farther and more sterling revivals." *

Things were not at all better, in the range of opera, at the two great patent theatres—Drury Lane and Covent Garden—than they were at the King's Theatre. At the former—until very late indeed in the season—there was no attempt whatever at anything like a musical entertainment of any kind; whilst at the latter, no other opera than the *Sonnambula* was given, in which Miss Romer † had been the heroine, at the close of 1834; but was now replaced by Malibran—a change most decidedly for the better—who had returned after an absence of two years, and at once drew forth the following remarkable manifestation of feeling from one whose criticisms were not generally written in so energetic or complimentary a strain :—

"Malibran comes back, and one feels in a moment, not

---

* See *Athenæum* for 1835, p. 651.

† See p. 246.

only the force of *her* song, but the force of that which says,—

> " On court de belle en belle,
> Mais on revient toujours
> A ses premiers amours."

First among the first, to our thinking, she was and is. The greatest compliment that can be paid to her singing is to say that it is equal to her acting; the greatest to her acting, that it is worthy of her singing. Both are close upon perfection; and taking the extraordinary combination of the two in one person into consideration, her performance may, on the whole, be described as reaching it. We cannot say more; we dare not say less. We may notice other performances—*hers* we have only to record; for criticism, whose province it is to teach others, goes to school to learn of Madame Malibran." *

No less commendatory were the remarks of the *Times* of Tuesday, May 19th, which I am constrained to reproduce, because of the hour being so soon at hand when the musical world was suddenly to be deprived of the talent of this remarkable woman, whilst she was still in the zenith of her fame :—

"Madame Malibran," says the *Times* critic, "appeared last night in the character of la Sonnambula in Bellina's opera, a part which she has made so perfectly her own, and in which she displays such astonishing excellence, as to make all competition with her a very dangerous experiment. Her performance of this part is too well known to require any detailed criticism ; but it would be unjust to pass it by without characterizing it as one of the most perfect and exquisite specimens

---

* See *Athenæum* for 1835, p. 397.

of scenic art of which the actual stage can boast. As a piece of acting merely, it is the perfection of truth and simplicity. The *naïveté* of the earlier scenes; the pathetic force of those in which Amina suffers the agonies of despair, and the shame and horror of imputations of which she is wholly innocent; and the sleep-walking scenes, where her waking fancy presents strange and busy contrasts to the slumber in which her physical senses are bound,—give full scope for the extraordinary skill of the actress. The play is of that peculiar construction that it may be said to have only this one part in it. All the others are so decidedly subordinate, that they command the slightest possible attention, and the whole interest is concentrated in the single character of the heroine. One listens to the others with impatience, and after the representation is finished, it is impossible to recollect anything of them, but that they interfered with the more absorbing interest created by the fair and touching sleep-walker. But, delightful as the acting of Madame Malibran is in this character, it is inferior to the consummate ability with which the vocal part of the performance is executed. It is almost impossible to conceive anything of this description superior to it. The purity of her voice, the accuracy and facility of her execution, the profusion of gracefulness, and the intensity of feeling which she displays, give charms to the whole representation, which seem to reach, as nearly as human genius can reach, the highest point of excellence. Among the very best singers of Europe—and they may soon be reckoned, although good singers are sufficiently numerous—one of the first places belongs to Madame Malibran; and of all the parts she has yet played in England, this of la Sonnambula is her *capo d' opera.* At the end of the second act the force of

Madame Malibran's exertions appeared to have exhausted her. She remained for some moments in the arms of the attendants, apparently insensible. The alarm of the audience was, however, immediately afterwards dissipated by her appearing before the drop, and acknowledging the plaudits with which she was greeted."

The other characters on this occasion of Madame Malibran's return to the English stage—which are spoken of so slightingly —were tolerably filled by Mr. Seguin (Count Rodolfo), Mr. Templeton (Elvino), Mr. Duruset (Alessio), and Miss Betts (Lisa). Malibran, who entered heart and soul into every character she undertook, was reduced almost to despair at first by the stupidity and *gaucherie* of Mr. Templeton, who had not the slightest idea of acting. It was enough for him—as it was also for Rubini and Ivanhoff—to walk on and off and about the stage, coming in with his part at the proper cues, and singing at his best. But this did not suit Madame Malibran. At the first rehearsal she bore this imperturbability of manner with some degree of patience, thinking that she could rouse "the man," as she called him, into something like enthusiasm by her own manner. But when, at the next and the succeeding *répétition*, she found him "no better than a stick," she suddenly seized him by the arm, and hissed into his ear, "Good heavens, sir, don't you know you are my lover ? You must make love to me with some show of passion in the first act, and in the second you must pull me about the stage as if you would tear me into little bits." "But," replied Mr. Templeton, as meekly as a lamb, "but, madame, I shall hurt you." "And what if you do ?" screamed out the impetuous woman. "Never you mind. That's my affair ; and if you don't do it"—suiting the action to

the words by stamping her pretty little foot—"by heaven, I'll
kill you!"   And Mr. Templeton so evidently thought she was
in earnest that he made an effort, and from that moment gradually grew into as respectable an actor as he was a singer,
although he needed and experienced at times that rousing
which compelled him to act up at his best to the one single
human being that could ever have done anything with him.
It is only recently that I heard of this gentleman being alive
and well, and of tears having been brought into his eyes at the
mention to him of the witching name of Malibran.   And no
wonder, for to have known her was to love her.   She had
many faults—who of human birth and nature is without them?
—but she had that marvellous fascination about her that drew
all who heard her to her feet, without so much as producing a
breath of envy or of depreciation against her on the score of
talent, amiability of disposition, or goodness of heart.

On the 28th of October another remarkable event in the
annals of English opera took place—the production at Drury
Lane of an entirely original three-act opera, entitled the *Siege
of Rochelle*, by Mr. Balfe, who was announced as a "native of
Ireland, who had been for some years pursuing his studies in
Italy, and was expected to remain in England, provided that
encouragement was afforded to which, on account of his talents,
he was justly entitled."   The most unqualified approval of this
work was immediately expressed, as it deserved to be, the
music being spoken of "as entitling him to fairly take his
stand as a native composer amongst the more distinguished
living musicians.   In spite of the libretto of this opera being
"somewhat weak," and the poetry—save the mark!—a degree
below the style of the bellman's verses, it met with a most

decided success, and had a considerable run." I saw it, after the first night's presentation, several times, but failed to continue so much pleased as at first, because of a certain prettiness which pervaded almost every "number," having a cloying effect, and being much more of an *ad captandum* appeal to the senses than as demonstrating depth of thought or manifestation of genius. Mr. Balfe was fortunate in having as strong a cast as the times could possibly have afforded him, as will be perceived when it is said that it embraced the talent of Miss Shirreff (Clara), who had made a remarkable progress since her last appearance in London—in the *Gustave*,* if I rightly remember—Mr. Wilson (Marquis de Valmour), Mr. H. Phillips (Michel), and Mr. Paul Bedford (Azino).

And now I arrive at an event in the " Musical Recollections of the last Half Century " which cannot be passed over briefly or lightly, since a very large amount of the progress which was then beginning, and is still rapidly increasing in this country, may be traced thereto—the first concert ever given by M. Julius Benedict in London. It was amongst the many pleasurable musical events of my life to have been present at that "benefit," which was given at the concert-room of the King's Theatre, on Wednesday, July 15, 1835, under circumstances than which few have been more favourable in the annals of musical events. The selection of music at this concert was " varied and excellent. M. Benedict himself played a pianoforte concerto of great merit, composed by himself," manifesting " a lightness and dexterity " of finger, combined with a singular degree of firmness and spirit ; whilst his overture to *Raoul de Créqui* proved him to be a musician not only of the promise he has ever

* See p. 282.

since fulfilled, but of an original and decided stamp. M. Benedict was most fortunate in his assistant associates on this occasion ; for Malibran came to his aid, and never more greatly excelled than in the celebrated music lesson of Gnecco, with Lablache, or was more charmingly fantastic and skilful than in "La Cadence de Diable," a *concertante* with De Beriot, who was, also playing his best. Ivanhoff and Balfe sang Rossini's charming duett, the best specimen of his last collection, "I Marinari," beautifully, and Rubini introduced a new grand air by Raimondi. The rest of the music, with trifling exceptions, was most interesting, and carefully performed, more especially the "Ebben ti feresci" from *La Gazza Ladra*, in which Grisi and Malibran left an impression so strong that it can never be obliterated, and must always be considered as the most splendid and inspired performance of its kind that was ever heard ; for each of these gifted women was evidently incited to do her utmost, not to rival, but to keep pace with her companion. The consent of their voices in the passages *a due* was more delicious than can be described ; and in the final movement, Malibran's flashes of sudden enthusiasm, and Grisi's more sustained displays of passion and brilliant execution combined— as they had rarely, if ever, been combined before—carried their hearers to a higher pitch of delight than it is easy to record.* In addition to the several above-named artistes, Madame Stockhausen and Tamburini † also gave their services.

The advent of M. Benedict to England, as I have already intimated, was so important an event, that I feel it to be incumbent to give a brief account of his remarkable career, from

---

* See *Athenæum* for 1835, p. 552.

† See pp. 184, 235.

its earliest commencement to the present time, before passing on to a notice of other topics, those of the Philharmonic Society in particular, of the season of 1835, at which I was present, and of which I retain the liveliest remembrance, as well as the notes that were then regularly made, with no idea whatever of future publication, but simply for private gratification.

Julius Benedict was born at Stuttgard, on the 27th November, 1805, and at a very early age gave such large indications of musical promise and proficiency, that he became, on reaching his ninth year, the pupil of Abeille for the pianoforte and harmony. Under this master he made the most rapid advances, and at thirteen years of age produced a Cantata of sufficient merit, on the occasion of the death of Queen Catherine of Wurtemberg, to assure those who heard its performance of the brilliant career that was before him. His native town not furnishing him with sufficient opportunities for rapid advancement, he was induced in 1820 to visit Munich, whence he proceeded to Weimar, where, placing himself under Hummel, he continued to avail himself for eight months of that celebrated *maestro's* tuition. Weimar, however, was much too contracted a locality for the development of the youthful musician's powers; he therefore speedily sought a larger sphere at Dresden, and became the pupil of Carl Maria von Weber, who accepted him simply on account of his talent, since that celebrated composer had hitherto refused to receive any *élèves* under his care, because of the annoyance the drudgery of teaching occasions. The relation between master and pupil may be easily understood, when it is said that Julius Benedict not only remained four years at Dresden, but accompanied Weber to Berlin and Vienna, witnessing the first performance (1821) of *Der Freischütz* at the former, and of the

Euryanthe (1823) at the latter, capital. Impressed with a high consideration of his *protégé's* talent, and assured of his competency to undertake the highest duties of his profession, Weber procured for him in 1825 the important post of Musical Director at Vienna, under Duport, where the discharge of his duties was so efficient that he exchanged that situation for one of greater prominence at Naples, under Barbaja,* where he filled the office of *maestro al cembalo* and conductor both at the San Carlo and Fondo theatres.

Although the demands of his position now drew largely upon his time, Julius Benedict found sufficient leisure for composition, and having already produced the music of two ballets, *Enea nel Lazio*, and *Le Minière de Beaujon*, besides a considerable number of vocal and pianoforte pieces, he brought out (1827) his first opera, *Giacinta ed Ernesto*, the cast of which included Mdlle. Unger, the Neapolitan *buffo* Casaccia, Fioravanti, and Rubini. The success of this work was sufficient to induce him once more to devote himself to the same range of musical creation, the result of which was another opera, *I Portoghesi a Goa*, which, interpreted by Mdlle. Adelaide Tosi, Winter, Benedetti, and Lablache, added considerably to his already-established celebrity. The fame of the young *maestro* having now become established, he was induced, soon after the reception of his second effort, to make a tour through Italy, during which he gave concerts at Naples, Lucca, and Milan, and proved himself to be an accomplished pianist no less than a brilliant composer.

From Italy Julius Benedict was once more drawn towards the place of his birth, where the reputation he had legitimately

* See pp. 262, 263, 284.

earned from the most severe of musically critical countries had already gained for him great renown, to be immediately enlarged upon the performance of his opera in German. From Stuttgard he once more wended his way to Dresden and Berlin, and having there "won golden opinions" from those who witnessed the fulfilment of their prognostications of his celebrity, he determined to spend the winter in Paris, making the progress of his art the chief occupation of his residence in that then captivating city. In March, 1831, he returned to Naples, and not long afterwards had the good fortune to make the acquaintance of Madame Malibran, who, with her usual appreciation of talent, at once foretold his future career, and set herself to assist him in achieving its advantageous results. By the inducement of this gifted *artiste*, he proceeded to Bologna in 1832, and visited England in 1835. Immediately on his arrival in London, he took a position at his first concert, as I have already related,* which was the most successful of the season of that year. Although his reception was all he could have desired, he was not induced immediately to fix his residence in England; but, intending to return to Italy, he passed part of the winter of 1835–6 in Paris.

In the spring of 1836 *buffo opera* was initiated at the Lyceum Theatre, and Julius Benedict was selected as *chef-d'orchestre* simply on account of the talent he had exhibited during the preceding summer. From London he set out again for Naples, where, soon after his arrival, an operetta, *Un Anno ed un Giorno*, one of the most felicitous of his creations, was performed for the *début* of Frederic Lablache, the worthy and estimable son of the great *basso profondo*. Re-

* See above, p. 322.

turning to London in the winter of 1837, he brought this successful operetta with him, and gave it at the Lyceum Theatre, where he again occupied the position of musical composer and conductor.

Having now permanently established himself in London, Julius Benedict commenced the arduous duties of his profession with his wonted energy; but, finding that no *maestro* can exist in our cold climate merely as a composer, he also devoted his immediate attention to tuition. In spite of the tax upon his time and patience this occupation necessitated, he threw off no less than three operas between the years 1838 and 1846, *The Gipsy's Warning*, *The Bride of Venice*, and *The Crusaders*, the success of which was quite as much of European as of English celebrity. From 1844 to 1846 Julius Benedict occupied the post of musical composer at Covent Garden, first under the direction of Madame Vestris and Mr. Charles Mathews, and afterwards of Messrs. Charles Kemble and Bunn, and raised the character of that theatre by the taste, tact, and judgment he manifested in the management of the operatic department.

Amongst the great triennial musical *réunions*, that of Norwich has always held a prominent rank. It was, therefore, as high a compliment as could possibly have been paid to M. Julius Benedict when the committee requested him to undertake the distinguished office of conductor of the Festival of 1845—a position he still continues to occupy, to the satisfaction of the committee as well as for the advancement of art. In this year, notwithstanding the arduous nature of his numerous professional avocations, he made several journeys through the United Kingdom with the principal Italian vocalists, acting as pianist and conductor at a series of highly successful concerts. On the opening of the Philharmonic Hall at Liverpool in 1849, his acknowledged talent secured for him the direction of several grand concerts, by which the erection of that building was inaugurated.

In 1850 Julius Benedict accompanied Mdme. Lind-Goldschmidt (then Jenny Lind) to the United States and Cuba, where he remained nearly twelve months, during which time he conducted no less than one hundred and twenty-two concerts in all the principal cities and towns of the American continent. On his return to Europe, severe domestic affliction befell him by the death of a son through an accident from the falling of the funnel of a steamboat on the Rhone, and soon afterwards by the decease of his amiable and accomplished wife. Gradually, however, listening to the claims of his art, Julius Benedict proved to the world, in 1857, that he had lost none of his pristine talent, by the manner in which he wrote an overture and incidental music to the tragedy of *Macbeth*, which was played at Her Majesty's Theatre on the occasion of the marriage of the Princess Royal with the Crown Prince of Prussia, January 25th, 1858. From that period to the present he has been indefatigably prosecuting his labours, conducting, during the seasons of 1859 and 1860, Italian operas at Drury Lane and Her Majesty's Theatres conjointly with Signor Arditi. During this engagement he composed the recitatives and arranged Weber's *Oberon* for the Italian stage, an adaptation that has deservedly won the highest encomiums. Amongst the more recent works by which he has increased his fame, the following may be especially mentioned :—"Undine," "Richard Cœur de Lion," and "Sta. Cecilia"—Cantatas written for the Norwich Festivals of 1860, 1863, and 1866; and the *Lily of Kil-*

larney, brought out at the Royal English Opera in 1862. He also undertook in 1864 the composition of a grand opera under the title of *Esmeralda,* the libretto of which is founded upon Victor Hugo's celebrated novel, and produced the oratorio of *St. Peter* at the Birmingham Festival of 1870 ; besides several other works of considerable importance.

Julius Benedict, now a " naturalised Englishman," received the honour of knighthood the year before last, and permanently resides in London, where he deservedly enjoys the good opinion of musicians, having won for himself the warmest friendships both within and without the circle of a profession he has adorned by his works and promoted by his unremitting assiduity.

The concert season—like that of the King's Theatre—of 1835 was perhaps "the dullest of the dull" that may ever have been remembered. At the first four of those given by the Philharmonic Society—with the exception of Spohr's Symphony, "Die Weihe der Töne," known in this country by the incorrectly translated title, "The Power of Sound," which was played at the first—there was no novelty whatever, either instrumental or vocal, presented ; and so little was that composition understood—although its difficulties were overcome with great ease under Sir George Smart's direction—that it was not repeated.

The fifth concert, at the end of April, presented some features, however, of a more exciting character ; for Mr. Neate played Hummel's concerto in A minor, in the performance of which parts were carefully finished ; but, on account of its wanting that light and shade which the composer imparted to its interpretation,* it did not in the slightest degree move the pro-verbially coldest of audiences that ever assembles anywhere in Europe. In the second act, a septett by Neukomm,† elicited some applause, but afforded nothing else than a fulfilment of the old proverb, *beaucoup de talent, pas de génie.* The vocal portion of this concert was intrusted to Grisi, Rubini, Lablache, and this alone enlivened a performance which had well nigh been amongst the heaviest at which any *habitué* had ever "assisted." Grisi sang—will her version of the final bravura from Rossini's *La Donna del Lago* ever be forgotten?—with greater ease and brilliancy than ever; Rubini more than confirmed the good opinion in which he was universally held as a pure and legitimate singer of classical music, by the really impassioned manner with which he gave the "Cara imagine" from the *Zauberflöte;* and Lablache gained a unanimous encore for his rendering of the great *scena* of Mephistopheles, Va sbramando"—one of the grandest songs that ever was written—from Spohr's *Faust*—an opera that has been eclipsed in modern times by Gounod's work under the same title, which, although a charming combination of innumerable plagiarisms, admirably put together, is no more to be compared with the creation of his gifted German predecessor than anything he himself has ever produced—before or since he constructed the delicious musical idyl of the second act—can be said to have entitled him to the name and reputation of a master after the sublime type. To have heard Lablache declaim Spohr's *scena,* was to have been brought into contact with musical perfection. The intensity of passion he threw into every note, combined with the grandeur of his magnificent organ, produced an effect

* See p. 191.   † See p. 245.

which never has been, and, in all probability, never will be, surpassed. The only expression that can give the slightest notion of Lablache's version is, that it was perfectly "fiendish;" just, in fact, as the character represented can only be imagined to be. Three such specimens as these, nay, even the latter in itself, might have been deemed more than sufficient for one performance ; but the "climax was capped," as brother Jonathan expresses his idea of anything superlatively great, when the three joined in the trio "Di parli d'amore," which brought the performance to an end with unwonted *éclat.*

The sixth Philharmonic was graced by an event which can by no means be overlooked : the performance by William Sterndale Bennett—our own highly-esteemed countryman, and thoroughly genuine musician—on Monday, May 11, of a pianoforte concerto composed and played by himself, as it was the next day stated in the *Times,* " so as to indicate execution at once correct and tasteful in the highest degree,"

The early career of this eminent musical composer, like that of many others of his countrymen in science, art, and commerce, was of a chequered character. Born in 1816, at Sheffield, in Yorkshire, he had the misfortune to lose not only his father—Robert Bennett, a musician of more than average ability, and the organist of the parish church of that town—but his mother also, at so early an age that he has scarcely any recollection of them. Not very long after this very severe loss—indeed, whilst he was only three years old—he was taken charge of by his grandfather, John Bennett, who held the appointment of vicar choral, or lay clerk, in King's College, Cambridge. Having discerned the dawning of musical genius in his interesting *protégé,* and with the view to make the acquirement of its theory and practice a means for the future livelihood of the somewhat precocious boy, John Bennett entered him as a chorister of his own college when he had reached his eighth year, the age at which boys are usually admitted into cathedral and collegiate choirs—those nurseries of musical, as they ought also to be, agreeably to the statutes of founders and benefactors, but which they now are not, of classical education. Here William Sterndale Bennett's progress was so rapid, and his talent so obvious, that he attracted the attention of the Rev. W. F. Hamilton, a member of Peter House, and speedily secured his patronage. This gentleman, being persuaded that the gifted chorister of King's could have no chance of rising to future eminence if he remained merely as a singing-boy in the choir of that college, neglected as to his musical, no less than as to his ordinary, education, made interest with the authorities of the Royal Academy of Music, then but recently established in Hanover Square, London, who admitted him into that Institution at the earliest moment its rules permitted—ten years of age—and forthwith took charge of his studies. In entering this musical seminary, it is customary for a pupil to make choice of the instrument which he purposes to adopt as his speciality in after-life. This choice, however, not precluding the possibility of change at some future time, William Sterndale Bennett, after a short time, gave up the violin as his instrument, and finally abandoned it for the pianoforte. The usefulness of his first selection was, however, of considerable service to him in the prosecution of his studies, since it not only gave him a greater insight into the means of writing for stringed instruments, but enabled him, by the correct judgment of the ear, to decide at once as to the key-note of any chord, and even of any single note, which might be struck. This peculiarity is indeed possessed by violin players in a much more accurate degree than by those of any other instrument ; and it needs no elaborate proof to indicate how highly important and advantageous the acquirement of such a facility must be to any musician who makes composition his study and pursuit.

The violin having been discarded for the pianoforte, William Sterndale Bennett now assiduously applied himself to obtain a mastery of the mechanical difficulties of the latter instrument. In his practice he had at first the assistance of Mr. William Holmes, an accomplished pianist of acknowledged merit. Under that gentleman's tuition his progress was so rapid that he was speedily transferred to the care of Mr. Cipriani Potter,* who had been the pupil of Attwood, Calcott, and Crotch, all eminent English musicians in their respective departments, with whom he was afterwards most worthily to be compared. Mr. Potter was not only competent to instruct the young pianist in the sound method of musical practice peculiar to this country, but, having pursued his own studies in Germany after he had been parted with by the English "worthies" with whom he had in earlier life been associated, and having also enjoyed the friendship, advice, and assistance of Beethoven, he was able to instil into his juvenile pupil's mind those comparatively modern adaptations which especially belong to the German school, and are of incomparable value. This Mr. Potter did with uncompromising fidelity, whilst, from the perseverance of his pupil, he was able to prognosticate his future celebrity.

* See p. 76.

During the time, however, that William Sterndale Bennett was prosecuting his design of becoming a well-skilled pianist under such competent instructors as Mr. William Holmes and Mr. Cipriani Potter, he did not omit to give his attention to the study of the theory and rules of composition. Here, again, he was singularly fortunate in obtaining the aid of Mr. Charles Lucas,* himself one of the earliest and most accomplished pupils whom the Royal Academy of Music "built" for the profession. Afterwards he became the pupil of Dr. Crotch in the department of theory ; but he obtained very little assistance or tuition from that professor, who, upon his retirement from the Royal Academy, transferred him to Mr. Cipriani Potter, in whose competency and earnestness he was able to place the utmost confidence.

No sooner had the crude system of musical notation and the strict rules of harmony been mastered, than William Sterndale Bennett turned his attention to composition, and produced, as one of the first specimens of his talent, that which was afterwards to give him more perhaps of a continental than of a native renown—a Symphony written upon the models of Haydn and Mozart. This Symphony was much admired, not only for the freshness of its phases, but on account of the cleverness of instrumentation by which every *motivo* was coloured. The fertility of William Sterndale Bennett's musical invention, whilst under Mr. Charles Lucas's tuition, was considerable. He was incessantly at work, and produced in rapid succession a series of fugues, as well as an overture to the *Tempest*, which indicated unquestionable talent and the largest promise. Amongst the most noteworthy of the specimens he was then

* See pp. 185, 186.

constantly throwing off at brief intervals, his pianoforte concertos in D minor, E flat, and C minor may be particularly mentioned. These concertos were written whilst he was Mr. Potter's pupil, and the two latter were performed at concerts of the Philharmonic Society by the special invitation of the directors, contributing to his rising reputation, and indicating that a brilliant career was before him. He also had written two pianoforte concertos in F minor, an overture entitled "Parasina," and an instrumental sestet for pianoforte, two violins, viola, violoncello, and double-bass, before he had completed his twentieth year. But very few of these specimens have been published; and as they have been laid aside because of the modesty of the composer, rather than on account of any imperfection of structure, their very existence is forgotten, although there is not one amongst them that will not bear comparison with similar efforts of several of the best and oldest masters.

In the year 1836, after he had left the Royal Academy of Music, having published several of his early compositions, William Sterndale Bennett had the good fortune to make the acquaintance and win the esteem and regard of Mendelssohn. By the invitation, and at the earnest entreaty, of that great and accomplished *maestro*, he was induced to visit Germany, and take up his residence at Leipsic, where several of his works, particularly his overtures the " Naiades " and " Waldnymphe "— written after he left England—and his pianoforte concerto in C minor, were performed at the celebrated Gewandhaus Concerts under Mendelssohn's own personal direction. So great is its popularity, that the former of these compositions is constantly played at Leipsic, no less than in every other town of Germany where purely classical music is cultivated; indeed, no "scheme" of thoroughly acknowledged merit or character is ever drawn for the best German instrumental concerts without the " Naiades " overture forming one of its chief features.

In spite of the promise indicated by his compositions, and the assurance of success if he could but enjoy the benefits of continental experience, the world had hitherto not smiled very benignantly upon the rising professor. His published compositions were much too classical to command a rapid sale, and but for the liberality of Messrs. Broadwood and Sons, the world-renowned pianoforte-makers,* it is doubtful whether the juvenile aspirant could have even accepted the patronage of Mendelssohn. They, however, stepped in to his assistance, and sent him on his way, with such encouragement as only delicacy of feeling and kindness of heart can proffer. They had confidence both in the integrity and the talent of William Sterndale Bennett, and they have not been disappointed in him, either as a man or as a musician.

Whilst residing in Germany, where he remained during the years 1837 and 1838, William Sterndale Bennett often played in public at the Gewandhaus Concerts—his own concerto in C minor most frequently—and also brought out several of the overtures he had previously written, but not published in England, all of which, especially the " Naiades," as has been mentioned, being most favourably received. At the end of two years—years of intense application and study—he returned to London, where he established himself, and at once obtained the highest reputation as a composer, a pianist, and a teacher of music. At this time he had the good fortune to make the acquaintance and win the affections of Miss Wood—the daughter

* See p. 156.

of Captain Wood, an officer in the Royal Navy, who resided at Southampton—herself an accomplished pianist from having had the advantage of being instructed by Mrs. Anderson. A few years after William Sterndale Bennett's return to London he married this lady, with whom he lived in the most perfect harmony and affection of married life until the year 1862, when, after several months of severe affliction, she died, to the almost inconsolable grief of her husband and three children—two sons and a daughter—who survive her. Whilst paying his addresses to this lady, he wrote an overture—amongst the most facile and elegant of his several orchestral preludes—now well known from being annexed to his popular Cantata, the *May Queen*, composed expressly for the Musical Festival at Leeds in 1858, which he himself conducted. This overture, to which he had at first given the title "Marie-le-Blois," had not been previously published.

Soon after his return from Germany, and his establishment in London, William Sterndale Bennett brought out his overtures, the "Naiades," and "Wood Nymphs," better known at Leipsic by its German title, "Waldnymphe," and afterwards that which he had entitled "Parasina," previously to his leaving England. These orchestral preludes contain many elegant and original specimens of part writing, and fully confirm Mendelssohn's judgment respecting their merit. After producing these compositions, he gave his attention almost exclusively to tuition, and has rarely devoted himself to the higher department of his profession, except when any special occasion has called for the exercise of his powers.

Independently, however, of his high standing as a London musician, and till within the last three or four years as the conductor of the Philharmonic Society, William Sterndale Bennett also holds the highly honourable office of Professor of Music in the University of Cambridge. To this professorship he was unanimously elected in 1856, upon the death of Dr. Walmsley. The duties which devolve upon him in this office are not, however, onerous, being chiefly confined to the examination of exercises for musical degrees, and to conducting two or three concerts during the winter and spring terms.

Of late years, with the exception of the Cantatas written to order—the *May Queen* for Leeds; that for the opening of the great International Exhibition of 1862; the fantasia-overture, "Paradise and the Peri," for the Jubilee Concert of the Philharmonic Society; and his Ode for the installation of the Duke of Devonshire as Chancellor off the University of Cambridge —the last three works all thrown off in 1862—William Sterndale Bennett has published nothing of note; neither has he prepared any other works upon the theory and study of music than his "Classical Practice for the Pianoforte," which appeared in 1841, and a "Discourse upon Harmony," which followed in 1849. Truly, therefore, may every lover of music indorse the following remarks, recently made respecting him by another eminent musical professor, Herr Ernst Pauer : "For myself, I must be permitted to express my regret that this accomplished master now writes so little, and leaves an expectant public without fresh publications. Has the minstrel hung up his lyre for ever ? It is to be hoped not." At the installation of the Marquis of Salisbury as Chancellor of the University of Oxford, and successor to the late Earl of Derby, during the Commemoration (June 22nd) of 1870, the degree of D.C.L. was conferred upon William Sterndale Bennett, *honoris causâ ;* and at the close of the year before last the honour of knighthood was granted him by her most gracious Majesty, at the same time that the like distinction was awarded to M. Julius Benedict.*

The seventh Philharmonic Concert, May 25th, was one of the most unequal that it ever was the misfortune of the subscribers to listen to; for the two Symphonies—Spohr's in E flat and Beethoven's in D—the latter of which threw the former wholly into the shade—Mendelssohn's *Midsummer Night's Dream* and Beethoven's *Fidelio*, were so slovenly played under Mori's † leading, that it was suggested " there was a fine opening just then for a new leader in London, as it was impossible that he, who by no means satisfied the critics in this capacity, could bear the weight of everything upon his shoulders, especially as other veteran performers were retiring, or should do so." ‡ A Belgian violoncellist, M. Servais, *débuted* on this occasion, but made little or no impression, his tone being thin and wiry, and "his execution, although considerable, by no means neat or perfect, and being carried to an extremity made both his expression and his brilliancy *troppo caricato* to enable him to deserve the name of an *artiste* in the highest sense." § M. Servais laboured under this especial disadvantage, that Lindley "still held his own against all comers," so that if he— or any other violoncellist—could have played like an angel, they would have failed to satisfy the public taste. Because M. Servais manifested that unusual manner of producing his tone which has come into fashion, not quite meritoriously, since Piatti in a measure took the place that Lindley vacated, the public were warned that " there was so much danger of music

<hr>

* See p. 329.   † See pp. 108, 109, 149.
‡ See *Athenæum* for 1835, p. 419.   § See *Athenæum* for 1835, p. 419.

being corrupted, if not utterly destroyed, by extravagance and whimsicality, that it could not be too decidedly laid down that no forced effects, no passion pushed to its extreme, or delicacy refined into super-delicacy, deserved to be admired, although they might be excused in consideration of the talent of the performer." * The fact was, that M. Servais produced his tone by that intense pressure of the fingers which has since been better understood by the term *vibrato*, and this was at once denounced to be spasmodic, and a not altogether creditable trick. " Dear old Bob," as Lindley was called, brought out all his tone like the rolling notes of an organ, with no effort that was painful to the eye and not altogether satisfactory to the ear. There was no inordinate pressure used by him to bring out note after note, such as is invariably witnessed in the present day.   He could crack a nut between the tips of his fingers and the finger-board by simple pressure, and the effect of his tone being always smooth, there was no tremulousness whatever apparent in his playing.   It was the same with Dragonetti's contre-basso playing.   His left hand was more like a claw than anything else in the world; and as he and his *confrère* of upwards of thirty years—to speak quite within the mark—played everything placed before them with the utmost ease and purest tone as to sound—as I have heard Sir M. Costa again and again say—like the pedals of a grand old organ, nothing inferior would or could be accepted in their place or room.   If it ever happened that these two orchestralists were absent, it was at once perceived.   True indeed that Lindley did not make his instrument always " sing," as violoncellos now-adays invariably do in such passages as Weber, Meyerbeer,

* See *Athenæum* for 1835, p. 419.

and Gounod have written for them; but this is to be accounted for by the fact that, in the times of my own earliest remembrance, the strings were universally thicker than they are now.

If at the Philharmonic Concert, out of which the above remarks have originated, M. Servais's violoncello performance did not generally satisfy, it was very far from being the case as respected M. De Beriot, who played—as he almost invariably did—a composition (a concerto) of his own with the utmost brilliancy. It seemed, indeed, that this " was the *one thing* of the season, and as if his tone was brighter and purer, as well as more delicate and genuine, and his execution more brilliant than ever." * Thoroughly do I endorse this opinion, for it was the last time but one I ever heard him play—an event on that account the more permanently fixed in my memory. The vocalists on this occasion were Madame Caradori and M. Ivanhoff,† both of whom were rapidly declining in power. The former like a genuine *artiste,* managed to cover the defects which time had made upon her once pure and sympathetic organ; but the other tried to make the song " Vivi tu," with which he at one time enchanted every one, effective by noise rather than refinement, so that the saying was indeed painfully verified " that familiarity breeds contempt." H. Phillips had the bad taste to attempt to " measure weapons " with Lablache— by selecting Spohr's *scena* ‡—of whose manner the remembrance was much too recent not to induce every one to feel that the Englishman's version was as imperfect as it was impertinent. The music, in the first place, was wholly beyond

* See *Athenæum* for 1835, p. 419.
† See pp. 116, 294.   ‡ See p. 330.

his reach ; and in the next, it was altogether unsuited to his heavy and somewhat mechanical style.

At the eighth and last Philharmonic Concert of this year I heard M. Herz, a German pianist of a large continental reputation, but except possessing considerable brilliancy of finger, having very little besides to claim consideration. This well-known and successful musician was an Austrian by birth, having been born at Vienna, January 6, 1804. His studies were commenced at Coblentz under his father, who rather taught him by means of certain elementary treatises then in vogue, than by any remarkable gifts or talents of his own. His progress was, however, so rapid, even under those manifest disadvantages, that at eight years of age he played the " variations of Hummel " (Op. 8) at a public concert, and obtained considerable applause.

In order to strengthen his left hand, which showed signs of weakness, his father set him to learn the violin, which, as an expedient, was eminently successful. Urged by his master, M. Hunten, an organist at Coblentz, to commit his ideas to writing, Herz, at the early age of eight and a half, wrote his first composition for the pianoforte—a remarkable feat, seeing that he had been only three months under the tuition of that instructor. This and other indications of future promise at once induced his father to take him to Paris, where he was entered as a pupil of the Conservatoire, April 19th, 1816, under Pradher, then an eminent professor of the instrument the young pupil was ere long to make essentially his own. Rising from his sick-bed, to which he had been confined by an attack of small-pox, to attend the Conservatoire examination, he obtained the first prize for his manner of playing Dussek's

12th concerto and "a study," by Clementi ; and from this event
the remarkable popularity he enjoyed throughout the whole of
his career may be dated. Not satisfied, however, with the progress he had made, he still pursued his studies—at first, for
theory, under M. Dourlen, and afterwards under Reicha. Upon
hearing Moscheles, on that "master's" arrival in Paris, Herz at
once adopted his method, when his own style immediately
became more brilliant, light, and elegant. The result of this
was that his compositions for the pianoforte became at once the
rage, not only in Paris, but throughout all Europe, which lasted,
with more or less extension, for the next twelve years. The
time had now arrived for the young pianist to exhibit his
talent upon a wider field than even Paris afforded ; and therefore, in 1831, in company with the celebrated violinist Lafont,
he made a tour through Germany, giving concerts in most of
the principal towns and cities. In 1835 he came to London,
and played, not only, as I have said, at the last Philharmonic
Concert of that year,* but at other *réunions*, both public and
private, besides giving a concert on his own account, at which
he introduced several hitherto unheard works of somewhat too
much of an *ad captandum* character, although they were generally pronounced to be models of a new and brilliant style, that
was likely to supersede the more solid system of pianoforte-
playing which had for its interpreters such "masters" as
Hummel,† Moscheles,‡ J. B. Cramer,§ Field,‖ Cipriani Potter,¶
and several others of corresponding excellence and merit.
Herz's success, however, was even greater at Dublin and Edinburgh than it had been in London, the musical public in those

<hr>

* See p. 342.   † See p. 191.   ‡ See p. 77.
§ See p. 72   ‖ See p. 244.   ¶ See p. 76.

cities having been influenced much more by dash and brilliancy than by solidity of manipulation. Not satisfied with earning money almost with the same rapidity as he executed the most difficult passages, Herz became a pianoforte manufacturer with Klepfer at Lyons and Paris, and very speedily lost nearly all he had gained by the pursuit of his more legitimate calling.

Not convinced, however, that pianoforte playing and pianoforte making were never likely to accord, upon dissolving partnership with Klepfer, he set up for himself in the latter occupation, and speedily completed the ruin that partnership had commenced. To recruit his diminished resources he resolved to visit America, where he naturally anticipated that he would be well received, because his music was as warmly accepted there as it had hitherto been in Europe. Nor was he disappointed; for in the course of three times visiting the chief towns of the States, he gave no less than *four hundred* concerts, the profits arising from which must have been enormous. From the States he went to the Havanna, Vera Cruz, and Mexico; after which he proceeded to Peru, Chili, and California, whence he returned by way of Valparaiso and Lima, finally arriving at Paris in 1851, after five years' absence from that capital. Here he again set to work to perfect the manufacture of pianos, which had been carried on at a considerable loss during the period of his lengthened travels. Success now attended this business; and to its requirements, with the exception of making an occasional holiday to visit and give concerts in Spain, Belgium, Holland, the towns on the Rhine, Poland, and Russia, Herz devoted his almost entire attention.*

* See Fétis's *Biographic Universelle des Musiciens*, tom. iv. pp. 316-17.

Of late years, little or nothing has been heard of him, whilst his compositions, about which all the world once ridiculously raved, are equally forgotten. For my own part, I have always regarded Herz as one of the most unsatisfactory players and frivolous composers for his instrument the world has ever met with. If at any time the saying was realized of "a man going up like a rocket, and coming down like a stick," it assuredly was so in his case. I really believe that Herz could play no other music than his own—at least I did not hear him attempt anything else, and assuredly I know of no one of his contemporaries who could say that he was ever believed to do so. If he at any time tried this experiment, it must have been a miserable *fiasco*. He had neither the genius nor the disposition to understand the grand masters ; and thus, unlike that race of musicians, it must be said—in the words of a once popular ballad, now alike universally forgotten—

> " O no, we never mention him,
> His name is never heard ! "

END OF VOL. L

BRADBURY, EVANS, AND CO., PRINTERS, WHITEFRIARS.

TINSLEY BROTHERS' NEW BOOKS.

Notice.—Now ready, a new and important Book of Travels, by Captain BURTON, F.R.G.S., and Mr. C. F. TYRWHITT DRAKE, F.R.G.S., &c., entitled

UNEXPLORED SYRIA. With a New Map of Syria, Illustrated,
Inscriptions, the "Hamah Stones," &c. 2 vols., 8vo.

"The work before us is no common book of travels; it is rather a series of elaborate, and at the same time luminous, descriptions of the various sites visited and explored by the authors, either together or singly, and of the discoveries made there by them."—*Athenæum.*

THE LIFE AND TIMES OF ALGERNON SYDNEY,
Patriot, 1617—1683. By ALEXANDER CHARLES EWALD, F.S.A., Senior Clerk of Her Majesty's Public Records, author of "The Crown and its Advisers," "Last Century of Universal History," &c. 2 vols., 8vo.

THE LIFE and ADVENTURES of ALEXANDER DUMAS.
By PERCY FITZGERALD, author of "The Lives of the Kembles," "The Life of David Garrick," &c. 2 vols., 8vo.

ZANZIBAR. By Captain R. F. Burton, author of " A Mission
to Geléle," "Explorations of the Highlands of the Brazil," "Abeokuta," "My Wanderings in West Africa," &c. 2 vols., 8vo, 30s.

"We welcome with pleasure this new work from the prolific pen of the accomplished traveller in all four quarters of the globe. . . . The information furnished is unquestionably very valuable and interesting."—*Athenæum.*

THE LIFE AND TIMES OF MARGARET OF ANJOU.
By Mrs. HOOKHAM. 2 vols., 8vo.

"Let Mrs. Hookham's history be as largely circulated as possible, and earnestly read in every home."—*Bell's Weekly Messenger.*

THE COURT OF ANNA CARAFA; an Historictl Narrative.
By Mrs. ST. JOHN. 1 vol., 8vo.

"Mrs. St. John always writes with grace and point. Not even in 'Masaniello of Naples' have her command of language and her epigrammatic style been more commendable than in the handsome volume before us."—*Standard.*

MILITARY MEN I HAVE MET. By E. DYNE FENTON,
author of "Sorties from Gib." With Twenty Illustrations. 1 vol., 8vo, 7s. 6d.

"Captain Fenton, encouraged by the very favourable reception which, with hardly an excep tion, his first essay in military writing was received, has wisely ventured on another volume, in which he sketches, with all the brevity, and not unfrequently with much of the wit, of Theophrastus, portraits of the military men he has met with in his military career . . . The illustrations by Sambourne are excellent and laughter-moving."—*Bell's Weekly Messenger.*

THE NEWSPAPER PRESS: its Origin, Progress, and Present
Position. By JAMES GRANT, author of "Random Recollections," "The Great Metropolis," &c., and late Editor of the *Morning Advertiser.* 2 vols., 8vo, 30s.

BARON GRIMBOSH, Doctor of Philosophy, and sometime
Governor of Barataria. A Record of his Experience, written by Himself in Exile, and published by authority. 1 vol., 8vo.

"Grimbosh in Barataria is surrounded by certain councillors and others, whose identity ie transparent through their pseudonyms. A couple of hours may be well spent in taking in ths wit, the wisdom, the fun, and the folly which flare up about them."—*Athenæum.*

TINSLEY BROTHERS, 18, CATHERINE STREET, STRAND.

Now ready, in 2 vols. 8vo,

THE

RECOLLECTIONS AND REFLECTIONS

OF

J. R. PLANCHÉ,

(SOMERSET HERALD):

A PROFESSIONAL AUTOBIOGRAPHY.

OPINIONS OF THE PRESS.

"His volumes are both amusing and instructive, and may be honestly recommended not merely as agreeable light reading, but as valuable contributions to the history of the stage."—*The Times.*

"To the portions of his book which will chiefly interest the general reader we have scarcely adverted at all, simply because we know not how to deal with them. So many and so good are the anecdotes he relates, that two or three could not be taken from the rest by any process more critical than the toss of a halfpenny. We will only state that he is perfectly familiar with stories already in print, and scrupulously avoids beaten ground. That nothing may be wanting to the attraction of his volumes, they are adorned with several facsimiles of quaint sketches by Thackeray, Alfred Crowquill, and Maclise."—*Saturday Review.*

"We have only now to leave Mr, Planché and his book to an appreciating public. There are few men who have amused and delighted the public so long as he has done, and perhaps there has never been a dramatic writer who has been so distinguished as he has been for uniting the utmost amount of wit and humour with refinement of expression and perfect purity of sentiment."—*Athenæum.*

"A man of such varied accomplishments, and whose genial character has made him a favourite in the good society of his time, must have a large store of agreeable Recollections and Reflections, the title of his autobiography, just published. The two volumes are full of interesting personal anecdotes, which cannot hurt the feelings of the living or the reputation of those departed, and which are related with discretion and good taste."—*Illustrated London News.*

"We can only for the present strongly recommend all our readers to seek for themselves the amusement we have so plentifully discovered upon nearly every page of Mr. Planché's 'Recollections.' There are hundreds to whom Mr. Planché's name alone is such a tower of strength, that they will send for the book before they even inquire what its contents may be."—*Era.*

"The moment the two volumes came to hand we sat down to their consideration, and did not leave them until we had devoured their contents, each chapter, like jealousy, increasing 'the meat' on which we 'fed' without satisfying our appetite inasmuch as, when we had come to the end, we were eagerly inclined—like poor Oliver Twist in Dickens's admirable novel —to ask for more."—*Bell's Weekly Messenger.*

"For upwards of half a century he has sedulously laboured to entertain the public, after a most pleasant and cultivated fashion, figuring prominently the while in literary and artistic society. His memories are thoroughly interesting and amusing."—*Pall Mall Gazette.*

"Here, however, we must stop, and have not space to do more than commend to our readers this very interesting and valuable budget of 'Recollections and Reflections.'— *Builder.*

"Mr. Planché writes in a lively and pleasant style, and having plenty to tell, knows how to tell it. His book, indeed, is a valuable contribution to the materials of theatrical history." —*Spectator.*

"That the labours of this veteran author, dramatist, and antiquarian may shortly be made public, and that he may long enjoy the favour he has fairly earned, is our sincere wish, as we once more recommend his book to our readers."—*Era.*

TINSLEY BROTHERS, 18, CATHERINE STREET, STRAND.

TINSLEY BROTHERS' LIST OF NEW BOOKS.

A New and Important Book of Travels.

Unexplored Syria. By Capt. BURTON, F.R.G.S.,

and Mr. C. F. TYRWHITT DRAKE, F.R.G.S., &c. With a New Map of Syria, Illustrations, Inscriptions, the 'Hamah Stones,' &c. 2 vols. 8vo, 32s.

"The work before us is no common book of travels. It is rather a series of elabora'e, and at the same time luminous, descriptions of the various sites visited and explored by the authors, either together or singly, and of the discoveries made there by them. . . . The present joint production of Cap'ain Burton and Mr. Tyrwhitt-Drake is therefore most opportune, on account of the material additions it makes to our acquaintance with a region which, notwithstanding the deep interest it excites, is still but imperfectly explored."—*Athenæum*.

"While these magnificent volumes, with their original plans and sketches by Mr. Drake, the unrivalled map of Northern Syria, and the luxurious print, are triumphs of typography, they are at the same time enduring monuments of the energy and enterprise of our countrymen."—*John Bull*.

"The book must be pronounced to be valuable for its information."—*Spectator*.

The Recollections and Reflections of J. R. PLANCHE

(*Somerset Herald*). A Professional Autobiography. 2 vols. 8vo, 25s.

"Besides illustrations of social and dramatic life, of literature, and of authors, Mr. Planché gives us record of travels, incidents of his *other* professional life as a herald, and reflections on most matters which have come under his notice. We have only now to leave Mr. Planché and his book to an appreciating public. There are few men who have amused and delighted the public as long as he has done; and perhaps there has never been a dramatic writer who has been so distinguished as he has been for uniting the utmost amount of wit and humour with refinement of expression and perfect purity of sentiment."—*Athenæum*.

"We have here two goodly octavo volumes full of amusing and often instructive gossip. To the portions of his book which will chiefly interest the general reader we have scarcely adverted at all. simply because we know not how to deal with them. So many and so good are the anecdotes he relates, that two or three could not be taken from the rest by any process more critical than the toss of a halfpenny."—*Saturday Review*.

Uniform with the above,

Musical Recollections of the Last Half-Century.

2 vols. 8vo.

The Life and Times of Algernon Sydney, Patriot,

1617—1683. By ALEXANDER CHARLES EWALD, F.S A., Senior Clerk of Her Majesty's Public Records, author of "The Crown and its Advisers," "Last Century of Universal History," &c. 2 vols. 8vo.

The Life and Times of Margaret of Anjou. By

Mrs. HOOKHAM. 2 vols. 8vo, 30s.

"Let Mrs. Hookham's history be as largely circulated as possible, and earnestly read in every home."—*Bell's Weekly Messenger*.

"The collection of the materials has evidently been a laborious task; the composition is careful and conscientious throughout, and it contains a great deal that is valuable and highly interesting."—*Pall Mall Gazette*.

TINSLEY BROTHERS, 18 CATHERINE STREET, STRAND.

TINSLEY BROTHERS' LIST OF NEW BOOKS.

Baron Grimbosh: Doctor of Philosophy and some-
time Governor of Barataria. A Record of his Experiences, written
by himself in Exile, and Published by Authority. 1 vol. 8vo, 10s. 6d.

"Grimbosh, in Barataria, is surrounded by certain counsellors and others,
whose identity is transparent through their pseudonyms. A couple of hours may
be well spent in taking in the wit, the wisdom, the fun, and the folly, which flare
up about them, from the overture to the fall of the curtain."—*Athenæum*.

The Court of Anna Carafa: an Historical Narra-
tive. By Mrs. ST. JOHN. 1 vol. 8vo, 12s.

"Apart from the interest which centres around the fair Duchess of Medina, we
obtain much curious and valuable information concerning the political intrigues
of Spain and Italy during the first half of the seventeenth century. This is a
deeply interesting and highly instructive volume."—*Court Journal*.

The Newspaper Press: its Origin, Progress, and
Present Position. By JAMES GRANT, author of "Random Recollec-
tions," "The Great Metropolis," &c., and late Editor of the *Morning
Advertiser*. 2 vols. 8vo, 30s.

"It was natural that such a man, to whom the press had been, as it were, the
atmosphere he had breathed for half a lifetime, should think of recording what
he personally knew, or had historically gathered, concerning that unique institution."—*Standard*.

Under the Sun. By GEORGE AUGUSTUS SALA, author
of "My Diary in America," &c. 1 vol. 8vo, 15s.

"We can loiter pleasantly enough with him in the streets and lanes, on the
wharfs and courtyards, and we find much to entertain us in his picture of the
humours of Havana."—*Athenæum*.

Military Men I have Met. By E. DYNE FENTON,
author of "Sorties from Gib." With Twenty Illustrations. 1 vol.
8vo, 7s. 6d.

"Captain Fenton, encouraged by the very favourable reception which, with
hardly an exception, his first essay in military writing received, has wisely ventured on another volume, in which he sketches, with all the brevity, and not unfrequently with much of the wit, of Theophrastus, portraits of the military men he
has met with in his military career . . . . . The illustrations by Sambourne are
excellent and laughter-moving."—*Bell's Weekly Messenger*.

The Life and Adventures of Alexander Dumas. By
PERCY FITZGERALD, author of "The Lives of the Kembles," &c.
2 vols. 8vo.

Paris after Two Sieges. Notes of a Visit during
the Armistice and immediately after the Suppression of the Commune.
By WILLIAM WOODALL. 1 vol. *[Just ready.*

Judicial Dramas: Romances of French Criminal
Law. By HENRY SPICER. 1 vol. 8vo, 15s.

The Retention of India. By ALEXANDER HALLIDAY.
1 vol. 7s. 6d.

TINSLEY BROTHERS, 18 CATHERINE STREET, STRAND.

WORKS BY CAPTAIN BURTON, F.R.G.S. &c.

A New Book of Travels.

Zanzibar. By CAPTAIN R. F. BURTON, author of
"A Mission to Geléle," "Explorations of the Highlands of the Brazil,"
"Abeokuta," "My Wanderings in West Africa," &c. 30*s*.

"We welcome with pleasure this new work from the prolific pen of the accomplished traveller in all four quarters of the globe. The information furnished is unquestionably very valuable and interesting."—*Athenæum*.

Explorations of the Highlands of the Brazil; with
a full account of the Gold and Diamond Mines; also, Canoeing down
Fifteen Hundred Miles of the great River, Sao Francisco, from
Sabarà to the Sea. In 2 vols. 8vo, with Map and Illustrations, 30*s*.

A Mission to Geléle. Being a Three Months'
Residence at the Court of Dahomé. In which are described the
Manners and Customs of the Country, including the Human Sacrifice,
&c. 2 vols., with Illustrations, 25*s*.

Abeokuta; and an Exploration of the Cameroons
Mountains. 2 vols. post 8vo, with Portrait of the Author, Map, and
Illustrations. 25*s*.

Wit and Wisdom from West Africa; or a Book of
Proverbial Philosophy, Idioms, Enigmas, and Laconisms. Compiled
by RICHARD F. BURTON, author of "A Mission to Dahomé," "A
Pilgrimage to El-Medinah and Meccah," &c. 12*s*. 6*d*.

My Wanderings in West Africa; from Liverpool
to Fernando Po. 2 vols. cr. 8vo, 21*s*.

Letters from the Battle-fields of Paraguay. With
Map and Illustrations, 18*s*.

The Nile Basin. With Map, &c. post 8vo, 7*s*. 6*d*.

WORKS BY GEORGE AUGUSTUS SALA.

My Diary in America in the Midst of War. In
2 vols. 8vo, 30*s*.

Notes and Sketches of the Paris Exhibition. 8vo, 15*s*.

From Waterloo to the Peninsula. 2 vols. 8vo, 24*s*.

Rome and Venice, with other Wanderings in Italy,
in 1866–7. 8vo, 16*s*.

Accepted Addresses. 1 vol. cr. 8vo, 5*s*.

History of France under the Bourbons, 1589-1830.
By CHARLES DUKE YONGE, Regius Professor, Queen's College, Belfast. In 4 vols. 8vo. Vols. I. and II. contain the Reigns of Henry IV., Louis XIII. and XIV.; Vols. III. and IV. contain the Reigns of Louis XV. and XVI. 3*l*.

The Regency of Anne of Austria, Queen of France,
Mother of Louis XIV. From Published and Unpublished Sources. With Portrait. By Miss FREER. 2 vols. 8vo, 30*s*.

The Married Life of Anne of Austria, Queen of
France, Mother of Louis XIV.; and the History of Don Sebastian, King of Portugal. Historical Studies. From numerous Unpublished Sources. By MARTHA WALKER FREER. 2 vols. 8vo, 30*s*.

The History of Monaco. By H. PEMBERTON. 12*s*.

The Great Country: Impressions of America. By
GEORGE ROSE, M.A. (ARTHUR SKETCHLEY). 8vo, 15*s*.

Biographies and Portraits of some Celebrated
People. By ALPHONSE DE LAMARTINE. 2 vols. 25*s*.

Memoirs of the Life and Reign of George III.
With Original Letters of the King and Other Unpublished MSS. By J. HENEAGE JESSE, author of "The Court of England under the Stuarts," &c. 3 vols. 8vo. £2 2*s*. Second Edition.

The Public Life of Lord Macaulay. By FREDERICK
ARNOLD, B.A. of Christ Church, Oxford. Post 8vo, 7*s*. 6*d*.

Memoirs of Sir George Sinclair, Bart., of Ulbster.
By JAMES GRANT, author of "The Great Metropolis," "The Religious Tendencies of the Times," &c. 8vo. With Portrait. 16*s*.

Memories of My Time; being Personal Remini-
scences of Eminent Men. By GEORGE HODDER. 8vo. 16*s*.

Lives of the Kembles. By PERCY FITZGERALD,
author of the "Life of David Garrick," &c. 2 vols. 8vo. 30*s*.

The Life of David Garrick. From Original Family
Papers, and numerous Published and Unpublished Sources. By PERCY FITZGERALD, M.A. 2 vols. 8vo, with Portraits. 36*s*.

The Life of Edmund Kean. From various Pub-
lished and Original Sources. By F. W. HAWKINS. In 2 vols. 8vo, 30*s*.

Our Living Poets: an Essay in Criticism. By
H. BUXTON FORMAN. 1 vol., 12*s*.

Johnny Robinson: The Story of the Childhood and
Schooldays of an "Intelligent Artisan." By the Author of "Some Habits and Customs of the Working Classes." 2 vols. 21*s*.

Letters on International Relations before and during
the War of 1870. By the *Times* Correspondent at Berlin. Reprinted,
by permission, from the *Times*, with considerable Additions. 2 vols.
8vo. 36*s.*

The Story of the Diamond Necklace. By HENRY
VIZETELLY. Illustrated with an exact representation of the Diamond Necklace, and a Portrait of the Countess de la Motte, engraved
on steel. 2 vols. post 8vo, 25*s.* Second Edition.

English Photographs. By an American. 8vo, 12*s.*

Travels in Central Africa, and Exploration of the
Western Nile Tributaries. By Mr. and Mrs. PETHERICK. With
Maps, Portraits, and numerous Illustrations. 2 vols. 8vo, 25*s.*

From Calcutta to the Snowy Range. By an OLD
INDIAN. With numerous coloured Illustrations. 14*s.*

Stray Leaves of Science and Folk-lore. By J. SCOF-
FERN, M.B. Lond. 8vo. 12*s.*

Three Hundred Years of a Norman House. With
Genealogical Miscellanies. By JAMES HANNAY, author of " A
Course of English Literature," "Satire and Satirists," &c. 12*s.*

The Religious Life of London. By J. EWING RITCHIE,
author of the " Night Side of London," &c. 8vo. 12*s.*

Religious Thought in Germany. By the TIMES
CORRESPONDENT at Berlin. Reprinted from the *Times.* 8vo. 12*s.*

Mornings of the Recess in 1861-4. Being a Series
of Literary and Biographical Papers, reprinted from the *Times*, by
permission, and revised by the Author. 2 vols. 21*s.*

The Schleswig-Holstein War. By EDWARD DICEY,
author of " Rome in 1860." 2 vols. 16*s.*

The Battle-fields of 1866. By EDWARD DICEY,
author of " Rome in 1860," &c. 12*s.*

From Sedan to Saarbrück, viâ Verdun, Gravelotte,
and Metz. By an Officer of the Royal Artillery. In one vol. 7*s.* 6*d.*

British Senators; or Political Sketches, Past and
Present. By J. EWING RITCHIE. Post 8vo, 10*s.* 6*d.*

Prohibitory Legislation in the United States. By
JUSTIN MCCARTHY. 1 vol., 2*s.* 6*d.*

The Idol in Horeb. Evidence that the Golden
Image at Mount Sinai was a Cone and not a Calf. With Three Ap-
pendices. By CHARLES T. BEKE, Ph.D. 1 vol., 5*s.*

TINSLEY BROTHERS, 18 CATHERINE STREET, STRAND.

Ten Years in Sarawak. By CHARLES BROOKE, the
"Tuanmudah" of Sarawak. With an Introduction by H. H. the
Rajah Sir JAMES BROOKE ; and numerous Illustrations. 2 vols. 25*s.*

Peasant Life in Sweden. By L. LLOYD, author
of "The Game Birds of Sweden," "Scandinavian Adventures," &c.
8vo. With Illustrations. 18*s.*

Hog Hunting in the East, and other Sports. By
Captain J. NEWALL, author of "The Eastern Hunters." With numerous Illustrations. 8vo, 21*s.*

The Eastern Hunters. By Captain JAMES NEWALL.
8vo, with numerous Illustrations. 16*s.*

Fish Hatching; and the Artificial Culture of Fish.
By FRANK BUCKLAND. With 5 Illustrations. 5*s.*

Incidents in my Life. By D. D. Home. In 1
vol. crown 8vo, 10*s. 6d. Second Series.*

Con Amore; or, Critical Chapters. By JUSTIN
MCCARTHY, author of "The Waterdale Neighbours." Post 8vo. 12*s.*

The Cruise of the Humming Bird, being a Yacht Cruise
around the West Coast of Ireland. By MARK HUTTON. In 1 vol. 14*s.*

Murmurings in the May and Summer of Manhood:
O'Ruark's Bride, or the Blood-spark in the Emerald; and Man's Mission a Pilgrimage to Glory's Goal. By EDMUND FALCONER. 1 vol., 5*s.*

Poems. By EDMUND FALCONER. 1 vol., 5*s.*

Dante's Divina Commedia. Translated into English in the Metre and Triple Rhyme of the Original. By Mrs. RAM-
SAY. 3 vols. 18*s.*

The Gaming Table, its Votaries and Victims, in all
Countries and Times, especially in England and France. By ANDREW
STEINMETZ, Barrister-at-Law. 2 vols. 8vo. 31*s.*

Principles of Comedy and Dramatic Effect. By
PERCY FITZGERALD, author of "The Life of Garrick," &c. 8vo. 12*s.*

A Winter Tour in Spain. By the Author of "Altogether Wrong." 8vo, illustrated, 15*s.*

Life Beneath the Waves; and a Description of the
Brighton Aquarium, with numerous Illustrations. 1 vol., 2*s. 6d.*

The Rose of Jericho; from the French; called by
the German "Weinachts-Rose," or "Christmas Rose. Edited by the
Hon. Mrs. NORTON, Author of "Old Sir Douglas," &c: 2*s. 6d.*

The Bells: a Romantic Story. Adapted from the
French of MM. ERCKMANN-CHATRIAN. 1*s.*

TINSLEY BROTHERS'
SERIES OF SEVEN-AND-SIXPENNY WORKS.

HANDSOMELY BOUND IN BEVELLED BOARDS.

Poppies in the Corn; or Glad Hours in the Grave Years. By the Author of "The Harvest of a Quiet Eye," &c.

The Pilgrim and the Shrine; or Passages from the Life and Correspondence of Herbert Ainslie, B.A., Cantab.

Higher Law. A Romance in One Volume.

Moorland and Stream. By W. BARRY.

Maxims by a Man of the World. By the Author of "Lost Sir Massingberd."

The Adventures of a Bric-a-Brac Hunter. By Major BYNG HALL.

The Night Side of London. By J. EWING RITCHIE, author of "About London," &c. New and Enlarged Edition.

Some Habits and Customs of the Working Classes. By a JOURNEYMAN ENGINEER.

The Great Unwashed. By "THE JOURNEYMAN ENGINEER." Uniform with "Some Habits and Customs of the Working Classes."

Sunnyside Papers. By ANDREW HALLIDAY.

Essays in Defence of Women. Crown 8vo, handsomely bound in cloth, gilt, bevelled boards.

Places and People; being Studies from the Life. By J. C. PARKINSON.

A Course of English Literature. By JAMES HANNAY. *Suitable for Students and Schools.*

Modern Characteristics: a Series of Essays from the "Saturday Review," revised by the Author.

The Law: What I have Seen, What I have Heard, and What I have Known. By CYRUS JAY.

The King of Topsy-Turvy: a Fairy Tale. By the Author of "The Enchanted Toasting-Fork." Profusely illustrated and handsomely bound. 5s.

The Enchanted Toasting-fork: a Fairy Tale. · Profusely illustrated and handsomely bound. 5s.

TINSLEY BROTHERS, 18 CATHERINE STREET, STRAND.

TINSLEY BROTHERS' NEW NOVELS
AT EVERY LIBRARY.

Notice.—A New Novel by Harrison Ainsworth.

Boscobel: a Tale of the Year 1651. By WILLIAM HARRISON AINSWORTH, author of "Rookwood," "The Tower of London," &c. With Illustrations. 3 vols.

At His Gates. By Mrs. OLIPHANT, author of "Chronicles of Carlingford," &c.

The Vicar's Daughter: a New Story. By GEORGE MACDONALD, author of "Annals of a Quiet Neighbourhood," "The Seaboard Parish," &c.

A Waiting Race. By EDMUND YATES, author of "Broken to Harness," "Black Sheep," &c. 3 vols.

Valentin: a Story of Sedan. By HENRY KINGSLEY, author of "Ravenshoe," "Geoffry Hamlyn," &c. 2 vols.

Two Worlds of Fashion. By CALTHORPE STRANGE.

The Pace that Kills: a New Novel. 3 vols.

A Woman's Triumph. By Lady HARDY. 3 vols.

Erma's Engagements: a New Novel. By the Author of "Blanche Seymour," &c.

Dower and Curse. By JOHN LANE FORD, author of "Charles Stennie," &c.

Autobiography of a Cornish Rector. By the late JAMES HAMLEY TREGENNA. 2 vols.

The Scarborough Belle. By ALICE CHARLOTTE SAMPSON. 3 vols.

Puppets Dallying. By ARTHUR LILLIE, author of "Out of the Meshes," "King of Topsy Turvy," &c.

Under the Greenwood Tree. A Rural Painting of the Dutch School. By the Author of "Desperate Remedies," &c. 2 vols.

Coming Home to Roost. By GERALD GRANT. 3 vols.

Midnight Webs. By G. M. FENN, author of "The Sapphire Cross," &c. 1 vol. fancy cloth binding, 10s. 6d.

Sorties from "Gib." in quest of Sensation and Sentiment. By E. DYNE FENTON, late Captain 86th Regiment. 1 vol. post 8vo, 10s. 6d.

The Golden Lion of Granpere. By ANTHONY TROL-
LOPE, author of " Ralph the Heir," " Can You Forgive Her ?" &c.

Under which King. By B. W. JOHNSTON, M.P.
1 vol.

Under the Red Dragon. By JAMES GRANT, author
of " The Romance of War," " Only an Ensign," &c.

Hornby Mills; and other Stories. By HENRY
KINGSLEY, author of " Ravenshoe," " Mademoiselle Mathilde,"
" Geoffry Hamlyn," &c. In 2 vols.

Grainger's Thorn. By THOS. WRIGHT (the " Jour-
neyman Engineer"), author of " The Bane of a Life," " Some Habits
and Customs of the Working Classes," &c. 3 vols.

Church and Wife: a Question of Celibacy. By
ROBERT ST. JOHN CORBET, author of " The Canon's Daughters."
3 vols.

Not Easily Jealous: a New Novel. In 3 vols.

Rough but True. By ST. CLARE. In 1 vol.

Christopher Dudley. By MARY BRIDGMAN, author
of ' Robert Lynne,' &c. In 3 vols.

Love and Treason. By W. FREELAND. 3 vols.

Tender Tyrants. By JOSEPH VEREY. 3 vols.

Loyal: a New Novel. By M. A. GODFREY. 3 vols.

Fatal Sacrifice: a New Novel.

Old Margaret. By HENRY KINGSLEY, author of
" Ravenshoe," " Geoffry Hamlyn," &c. 2 vols.

Bide Time and Tide.. By J. T. NEWALL, author of
" The Gage of Honour," " The Eastern Hunters," &c. 3 vols.

The Scandinavian Ring. By JOHN POMEROY. 3 vols.

The Harveys. By HENRY KINGSLEY, author of
" Old Margaret," " Hetty," " Geoffry Hamlyn," &c. 2 vols.

TINSLEY BROTHERS, 18 CATHERINE STREET, STRAND.

Henry Ancrum: a Tale of the last War in New Zealand. 2 vols.

She was Young, and He was Old. By the Author of "Lover and Husband." 3 vols.

A Ready-made Family: or the Life and Adventures of Julian Leep's Cherub. A Story. 3 vols.

Cecil's Tryst. By the Author of "Lost Sir Massingberd," &c. 3 vols.

Denison's Wife. By Mrs. ALEXANDER FRASER, author of "Not while She lives," "Faithless; or the Loves of the Period," &c. 2 vols.

Barbara Heathcote's Trial. By the Author of "Nellie's Memories," &c. 3 vols.

Wide of the Mark. By the Author of "Recommended to Mercy," "Taken upon Trust," &c. 3 vols.

Title and Estate. By F. LANCASTER. 3 vols.

Hollowhill Farm. By JOHN EDWARDSON. 3 vols.

The Sapphire Cross: a Tale of Two Generations. By G. M. FENN, author of "Bent, not Broken," &c. 3 vols.

Edith. By C. A. LEE. 2 vols.

Lady Judith. By JUSTIN MCCARTHY, author of "My Enemy's Daughter," "The Waterdale Neighbours," &c. 3 vols.

Only an Ensign. By JAMES GRANT, author of "The Romance of War," "Lady Wedderburn's Wish," &c. 3 vols.

Old as the Hills. By DOUGLAS MOREY FORD. 3 vols.

Not Wooed, but Won. By the Author of "Lost Sir Massingberd," "Found Dead," &c. 3 vols.

My Heroine. 1 vol.

Sundered Lives. By WYBERT REEVE, author of the Comedies of "Won at Last," "Not so Bad after all," &c. 3 vols.

TINSLEY BROTHERS, 18 CATHERINE STREET, STRAND.

The Prussian Spy. By V. VALMONT. 2 vols.

The Nomads of the North: a Tale of Lapland. By J. LOVEL HADWEN. 1 vol.

Family Pride. By the Author of "Olive Varcoe," "Simple as a Dove," &c. 3 vols.

Fair Passions; or the Setting of the Pearls. By the Hon. Mrs. PIGOTT CARLETON. 3 vols.

Harry Disney: an Autobiography. Edited by ATHOLL DE WALDEN. 3 vols.

Desperate Remedies. 3 vols.

The Foster Sisters. By EDMOND BRENAN LOUGHNAN. 3 vols.

Only a Commoner. By HENRY MORFORD. 3 vols.

Madame la Marquise. By the Author of "Dacia Singleton," "What Money Can't Do," &c. 3 vols.

Clara Delamaine. By A. W. CUNNINGHAM. 3 vols.

Sentenced by Fate. By Miss EDGCOMBE. 3 vols.

Fairly Won. By Miss H. S. ENGSTRÖM. 3 vols.

Joshua Marvel. By B. L. FARJEON, author of "Grif." 3 vols.

Blanche Seymour. 3 vols.

By Birth a Lady. By G. M. FENN, author of "Mad," "Webs in the Way," &c. 3 vols.

A Life's Assize. By Mrs. J. H. RIDDELL, author of "George Geith," "City and Suburb," "Too much Alone," &c. 3 vols.

Gerald Hastings. By the Author of "No Appeal," &c. 3 vols.

Monarch of Mincing-Lane. By WILLIAM BLACK, author of "In Silk Attire," "Kilmeny," &c. 3 vols.

TINSLEY BROTHERS, 18 CATHERINE STREET, STRAND.

The Golden Bait. By H. HOLL, author of "The King's Mail," &c. In 3 vols.

Like Father, like Son. By the Author of "Lost Sir Massingberd," &c. 3 vols.

Beyond these Voices. By the EARL OF DESART, author of "Only a Woman's Love," &c. 3 vols.

The Queen's Sailors. A Nautical Novel. By ED-WARD GREEY. 3 vols.

Bought with a Price. By the Author of "Golden Pippin," &c. 1 vol.

The Florentines: a Story of Home-life in Italy. By the COUNTESS MARIE MONTEMERLI, author of "Four Months in a Garibaldian Hospital," &c. 3 vols.

The Inquisitor. By WILLIAM GILBERT, author of "Doctor Austin's Guests," &c. 3 vols.

Falsely True. By Mrs. CASHEL HOEY, author of "A House of Cards," &c. In 3 vols.

After Baxtow's Death. By MORLEY FARROW, author of "No Easy Task," &c. 3 vols.

Hearts and Diamonds. By ELIZABETH P. RAMSAY, 3 vols.

The Bane of a Life. By THOMAS WRIGHT (the Journeyman Engineer), author of "Some Habits and Customs of the Working Classes," &c. 3 vols.

Robert Lynne. By MARY BRIDGMAN. 2 vols.

Baptised with a Curse. By EDITH S. DREWRY. 3 vols.

Brought to Book. By HENRY SPICER, Esq. 2 vols.

Fenacre Grange. By LANGFORD CECIL. 3 vols.

Schooled with Briars: a Story of To-day. 1 vol.

A Righted Wrong. By EDMUND YATES, author of "Black Sheep," &c. 3 vols.

TINSLEY BROTHERS, 18 CATHERINE STREET, STRAND.

Gwendoline's Harvest.   By the Author of " Lost Sir Massingberd," " Found Dead," &c.   2 vols.

A Fool's Paradise.   By THOMAS ARCHER, author of " Strange Work," &c.   3 vols.

George Canterbury's Will.   By Mrs. HENRY WOOD, author of " East Lynne," &c.   3 vols.

Gold and Tinsel.   By the Author of "Ups and Downs of an Old Maid's Life."   3 vols.

Sidney Bellew.   A Sporting Story.   By FRANCIS FRANCIS.   2 vols.

Ready-Money Mortiboy : a Matter of Fact Story.   3 vols.

Not while She Lives.   By the Author of " Faithless ; or the Loves of the Period."   2 vols.

A Double Secret and Golden Pippin.   By JOHN POMEROY.   3 vols.

Heathfield Hall ; or Prefatory Life.   A Youthful Reminiscence.   By HANS SCHREIBER, author of " Nicknames at the Playingfield College," &c.   10s. 6d.

Phœbe's Mother.   By LOUISA ANN MEREDITH, author of " My Bush Friends in Tasmania."   2 vols.

Strong Hands and Steadfast Hearts.   By the Countess von BOTHMER.   3 vols.

Saved by a Woman.   By the Author of "No Appeal," &c.   3 vols.

Home from India.   By JOHN POMEROY.   2 vols.

The Soul and Money : a New Novel.   1 vol. 7s. 6d.

Nellie's Memories : a Domestic Story.   By ROSA NOUCHETTE CAREY.   3 vols.

Clarissa.   By SAMUEL RICHARDSON.   Edited by E. S. DALLAS, author of " The Gay Science," &c.   3 vols.

Tregarthen Hall.   By JAMES GARLAND.   3 vols.